ALL THE GOLD IN CALIFORNIA

AND OTHER PEOPLE, PLACES, & THINGS

ALL THE GOLD IN CALIFORNIA

AND OTHER PEOPLE, PLACES, & THINGS

LARRY GATLIN
WITH JEFF LENBURG

A
JANET
THOMA
BOOK

THOMAS NELSON PUBLISHERS
Nashville
Printed in the United States of America

Published in Nashville, Tennessee, by Thomas Nelson, Inc., Publishers.

The Bible version used in this publication is THE NEW KING JAMES VERSION. Copyright © 1979, 1980, 1982, 1990, Thomas Nelson, Inc., Publishers.

Interior design by Brenda Pope, Pope Graphic Design.

Unless otherwise noted, all photos are courtesy of Larry Gatlin and the Gatlin family.

ALL THE GOLD IN CALIFORNIA. Words and Music by Larry Gatlin. © Copyright 1979 by MUSIC CORPORATION OF AMERICA, INC., and TEMI COMBINE INC. All Rights for TEMI COMBINE INC. Controlled by COMBINE MUSIC CORP. and Administered by EMI BLACKWOOD MUSIC INC. International Copyright Secured. Used by Permission. All Rights Reserved.

THE MIDNIGHT CHOIR. Words and Music by Larry Gatlin. © Copyright 1979 by MUSIC CORPORATION OF AMERICA, INC., and TEMI COMBINE INC. All Rights for TEMI COMBINE INC. Controlled by COMBINE MUSIC CORP. and Administered by EMI BLACKWOOD MUSIC INC. International Copyright Secured. Used by Permission. All Rights Reserved.

THE PRODIGAL SON. Words and Music by Larry Gatlin. © Copyright 1990 by MUSIC CORPORATION OF AMERICA, INC. International Copyright Secured. Used by Permission. All Rights Reserved.

ONE DREAM PER CUSTOMER. Words and Music by Larry Gatlin. © Copyright 1992 by MUSIC CORPORATION OF AMERICA, INC. International Copyright Secured. Used by Permission. All Rights Reserved

Library of Congress Cataloging-in-Publication Data

Gatlin, Larry.
    All the gold in California and other people, places, and things / Larry Gatlin ; with Jeff Lenburg.
      p. cm.
    ISBN 0-7852-7204-6
    1. Gatlin, Larry. 2. Country musicians—United States—Biography. I. Lenburg, Jeff. II. Title.
ML420.G28A3 1998
782.421642'092
[b]—DC21
            97-51912
                 CIP
                MN
              Rev.

Printed in the United States of America.

1 2 3 4 5 6 BVG 03 02 01 00 99 98

To my family with love and gratitude for their love, prayers, and support—Mom, Dad, Steve, Rudy, La Donna, Janis, Kristin, Josh, and T. C., too; to my extended family—the band, crew, and family and friends, good guys and gals, one and all; and to my universal family, you, the fans, for your unfailing love, devotion, and prayers all these years.
—*Larry Gatlin*

To Larry, for giving this "good ole boy" the opportunity of a lifetime, and to Texas Ruby Red, for always being there.
—*Jeff Lenburg*

Contents

$\mathscr{A}$CKNOWLEDGMENTS

My sincere thanks to Rick Blackburn, Lorianne Crook and Charlie Chase, D. J. McLachlan, Dr. Robert Ossoff, Dr. Joe Pursch, and Dr. Edward Stone.

Special thanks to Steve Medlin, Capitol Records, Nashville; Matt McConnell, Columbia Records, Nashville; Dixie Weathersby, the Country Music Association; Ronnie Pugh, Country Music Hall of Fame and Museum Library; Bob Mather, EMI Music Publishing; Kathy Gangwisch and Beckie Collins, Kathy Gangwisch & Associates; Karen Berry, the Gospel Music Association; Shirley Carter, Hood Junior High School; Bill Hallquist, K-Tel Records; Janet Lorenz, Margaret Herrick Library of the Academy of Motion Picture Arts and Sciences; Rhonda Armstrong, Middle Tennessee State University Library; Raymond Hayes and Milton Thompson, Odessa High School; George Collier, Platinum Records; Rita Latimer, Sam Houston Elementary School; Nathaniel Brewster, Sony Music Entertainment Inc.; the research staffs of ABC Entertainment, CBS Entertainment, and NBC Entertainment; and the staffs of College of the Desert Library, Hardin-Simmons University Library; Palm Desert Public Library, Rancho Mirage Public Library, University of Houston Library, and Westlake Public Library.

Very special thanks to my cowriter, Jeff Lenburg; to my agents,

ACKNOWLEDGMENTS

Mel Berger and Claudia Cross of the William Morris Agency; and to my editor, Janet Thoma of Thomas Nelson Publishers for their support and guidance; to my parents, Billie and Curley Gatlin; my wife, Janis, and my daughter, Kristin; and to our typist, Toni Scott, for their help and support in doing this book; and, most of all, to God Almighty for keeping me alive long enough to tell my story.

ℱOREWORD

Back in '70-somethin' a twenty-somethin' year old, wet-behind-the-ears, skinny kid from West Texas asked me to say somethin' nice on the back of his first album of self-penned tunes. On that occasion I wrote:

Once I was kind of a Pilgrim, and one night about seventeen years ago I was backstage at a show in California. Gene Autry was there. I was just trying to get started, experiencing a few disappointments and complaining a little bit about how hard success was in coming. Gene Autry patted me on the back, "Son, if it was easy, everybody would be doing it."

And now along comes this Pilgrim, Larry Gatlin. He's kind of a proud banner-bearer and the banner ain't his own. This Pilgrim has a heart for sale and soul in his songs, and the price is mighty cheap. But it's a hard row to hoe, even with his talent.

He shared some of these songs with me, even on the day he wrote them. I wish you could've looked down his throat with me. The first time I ever heard him sing "Sweet Becky Walker" and "Penny Annie" you would have seen soul, heard heart, and felt fine. He's everything a singer, everything a writer, everything a picker ought to want to be. If I had been born blind, I would have seen the Pilgrim. Then at the Frisco convention, Kris [Kristofferson] heard him and he was so good that everybody thought he was already arrived. Oh, how they profusely praised him, the Pilgrim just grinned at 'em.

So then I said to the Pilgrim, once he wayfared back my way, "You just might be too good to ever make it. Son, the world ain't exactly over-quota-ed with humble people like you who have talent and know how to handle it. I'm not sure what percentage of the folks are ready for you."

And then the Pilgrim said to me, "Well, if I make it, that's fine." And he added with that secret-weapon grin, "If I don't, it'll still be alright, 'cause I like to be around show folk."

And when I looked at him, he knew that I was secretly saying, "That's good, son, 'cause show folk like me need prime people like you to keep us inspired. You're a source."

So now this album sends him off sailing, wayfaring over the airwaves of the world. You should be so lucky that he should ever pass your way.

Fast forward to '90-somethin' and this fifty-somethin'-year-old, drier-behind-the-ears, slightly pudgier, and much more road-tested, little-bit-older kid from West Texas has asked me to say somethin' nice about his first book, *All the Gold in California and Other People, Places, and Things*. Well, again I say, "You should be so lucky that he should ever pass your way."

—*Johnny Cash*

$\mathcal{I}$NTRODUCTION

Somebody kick it off. One, two . . .

> *All the gold in California*
> *Is in a bank in the middle of Beverly Hills*
> *In somebody else's name*
> *So if you're dreamin' 'bout California*
> *It don't matter at all where you've played before*
> *California's a brand new game*

I can just hear someone saying, "Oh, please, God, no. Not another tell-all book written by a famous country singer."

Well, be of good cheer, brothers and sisters. God has answered your prayers because I ain't about to "tell all."

I may not tell you everything you want to know, but what I will tell you in this book is absolutely, positively, 100 percent true as I remember it. There are some things that have happened in my life, some things that I have done, some things that I have said, some things that I have felt, that I have only told God. (He already knew anyway.)

If you desperately want to know what they are, you'll have to ask Him. If He chooses to tell you, that's OK by me.

Keep the faith!
Larry

CHAPTER 1

ALL THE GOLD
IN CALIFORNIA

Tryin' to be a hero
Windin' up a zero
Can scar a man forever
Right down to his soul
Livin' on the spotlight
Can kill a man outright
'Cause everything that glitters
Is not gold.
—"All the Gold in California"

Some mystic or sage or philosopher may have somewhere, at some time in history, written something more perfectly true than this, but I have not.

I was a hero, for a while. Not a rock 'n' roll hero like my old buddy Ronnie Hawkins is always talking about, but a country music hero. A star. A celebrity. A somebody selling records, who traveled in private jets and long black limousines and lived in the spotlight, every minute of every day.

I was a hero because hard-working, God-fearing, honest-to-goodness, dyed-in-the-wool country music fans said I was, and I loved it.

My problem was, I loved it all too much.

1

Larry Gatlin, "Country Music Hero," stepped off the solid ground of faith and love and Coca-Cola and Butterfingers into a quicksand of anger and resentment and booze and drugs. Hero-to-zero in a matter of minutes, it seems, now as I look back.

The prodigal son decided to take his part of the inheritance and go into a Far Country, live the good life, drink the wine, dance every dance, and howl at the moon at every opportunity. The prodigal son of old ended up in a pigpen, eating the husks of corn that even pigs would not eat. This hero-to-zero Larry Gatlin ended up on his hands and knees, crawling on the floor of a Holiday Inn in Dallas, Texas, stuffing carpet lint into a freebase cocaine pipe.

It was late October 1984. I had been on a three-day binge, drinking and snorting cocaine with some very good friends I had known for about *thirty minutes* at the Holiday Inn in Dallas. My brothers and I were performing at the Star Garden Theater down the road.

It was the first time I had ever freebased cocaine. I stopped long enough to do our shows and then picked up right where I'd left off. I'm sure I was terrible, but fans stood up and applauded. They didn't seem to notice that Larry Gatlin was stoned out of his mind.

My brothers, Steve and Rudy, were afraid I was losing my mind. I had been on a four-day drug and alcohol rampage two weeks earlier in Fort Worth, Texas. Then I swore to them I would quit using, and for seventeen days I didn't do any cocaine. (I *was,* however, still drinking heavily.) That was until these friends arrived. To this day I don't remember their names. People like them just seemed to find me.

During those three days in Dallas, we went through all the money we had, drinking and snorting. I wrote them personal checks, withdrew cash from a local ready teller, and even borrowed money from a friend. I did what I had to do to keep the party going.

This time, however, everything was really out of control. Something was different, something I had never experienced before. The room was flashing by so fast my eyes could barely focus, and the sounds of the outside world reverberated so loudly in my brain I thought my head was going to explode. I lost all sense of reality and couldn't make heads or tails of where I was or what day it was. As hard as I tried, I couldn't make the spinning stop. The noise kept getting louder and louder. I started having serious withdrawals.

My supposed friends had left me on my hands and knees with a freebase pipe in one hand, crawling and picking lint out of the brown shag carpet. (I thought it was more cocaine.) By now my nose was dripping like a leaky faucet. My body was trembling and shaking all over, and sweating profusely. My heart was pounding hopelessly out of control, and I could barely keep my head up or breathe. I seriously thought I was going to die.

I crawled on my hands and knees into the bathroom. Looking up I caught a reflection in the mirror, and I saw the most hopeless, helpless, scared person I have ever seen. That person was me.

I don't know what the devil looks like. I don't know if he has horns and a tail. Or if he's hell-fire red, but I could not have been more frightened if I had seen the devil himself in that mirror.

Still on my knees I recoiled from the mirror, terrified.

It was then that I cried for help. "God, if You don't help me, I'm going to die."

Suddenly a mysterious force lifted me up. I tried to clear my head. I knew I had to get out of Dallas and get home to Nashville. God, in His infinite mercy, had given me a second chance. The rest was up to me.

•   •   •

My story is a tale that, to this day, many people still cannot understand: how could a famous country star who literally had everything—a loving and beautiful wife, two wonderful children, two fantastic brothers, two loving parents, a beautiful home, and a successful career—throw it all away?

The fact is, I can never change what happened. But of this much I'm sure: God has forgiven me, or I wouldn't be here to tell you about the miracle that is my life. And what a life it has been!

The places I have traveled—and I've been all over this great planet of ours—from Odessa, Texas, to Odessa, Russia (I didn't really get to Odessa, Russia. Is Moscow close enough?), from Midland to Mogadishu, and from Paris, Texas, to Paris, France.

The small towns, the big cities, the county fairs, the nightclubs, and the music halls, from the Ector Theatre in Odessa to the Greek Theatre in Los Angeles, Ford's Theatre in Washington, Radio City Music Hall, Madison Square Garden, and the Palace Theatre—from Podunk to Poughkeepsie.

And the people I have known, from Mary Jane Gentry, my high school American history teacher, to people making history—Presidents Carter, Ford, Reagan, and Bush; Prime Minister Margaret Thatcher; Generals Colin Powell and John Shalikashvili; Justices Sandra Day O'Connor and Clarence Thomas.

The greatest golfers the game has ever known—Arnold Palmer, Jack Nicklaus, Ben Crenshaw, Tom Kite, and Curtis Strange—and the spectacular courses I've played—Augusta National, Pebble Beach, Cypress Point, Pine Valley, and, yes, even St. Andrews.

The true legends of the business—and I have known and palled around with—Elvis Presley and "Ole Blue Eyes," Frank Sinatra; the "Man in Black," Johnny Cash, and his wife, June Carter Cash; Dottie West; Roger Miller; Willie Nelson; Kris Kristofferson; and Mickey Rooney.

One great thrill after another—gobs of number-one singles and Top 10 hits and countless awards—I've been blessed.

And the fans—what can I say? You've been there with me through it all—in good times and bad, through hits and misses, even when I was not in my *right* mind. I love you more than you'll ever know. You're simply the greatest.

The places, the people, the music, and the fans. I've been there, seen that, done that, met that one—I've done it all.

From the outhouse to the White House to the doghouse—that's my story. And guess what? It ain't over yet.

So let's get to it. How and where did this wonderful life begin? I thought you'd never ask.

PART ONE

$\mathcal{T}$EXAS

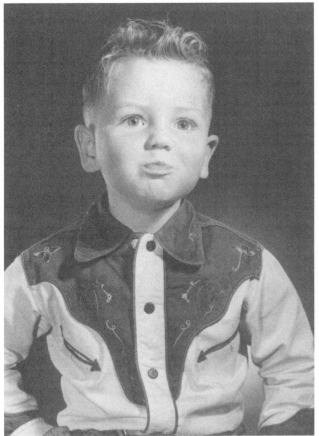

Dontcha just wanna pinch my cheeks?

PHOTO COURTESY OF TOM AGNEW STUDIOS

CHAPTER 2

Handsome couple—Mom and Dad

A Texas Boy, Born and Raised

I almost discovered America in the backseat of a dark green and silver 1936 Chevrolet on a flat, narrow, dusty, two-lane road, between Andrews, Texas, and Seminole, Texas. There are a lot of nice folks in Seminole. Actually, that's not entirely true. I promised to tell you the truth in this book, and I have already lied. There are only a few folks in Seminole, Texas, but they are *all* mighty nice.

Seminole is much like a hundred other small towns in Texas: slow, not much happening, pretty good high school football team, good plowable land, pretty girls, and big strong boys. Except for the nice folks, good high school football team, pretty girls, and big strong boys, Seminole only has two real claims to fame: Larry Gatlin and Tanya Tucker were born there, at Seminole General Hospital.

Mom and Dad were living in Andrews, Texas, at that time, but the town had no hospital, so I was born thirty miles down the road in Seminole. Dad was driving and cursing up a storm when the radiator started overheating.

He quickly pulled off the side of the road, popped open the hood, cursed some more, inspected the radiator—now almost bone dry—cursed again, threw up his hands, screwed the cap back on as best he could. It was no use—a total breakdown.

Fortunately, Dad had planned ahead and had some friends follow us just in case the radiator gave out. We hopped a ride with them to Dr. Tomb's clinic and hospital.

I was born Larry Wayne Gatlin, on May 2, 1948—an eight-pound, six-ounce bouncing baby boy with blue eyes and curly hair, and cuter than a bug from day one.

Life was a bit of a struggle because Dad did not make much money. He worked in the oil fields—he was a derrick man initially and worked on the drilling rigs—for Superior Oil Company in Andrews. He made $1.10 an hour and usually worked seven days a week, in the bitter cold of winter and the dead heat of summer. The drilling rigs operated twenty-four hours a day, seven days a week, and Dad did more than his share of the hard work. He always put food on the table, a roof over our heads, and clothes on our backs.

• • •

We Gatlins are kin to the man who invented the Gatling gun, the first machine gun of Civil War and Indian fighting fame or infamy, depending on which side of things you were on. According to my dad, when a bunch of Gatlings moved from North Carolina, Maryland, and Virginia to Texas, some of them dropped the terminal *g* because much of the local Spanish-speaking population didn't pronounce it.

On my mother's side of the family, I'm a direct-line descendant of the great Irish poet and playwright John Donne. (I love it. Machine guns and poetry—what a fitting metaphor for this chaotic, quixotic, neurotic, apostolic, alcoholic, incredibly fantastic thing called Larry Wayne Gatlin's life.)

Having said all that, I can assure you that not all of my relatives were lovely and poetic or trigger-happy Indian killers—far from it. Instead, they were, and are, probably the oddest bunch of characters you'll ever meet.

This is probably a good place to talk about my parents and their families and the valuable lessons that I learned from them, which helped mold me into the person I am today. I'll start with my mother's side and my mother first.

My mom was born Billie Christene Doan on December 21, 1929, in Megargel, Texas, to Clib and Nida Doan—Papa and Granny, to me. She was the tenth of twelve children. Eight of the twelve survived long enough for me to know them.

She grew up in Olney, Texas. Most of her family worked in the oil fields. They were poor and led simple lives, rooted in the traditional values of home, church, family, school, neighbors, and friends.

Much of what The Gatlin Brothers are today, musically and otherwise, we owe to our mother and Papa Doan. Papa stressed the importance of music early in my mother's life. He insisted that she start piano lessons in the second grade, even though they couldn't afford it. Thanks to a dedicated piano teacher, Iza Woods, and with a little help from God, Mom learned the fundamentals of playing piano and reading church music, and started playing for Papa at singing conventions long before she could even reach the pedals.

What can I say about my mom? That I love her. That's not enough. That she's the best mom you could have. It sounds trite and cliché— but it's true. No mother ever fought harder for her kids than my mom. She is really something. Oh yes, she is a very odd little duck. (Dad, don't get riled up and come whoop my butt—I don't mean anything negative by "odd little duck." You know it's true. That's probably why you married her instead of all those others. Also, Mom was the prettiest . . . and still is.)

My mother is as tough as the back wall of a shootin' gallery and yet as fragile as a flower. She is sweet and tender but will absolutely tear your head off if you mess with her kids. When my brothers and

I started our little singing careers, she would walk up to any preacher or show promoter and say something like, "You need to hear my kids sing. Your show would be much better with them on it."

Mom's a believer—always has been. Don't get me wrong, she didn't do it for *herself*. She did it for her kids.

On my mom's side of the family, there was nobody I was closer to than Papa and Granny Doan. Papa was, without a doubt, the all-time greatest grandfather and one of the all-time greatest people in the history of the world. Tall, quiet, funny, sweet, always smelling of Barbisol shaving cream—I can still see him, like it was yesterday, standing at the sink in the bathroom at his house on 206 West Kid Street in Olney, with a green coffee mug in one hand and a shaving brush in the other, stirring that concoction slowly at first, then faster, and finally brushing it onto his face.

Papa would take the straight razor and expertly remove every bit of the soap and every whisker from his face in about two minutes flat. One of the first great thrills of my life was when he turned to me one morning and said, "Gary Lynn, Tommy Carroll, Jimmy Ray, Larry Wayne . . ." (Papa had so many grandkids, he often got confused, so he would just start at the oldest and work his way down until he got to the right name.)

"Larry Wayne, do you think you can shave the back of my neck without cutting my head off?"

"Yes, Papa, I think I can."

"OK, just brush some of the soap on my neck and let's see."

He handed me the green mug and the brush and then brought a chair from the kitchen and sat down in front of me. I took the brush and slowly stirred it in the cup like I had seen him do so many times, and then I brushed some of that sweet-smelling shaving cream onto the back of his sun-browned, wrinkled old neck. That done, he handed me a Gillette safety razor and said, "Get after it, Gary Lynn, Tommy Carroll, Jimmy Ray, Larry Wayne. . . ."

Slowly, carefully, and lovingly, I shaved my papa's neck! I know it doesn't sound like a big deal to you, but to me, it was a *real* big deal.

I can still smell the shaving soap and my papa and that little bathroom in that house in Olney as if I were standing there now. It doesn't matter that Papa had taken the blade out of the old Gillette safety razor. (Looking back, I remember thinking, "These hairs *are not* coming off his neck!)

In Texas in the '20s, '30s, and '40s, all of the big oil companies—Sinclair, Texaco, Magnolia—sponsored company baseball teams. Papa was the catcher for the Sinclair Oil team. Everybody called Papa "Teapot" because of his last name's similarity to "dome." (There was a great scandal around that time involving a famous oil company at a place called Teapot Dome. And since Papa's last name was Doan—well, you get the idea.)

"Teapot," my grandfather, was a good player, to hear him tell it. I've heard some great stories about his heroics in the old oil league. He taught all of the grandkids to play baseball on a little makeshift diamond at the side of his house.

He also taught all the grandkids to drive a car and to sing. Papa had a beautiful tenor voice and could read music and direct the congregation in singing at church. One of Papa's favorite things was to go to "singing conventions." I remember on many occasions, we would pack a lunch and take off to some little town around Olney and go singin'.

On Sunday morning there would be the regular church service, then everybody would gather outside and bring out the food—fried chicken, potato salad, corn on the cob, blueberry cobbler. Everyone would eat and visit and have a great time, then they would all gather back in the church. The leader of the congregation would call on various people to come lead their favorite song from either the local church hymnal or from the Stamps-Baxter songbooks, which came out twice each year with new songs by Albert E. Brumley, Videt Polk, C. C. Stafford, and L. D. Huffstuttler.

Most of the folks in the congregation were good singers and directors, but nobody could sing as well or lead the singing the way Papa Doan could. He was the master of this deal and everybody knew it.

Granny Doan was one of the most unique people ever born. She was half Cherokee Indian, born in Oklahoma in 1895. Tough as nails and gentle as a lamb, her nickname was "Little Napoleon."

I remember so many things about her. She would get up at 4:30 every morning and make a pot of coffee that a spoon would stand straight up in. Granny Doan would drink a couple of cups of that "witches' brew" and then go outside and sweep the yard. I do not know why she did it. Leaves, gum, wrappers, dog droppings—she swept it all away every morning. There was almost no grass on either side of the sidewalk leading to the front door.

On cold winter nights she would warm my pillow in front of the gas heater in the front room of their little house. I would run and jump into bed, and she would fluff that pillow and pull those hand-made quilts up tight around my neck.

Every summer Granny would give me one—count it—one brand-new baseball. She would say firmly but lovingly, "Now, Larry Wayne, don't you go losing that ball. It's the last one I got, so take care of it."

I took care of that baseball as if it were a priceless diamond for the whole year. Every summer it was the same speech, same brand of ball, same line that it was "the last one."

For years I believed her, until, many years later, when Granny died, we opened her cedar chest—which was strictly off-limits while she was alive—and inside we found a box of one-dozen brand-new baseballs.

Then there was Uncle James—dear sweet Uncle James—one of the zaniest, funniest, and most creative cats to ever come down the pike. When he was eight years old, he would stand at the end of an upright piano and watch as my mom took her piano lessons. After the teacher would leave, Mom would struggle through the music, and when she was finished, Uncle James would sit down and rip right through the exercise like the dynamo that he was.

Uncle James left Olney for Dallas when he was seventeen and started playing piano in nightclubs. He was truly a great piano player. I mean, world-class jazz and gospel or whatever he wanted. Fastest right hand I've ever seen on a keyboard—bar none.

When we went to Olney to see Papa and Granny and the rest of the Doan clan, I always tried to spend as much time with Uncle James as possible. He opened up so many musical doors for me, introducing me to Ella Fitzgerald and Frank Sinatra, Tony Bennett and Billy Eckstein, Johnny Mathis and Sarah Vaughn, and other great pop and jazz singers. He had an old record player and hundreds of 78s and LPs. I played them for hours on end, every time I had the chance. Since then I've heard all those singers perform live, not just on scratchy old records. By introducing me to these greats and by playing the piano as I sang along, Uncle James had a tremendous impact on my singing style and phrasing.

The Gatlin side of the family is an altogether different story. Dad was the only son, born on May 14, 1927, to W. L. and Leona Gatlin in Mabank, Texas. They were a family of dirt-poor farmers who barely made ends meet. He was the second child—nine years younger than his sister Ruby Mae and eleven years older than his sister Ray Sylvia.

My father knew nothing but the hard way of life. His mother died of tuberculosis in 1942, when he was only fifteen, and his father was stricken by Parkinson's disease and was therefore unable to provide for his family financially.

My dad only went as far as the tenth grade before he had to leave school to help support his family because his father had become ill. He worked as a plowboy for some local farmers and did other hard labor to produce enough income to sustain them. (Even while serving in the Marine Corps during World War II, he sent half his salary home.)

• • •

Dad was the "enforcer" around the house and instilled in each of us a strong work ethic. He assigned us chores, and we quickly understood the value of hard work.

Dad was either working, out of work, between work, or looking for a job. He followed the rig—when the rig moved, so did we. In 1949, we moved to Olney when Dad accepted a job there. We lived in a one-bedroom, one-bathroom flat. I was a free-spirited, independent-minded, people-loving person with a strong will.

When I was two and a half, Mom got the shock of her life. I vanished. She searched every nook and cranny of our mobile home—under the bed, in the closets, under the kitchen sink—everywhere. Dad was working the 3 P.M. to 11 P.M. shift when Mom called him with the news.

"He's disappeared, Curley!"

"He's what?"

Mom called all the neighbors and launched a full-scale search. Neighbors checked with neighbors and people literally swarmed the area, looking for little lost Larry. In desperation, Mother hurried to Papa and Granny's home.

I had walked—all by myself—to Papa and Granny's for a short glass of Granny's homemade iced tea. They only lived a half-mile from our house—and how I remembered the way I will never know. I was only two-and-a-half years old.

Granny said, "He's right here. Drinkin' up a storm."

The next morning, Dad and I had one of those "man-to-man" talks—the first of many—something like, "Don't you ever scare your mother and me like that again, Son. Understand?"

The following day, I pulled another Svengali, and Mom immediately called Papa and Granny—only, this time, I wasn't there. She called around and, sure enough, she found me. I had walked to town, more than a mile from where we lived—no small feat for a two-and-a-half year old—to the Palace Drugstore to visit the pretty girls who ran the front counter.

Dad took me there all the time. The girls who worked at the drugstore loved to prop me up on the counter and feed me ice cream and sodas, just to hear me sing.

I didn't cause trouble, intentionally. I had a curious mind—still do—and once I got the hang of walking, I went wherever I wanted. It all seemed natural to me.

My life was good in Olney, and it was about to get better.

CHAPTER 3

Ride 'em cowboy.
Larry, Steve, and Rudy at about
eight, five, and three

ON THE GOSPEL TRAIL
WITH THE BLACKWOOD
BROTHERS
AND THE STATESMEN

Mom and Dad and I were living in Ballinger, Texas, when Steve was born. We had moved there from Olney when Dad got another job. Since Dad was working all hours of the day and night, and since babies generally do not announce in advance when they are going to show up, Mom decided that for the birth of her second child she wanted to be near Granny. Going into labor, alone, with no car and only a three-year-old boy to help, would not have been a pretty sight.

Don't get me wrong, my mom could have done this whole deal by herself. Luckily, she didn't have to.

Steven Daryl Gatlin was born in Olney, Texas, at Hamilton Hospital on April 4, 1951. Dad was somewhere working on a drilling rig so he was not there that day, but Granny—"Little Napoleon"—supervised everything and all went smoothly. Granny and Papa's house was only three blocks from the hospital so the day after the blessed event, I stole a newspaper out of the neighbor's yard and rode my tricycle to the hospital and took my mom the morning *Olney Enterprise.* I don't remember everything that happened but I do remember draggin' that tricycle up some steps in front of some big white columns, and I do remember a lady in white taking me to see my mom and new brother.

Mom brought Steve home to Papa and Granny's house, and then a few days after that, Dad got us all and we went back to Ballinger to George and Clemmie Mater's little rental house. The old German couple were not any relation to us, but they were always so sweet that Mom and Dad called them Grandma and Grandpa Mater and so I did too.

I remember well that little white house in Ballinger—small living room and kitchen and one small bedroom in the back. Steve's crib was in the front room, I think. We lived there for a while and then we moved somewhere. (We moved eight times the year Steve was born, following the oil field as Dad worked his backside off feeding and clothing and housing his rapidly growing family.)

Dad and I have always called Steve "Shib" because when people asked him his name when he was little, it always came out "Shib." Tough kid, old Shib. One night in Abilene we were singing in a little show at the Fair Park Auditorium. I remember there was a small electric fan at the side of the stage, and there was no wire cage over it.

On our way onto the stage to sing, Shib ran right into the fan. The metal blade tore up his pants and cut a real nasty gash in his knee. Bloodied knee and all, he proceeded to walk right out on stage and sing like a bird until our part was over. Then Mom ran him to the emergency room and a doctor stitched him up.

Rudy was born on August 20, 1952. Rudy Michael Gatlin—His

Mom and the boys

Rudeness, Cousin Rusty, Old Nub-Gub—now this boy is a real piece of work! He was sick from day one. He cried all the time. His face was red from sneezing his head off and the fact that everything he ate made him sick; he'd break out in a rash if Mom gave him regular milk, so they fed him goat's milk like some Bedouin prince.

We moved to Abilene in 1953 when Rudy was still a baby. Abilene is the biggest town on Interstate 20 (it was Highway 80 back then) between Fort Worth and Odessa and as such was a good job market for a driller. Dad worked for several companies at different jobs. The work was steady, and we were finally putting down some roots. Mom and Dad bought a little two-bedroom house at 250 Westridge Street.

Rudy Michael Gatlin was trouble from day one—always different, stiff necked, single-minded, and just a little bit off-center. He was a totally defiant little booger from the minute he hit the ground— and he hit the ground crying, believe me. He would mess up and Mom or Dad would tan his hide. Didn't do one bit of good. He would do whatever he wanted to do and then take his whoopin' and just look at you and wait for you to leave the room. Then, bingo, he'd do whatever it was that he'd just gotten blistered for, all over again.

My brothers, Steve and Rudy—ole Shib and Nub-Gub, respectively—are not just my partners or my brothers, they are my best friends. And if anyone tries to hurt either one of them, they're gonna have to come through me. I'm not really a tough guy or anything like that, but if you try to hurt my brothers, you better bring a sack lunch and a flashlight—you're gonna get hungry and it's gonna get dark before you go through Big Brother Larry to get to them.

• • •

In 1953 an event took place that would forever change my life. I went to my first gospel concert at the Fair Park Auditorium. Dad and Mom were members of a little gospel quartet (Mom played piano and Dad sang lead) with some really nice folks, Roy and Opal Owens. One night they invited Mom and Dad to go to the concert, so they got a baby-sitter for Steve and Rudy and me. Well, I will not say that I threw a fit when my parents started to leave without me (we did not throw fits in Curley Gatlin's house), but I did let it be known that I desperately wanted to go hear the music.

Steve and Rudy were too young to care. But I was not too young. And I did care. I wanted to go.

Finally, Mom said, "Well, Curley, let's take him with us. Those three boys are too much for one baby-sitter anyway."

So I got to go to the concert. It was the most infectious, the most moving, the most uplifting experience of my young life. Some of the greatest gospel artists ever to grace the planet sang that evening— The Blackwood Brothers (James, R. W., Bill Shaw, and Bill Lyles) and The Statesmen (Denver Crumpler, Jake Hess, Hovie Lister, Doy Ott, and Jim "Big Chief" Wetherington)—each of whom helped define Southern gospel music in the 1950s. I was overwhelmed, I was captivated, and I was completely won when James Blackwood sang "His Eye Is on the Sparrow," and when R. W. Blackwood sang "I Wanna Be More Like Jesus," and when Jake Hess sang "Prayer Is the Key to Heaven." I knew right then and there I wanted to be a gospel singer. (Country music, Broadway, and all the other music notwithstanding, that's what I really am—a gospel singer.)

It wasn't just the notes. It wasn't just the beautiful lyrics and soaring harmonies. It was the spirit. I knew in my heart that it was literally the "fire of God" letting me know beyond any doubt that this was my calling, this was my mission, and this was my life—to sing gospel music for people and help uplift them the way James and R. W. Blackwood, Bill Shaw, Bill Lyles, Denver Crumpler, Doy Ott, Jim Wetherington, Hovie Lister, and Jake Hess had uplifted and inspired a six-year-old boy.

The first real tragedy I experienced in my young life involved The Blackwood Brothers. In 1954, they were doing a concert in Clanton, Alabama. Before the show, R. W. Blackwood and Bill Lyles decided to take the promoter's son for his first airplane ride and then come back and pick up the rest of the quartet to fly to the next stop on their never-ending tour of America. Well, it was not to be a never-ending tour. It ended abruptly, tragically, when the plane fell to the ground during a trial run, killing R. W. and Bill and the little boy.

I cried for three days. I could not understand how God could let that happen. I had been told in church and Sunday school that God loved and protected everybody, and God would make sure that everything worked out OK in the end. Well, this was the end, and in my mind everything was not OK. It was the first time in my life that I remember questioning God—there would be many others. I was heartbroken and confused and sad beyond my years. My world had suddenly become a very dangerous and confusing place. I could not figure it out and no one could explain it to me. I was six years old and I was devastated.

•　　•　　•

In 1954, one month before I started first grade, our sister, La Donna Gayle Gatlin, was born in Abilene at Hendrick Memorial Hospital on August 18, our Granny Doan's fifty-ninth birthday.

Steve and Rudy and I were too young to go the hospital nursery to see her, so Dad had us wait under the big tree out in front. Five minutes later, he stuck our new baby sister out a window on the fourth floor. She was wearing a pink ribbon in her hair, and she was a sight to behold.

At that moment, someone started screaming loudly in the background from that opened fourth-floor window. "Curley Gatlin, you get that baby back in this room right now before I whoop you!"

It wasn't Mom doing all the screamin' and hollerin'. It was Granny Doan, Little Napoleon herself. If Mom had told Dad to bring La Donna back into the room, he would have probably laughed and said, "Now, Billie, honey, I'm not going to drop her."

My dad is big and strong and probably not afraid of the devil himself, but he was afraid of Granny, and he very quickly brought La Donna Gayle Gatlin, our new little sweetheart, back into the safety of the hospital room and saved himself a serious whoopin'.

I started first grade at Bonham Elementary School that September. I was not a very good student. I was a bit unruly and full of myself, and prone to arguments and fights. I almost never finished my schoolwork. It was boring. Numbers did not make sense to me, and the long hours cooped up inside made me really miserable. I wanted to play baseball and football and be out in the sunshine. The three Rs were not my cup of tea, and I was a troublemaker from day one.

I made it through first grade, and in second grade I found my true calling.

One day, Miss Backus, my teacher, said, "Larry, I've got to go down to the office. I'll be back in ten minutes. Go up to the front of the class and do something."

Her invitation was all I needed. I got up and sang. I told stories. I made up stuff and generally entertained the whole class for ten solid minutes. They laughed and applauded and I was hooked. There is no drug more powerful or more addictive than the applause, acceptance, attention, and adulation of an audience.

Miss Backus returned. "Larry, you can sit down now. I'm back."

Reluctantly, I returned to my seat.

Then she said, "Let's give Larry a big hand. He is very entertaining."

The whole class applauded. I smiled and took a prolonged bow and savored every moment. I was seven years old and I was the "star" of Miss Backus's second-grade class at Bonham Elementary School in Abilene, Texas.

I had no idea that this impromptu performance was the start of something big.

• • •

Every time The Blackwood Brothers and The Statesmen came to Abilene, we attended the concerts. Each time I heard them sing I felt that same calling to be a gospel singer, and I prayed that someday I would be able to sing and bring a smile to people's faces. Soon my prayers were answered.

On March 8, 1955, the Third Annual Cavalcade of Talent Contest was to be held at the Rose Field House at Hardin-Simmons University in Abilene. Mom knew how much I wanted to sing, so she decided to enter me in the show. On the day of the audition, Mom drove me to Hardin-Simmons University and brought along Aunt Nell and my brothers, Steve and Rudy, whom she intended to leave alone in the car while I auditioned.

At the sign-in desk, Aunt Nell told a woman who was associated with the show, "She's got two more in the car who can sing as good as he can."

Mom overheard the conversation and stepped right in. "They're too young."

The woman at the sign-in desk liked the idea of a boy trio, even though she had never heard us sing, and was rather persistent. "Let's see what they can do. They might make a nice novelty act."

Mom immediately nixed the idea. "Rudy's only two. He can't sing."

Aunt Nell made her case. "Oh, yeah. The other day, I saw them around the hi-fi, and they were all singin' the song on the record."

Mom reluctantly gave in and entered all three of us in the contest. I was six and a half, Steve was three and a half, and Rudy was two. It's true that we had sung together at times, but never on stage or in a contest. We auditioned anyway and Mom accompanied us on the piano. To our surprise, we were accepted for the show.

Mom was so excited she did everything up first class for our debut performance. She hired a local tailor, Dalton Galloway, to make identical Western costumes for us to wear in the show. We were hot stuff.

That night, Mom played the piano as we sang a medley of popular gospel songs. To our amazement, we won first prize in the elementary and junior high division.

When The Blackwood Brothers and The Statesmen returned to Abilene for another engagement, Aunt Nell went to bat for us. At the intermission, she cornered James Blackwood and said proudly, "I have three nephews who can outsing all of you guys."

James Blackwood, a kind and gentle man with a heart of gold, smiled sincerely. "Really? Well, bring 'em up here and we'll see if they can outsing all of us guys."

The microphone was taller than we were, so someone lowered it. Rudy still couldn't reach it.

Jake Hess, the lead singer for The Statesmen, came to Rudy's rescue. He brought an old wooden Dr Pepper crate to the stage and stood Rudy on it. Now we were in business.

Rudy, you're on the wrong "mic."
Smile, Mama.

With Mom accompanying us on the piano, we sang several popular gospel songs, including the first song we had ever learned, "I Woke Up This Morning Feeling Fine, I Woke Up with Heaven on My Mind." We performed flawlessly that evening until our closing number. While trying to hit the last note, Rudy fell off the Dr Pepper crate, and his head was the first thing that hit the floor (the boy ain't been right since that day). The audience went crazy. They stood to their feet and cheered for a whole minute.

Afterward, James Blackwood told them, "If I lived in this town and had a radio or TV show, I'd have these Gatlin kids on every week."

James Blackwood must have had his own personal pipeline to God, because the day after the show, Mom received a phone call from Slim Willett (Winston Moore was his real name) who hosted a local TV show, *The Slim Willett Show,* on KRBC-TV in Abilene, sponsored by Western Chevrolet. Slim was a talented country singer, a great salesman, and a hit songwriter—he wrote Perry Como's hit "Don't Let the Stars Get in Your Eyes."

Slim said to Mom, "I would like your boys as guests on my TV show," and offered to pay us $10 a week. Mom accepted.

Doing *The Slim Willett Show* was a lot of fun. It was also a real challenge. Back then, the show was broadcast live, and if you flubbed up everyone knew it. Rudy, who was only two, was easily distracted. The studio where we did the show had big TV lights, which attracted bugs like a magnet. The minute a bug would start crawling across the floor Rudy would go chase it, right in the middle of a song. Some of the cameramen got into the act too. They began rolling dimes and quarters toward Rudy; naturally, he would run off-camera to retrieve them, and we would have to keep singing without him. It was a hoot.

The Slim Willett Show did a lot for our career. We were hired to sing every Sunday on a religious radio program for a local radio station—for a mere ten cents a week—and on another popular local television program, *The Red Fox Show.* Church groups and other civic organizations also hired us to sing, paying us $35 or more for an appearance.

We didn't sing for the money. We sang because we loved to sing and to entertain people. But times were hard in Abilene and the money came in handy. We appeared on Slim Willett's program every other week for the next two years and sang at concerts, every other Saturday night, at Fair Park Auditorium. We soon became famous as The Gatlin Trio.

Abilene was where I had my first real home, where I discovered my love for gospel music, and where I started my singing career. My life couldn't have been more perfect, but that was all about to change.

CHAPTER 4

Heisman Trophy candidate: Larry Gatlin,
seventh grade

A STANDOUT IN MUSIC AND SPORTS

When the oil fields in Abilene played out and Dad was again out of work, he decided to pull up stakes and move us from Abilene to Olney, Mom's hometown. I was devastated. The intervening forty-plus years have not erased or even dulled my memory of that fateful day: Black Friday (as I call it), December 18, 1956.

I was sitting in Mrs. Owen's third-grade glass at Bonham Elementary when, all of a sudden, Dad was standing beside my teacher's desk. I had known all morning that he was coming to pick me up. I kept hoping and praying that a miracle would happen and that I would wake up and realize it was only a bad, bad dream.

Well, it was no dream. And there was no miracle.

Dad waited as I gathered my things. Then, fighting back tears, I said my good-byes and hugged Mrs. Owen (a nice lady and a good teacher) as I walked out the door, down the long open hallway and out the back entrance of the school to our 1953 white Chevy with the red hardtop and red fender skirts. Mom, Steve, Rudy, and La Donna were in the car waiting for us.

I sat in the backseat of that beautiful white Chevy, biting the inside of my jaw and trying to keep from crying out loud as Dad drove away from Bonham Elementary.

I was in such a state of shock, I really didn't say anything. I couldn't believe what was happening: I was leaving Abilene—the Mighty Warbirds football team; the First Assembly of God Church; all my friends and classmates; our weekly appearances on Slim Willett's television show—to go live in a little, one-horse, dried-up Podunk town.

Olney is approximately one hundred miles from Abilene. That day it seemed farther. It was the longest, saddest, coldest one hundred miles of my life.

Papa and Granny Doan lived in Olney. They had a small rental house next door to their own house at 206 West Kid Street. Dad and Mom decided that Mom, Steve, Rudy, La Donna, and I would stay in the rental house until Dad found a job. The oil business was booming farther west in Odessa, so he dropped us off in Olney and went to Odessa to look for a job.

A month later, in March of 1957, Dad came back for Mom, Steve, Rudy, and La Donna and moved them to Odessa, but he and Mom decided to leave me behind to finish the school year.

I really loved Papa and Granny. They were wonderful, funny, terrific, loving people, but I hated Olney. As the old saying goes, "Olney, Texas, may not be the end of the world, but you can sure see it from there." Most days I felt this way, and it showed. So when Mom and Dad came to visit me during Easter break, I convinced them to let me join them in Odessa. "Hallelujah! Good-bye, Podunk, U.S.A. Hello, West Texas!"

God certainly knew what he was doing, putting me in Odessa.

The next ten years would be ten of the happiest of my life. Odessa was not Abilene, but it was not Olney either—and that was good. No, that was great. Dad had a good job and "The Gatlin Quartet," as we were now called (after our sister, La Donna, joined the group), was once again singing together. (Hallelujah, again!)

We left Olney on the Saturday before Easter in 1957 and drove the 250 miles to Odessa. Our first little house in Odessa, at 3103 Eisenhower, wasn't big enough to cuss a cat in, but it was our house and we were all together. On Easter Sunday we went to church at Bethel Assembly of God Church at Forty-second and McKnight. We were the featured singers that day and would be every Sunday for years to come.

Reverend Perry Cowan, a good man and a good preacher, was the pastor of the church. I really liked him and his wife, Sister Pauline. I liked the church, the entire congregation, and especially the preacher's two daughters, Betty and Gay, upon whom I immediately turned all of my considerable eight-year-old charm. That's right, both of them.

School in Odessa was an adventure. One Monday morning in April 1957, I walked into the school office with my mom, and the office personnel enrolled me in Imogene Freer's third-grade class. What a lucky break for me. In Mrs. Freer's class I began a lifelong love affair with the English language, with books, and eventually with creative writing. The first day there I met my good friend Randy Walker.

In Odessa, we had music class every day. Our music teacher was a knockout named Jane Ann Clark. I had a crush on her for years. Miss Clark came to Mrs. Freer's room and brought a small record player. She played some songs and we all sang along.

When I started singing the harmony part, Miss Clark suddenly looked around the classroom, trying to find out who was singing tenor. I remember she looked puzzled as she walked up my aisle and stopped at my desk. I didn't really think anything about it. I had been singing harmony since I was five years old.

Miss Clark stood at my desk for a little while listening, and after the song was over, she asked "What is your name, young man?"

"Larry Gatlin."

"Where did you learn to sing harmony?"

I answered that I learned in church and at gospel singings and that I sang in a quartet with my two brothers and my little sister.

"Well, keep it up. You are very talented."

Life was good again. Odessa was a good place, and I felt right at home.

During fourth grade something else wonderful happened to me. Dr. Paul Peck, the choral director at Odessa College, wrote an operetta about a boy soprano, a young phenomenon, and I won the lead role in the production of *Bartholomeo Bonafacio*.

The story was about a boy soprano who becomes very famous singing all over the world, when suddenly, in the middle of his biggest song, "Brazil," his voice breaks on a high note. The boy blushes and tries again, to no avail. The audience leaves the concert very disappointed, and the youngster has to learn to deal with the fact that he cannot be a boy soprano forever. I toured all over West Texas and parts of New Mexico, singing in this wonderful operetta, with Dr. Peck and the Odessa College Choir.

•   •   •

I played a lot of football throughout elementary and junior high school, and during ninth grade I met a coach who would later play a pivotal role in my life: Coach Melvin Robertson. Coach Robertson, the backfield coach at Odessa High School, came to Hood Junior High to talk to the football players about playing in high school. He had a personality ten-feet tall and an incredible knowledge of the game of football.

After the meeting, he singled me out and said, "Gatlin, I saw you play this year, and you are a good little quarterback. You know, you can't throw the ball like Mike Campbell at Permian. But we are not gonna throw very much at Odessa High. We're gonna run the option and some sprint outs that will give you a chance to run, and I think you can be a good player. Come on out for football, and I'll help you."

He was excited and so was I. This meeting was the first of hundreds I would have with him.

Coach Robertson was true to his word. In 1963 I became the

quarterback of the junior varsity team at Odessa High School, under coaches Dick Brooks, Ray Newton, and Melvin Robertson who taught me the plays and game strategy. It helped that he was my biology teacher. We spent forty minutes every day on biology and fifteen minutes every day on football—formations, plays, and coverage.

One part of our final exam was a football problem where we had to diagram the proper defensive coverage of certain pass plays—pro right, drop back, sprint right. If you answered it correctly, he gave you an A on the exam. If you answered all the biology questions correctly, but not the football problem, he gave you a B+. (Yes, the young ladies in the class had to be able to diagram the defensive adjustments also.)

Football was definitely important to Melvin Robertson, to Odessa, Texas, and to me. (I made an A, by the way.)

Our junior varsity team went 10-1 and won the district championship that year. (San Angelo beat us early in the year, and we beat them in a rematch.) We had a great team and great players—Winston Beam, Darrell Byrd, Ray Goddard, Steve Hays, Mike Moore, Milton Thompson, and a slew of others.

Sports were an important part of my junior and senior high school years, but they never replaced music.

One of my favorite movies is *Mr. Holland's Opus*, starring Richard Dreyfuss. Dr. Maurice Alfred, director of the Odessa High School Choir, is my "Mr. Holland." Blending great voices with good voices, ordinary voices, and even some weak ones is a difficult task, but Dr. Alfred was a master at it. He took students with varying degrees of musical talent and turned them into what was generally considered the best high school choir in all of Texas at that time.

Dr. Alfred is a wonderful musicologist who knows all kinds of music—show tunes, classics, Latin music, jazz, blues, gospel—you name it. He worked us like dogs, but what great music we made under his direction! I'll never forget him or his wonderful wife, Glenna, who died in 1996 of cancer and was also a great influence in my life. She helped Dr. Alfred every spring with our high school's spring concert and with the staging of a twenty- to thirty-minute segment of a popular Broadway musical. They cast me as Sportin' Life in *Porgy and Bess,* my first school musical. Every time I sing for anyone, anywhere on this earth, these two wonderful people are part of my song.

CHAPTER 5

The Gatlin Quartet with Mom

$\mathscr{H}$EARTBREAK IN ODESSA

Through all of this, The Gatlin Quartet was alive and well and on the move. Our tour bus was a 1962 Rambler station wagon. We had a U-Haul trailer hitched to the back, where we carried our wardrobe and sound equipment. Usually, we left early on a Saturday morning and Mom drove all day until we reached our destination—sometimes for an engagement that night, followed by several more on Sunday (we often sang at more than one church on the same day). We stayed overnight, usually at a minister's home or at a nearby motel, then after our last engagement Sunday night we headed home.

Mom would drive all night, and most of the time we pulled into our driveway the following Monday morning. We would sleep in the back of the station wagon, and she would wake us in time to clean up, eat breakfast, and get to school. Our little road trips were a test of our endurance, willpower, and faith, but something else kept us going. I think it was the belief that God had a much greater plan for all of us and that this was only the beginning of something truly wonderful.

Mom kept us in line most of the time—not an easy thing to do with four rambunctious kids. Before an engagement, she'd tell us, "If you act up, or you are impolite or don't act like you should, they'll never ask us back. So behave yourselves and do things right."

To her credit, the people we sang for always asked us back.

Several other well-known country and gospel artists were struggling to make it around this time in West Texas. In 1959 we met one such artist who would later become a major musical force himself: the unforgettable Roy Orbison.

Steve and Rudy and La Donna and I were performing at the Ector Country Jaycees Talent Contest at the Odessa Coliseum. This event was a big deal in our area every year, and that year many up-and-coming singers and singing groups performed, including one promising act from nearby Wink, Texas: Roy Orbison and the Teen Kings.

Roy had one of the greatest voices I had ever heard. He and his group were very popular throughout West Texas and wowed the crowd that night with a medley of popular tunes. He was a tough act to follow, but we did our darndest to compete. We sang an old Red Foley favorite, "Peace in the Valley," and several other songs. To our surprise, we beat Roy's group for first prize. They won dinner for four at the Blue Star Chinese Restaurant, and we won a Shetland pony named Dan.

Roy was the lucky one. He and his boys enjoyed a wonderful five-course dinner at the Blue Star Chinese Restaurant, and we had to clean up horse manure in the backyard for almost a year until Dad thankfully sold Old Dan.

That same year Steve and Rudy and La Donna and I experienced another breakthrough in our career. The Wills Family, a famous gospel group, sang at the Methodist church one Sunday morning, and we went to hear them. The pastor asked us to sing. After the service, Calvin Wills came up to us and said, "That was some kind of singing."

We just smiled and Mom said, "Well, thank you." Then she invited Calvin and his sister, Lou Hildreth, and all the Wills family over for dinner, and we all ate Thanksgiving leftovers.

During dinner Calvin, who owned and operated Sword & Shield Records—a small, independent label featuring the recordings of many popular gospel groups—looked up from his delicious meal and said, "How about recording an album for us?"

He explained that several other groups had done really well by recording their own albums, and he thought we would too. My parents agreed, so we recorded our first album that year, *The Old Country Church*. The album was so successful we recorded three more albums after that, each featuring popular gospel standards, including "I'm Bound for That City" and "I'll Never Walk Alone."

Our little group became so popular that many churches outside the area (and the state) were interested in booking us. Mom contacted the pastors, and in the summer of 1962 we embarked on our first cross-country tour.

Mom, Steve, Rudy, and La Donna and I traveled everywhere in our Rambler station wagon with the little U-Haul trailer hitched to the back. We went through Texas and New Mexico, then Arizona, then California. Two years later, we went to California and New York (and the 1964 World's Fair, where we also sang), so we really put some miles on that ole car.

We saw plenty of beautiful countryside and met many wonderful people and experienced our share of funny moments along the way. But nothing compared—or came remotely close—to our stop in Tucson.

We arrived there the night before so we would be ready to sing at the Sunday morning service at the First Assembly of God Church. That morning we were all in our motel room, getting dressed to go to church, when suddenly there was a knock at the door. It was the pastor, Reverend Goodfellow (not his real name). We were more than a little surprised when he showed up at eight o'clock to give us a look-see.

Reverend Goodfellow was a pleasant man—between sixty and

sixty-five years of age—very fatherly and gentle, with a ready smile and friendly demeanor. He welcomed us to Tucson and told us that he and everyone at the First Assembly of God Church was excited about us coming to sing. Then he smiled at us, and we smiled back.

As he turned to leave, he suddenly stopped and looked back at my mother. Very gently, with no malice or condemnation in his voice, he said, "Sister Gatlin, I would ask you not to wear the string of pearls or other jewelry to our church this morning. We ask that none of our Christian sisters adorn themselves in any manner that might call attention to themselves. Thank you, Sister Gatlin, I know you will understand."

With that, Reverend Goodfellow turned and walked out the door.

Well, Mom reached up and unhooked the simple strand of pearls that Dad had given her as an anniversary gift, laid them on the dresser beside the bed, and shrugged her shoulders; we walked out of the room, got in the car, and drove to church.

When we got there, the first person we met was Sister Goodfellow, the pastor's wife. Well, folks, let me tell you the God's truth. She was wearing a corsage the size of Rhode Island. That hummer started just above her left bazoom and ended just below her left knee. It had flowers and ribbons, bells and whistles, some fruit salad and Lord knows what else. The darn thing had its own zip code.

If I hadn't known that the old girl was pushing seventy and a Pentecostal preacher's wife, I would have sworn she was the homecoming queen from the local high school. Steve, Rudy, La Donna, and I all had to bite the inside of our cheeks to keep from laughing out loud. That corsage was one for the record book, probably weighed ten pounds.

Sister Goodfellow was very sweet and gracious, and obviously she was a saintly woman full of love and compassion—and I know she meant well, and quite obviously, her husband did too. Lord knows we would not have wanted any of the good Christian brothers to be led to thoughts of forbidden, lustful pleasure by those pearls.

Many years down the road someone would aks my friend Willie Nelson, "What do you want on your tombstone?"

And Willie would reply, "He meant well."

Well, Brother and Sister Goodfellow, you meant well—and by the way, Willie's also a good fellow.

•   •   •

By this time my dad and I were having trouble with each other. Dad was then, and is now, an old-fashioned kind of guy—a former Marine and a strict disciplinarian.

It was a time of rock 'n' roll and Elvis and Roy Orbison, fast cars and short skirts and fuzzy cashmere sweaters with little bumps in front, and drive-in movies with fogged-up windows from heavy breathing in the backseat. To an old-fashioned guy like my dad, this was totally unacceptable. He thought a good parent was supposed to protect his sons and daughters from all this debauchery.

Well, protect us he did. We got out to go to church and school and to sing, and we played Little League games and stuff like that. But we didn't go to movies unless we all went together. Since our church, the Assembly of God, did not believe in dancing or mixed bathing (that's what they called swimming in those days), I was not allowed to go to the movies on Friday night with my buddies Mike Campbell, Randy White, and Danny Brinlee or to go swimming at Sherwood Park or the West County Swimming Pool. So things began to go south in my relationship with my father.

•   •   •

One of the highlights of my junior year was that I made the Texas All-State Choir for the first time. I had not made it as a sophomore.

My best buddy in the group was a senior named Clayton Bowles. He had made All-State Choir as a sophomore, junior, and senior. What a great guy, what a great singer.

The choir stayed at the Statler Hilton Hotel in downtown Dallas, and I roomed with Clayton for an entire week. What a wonderful week it was. The music was fantastic and the voices—my Lord—what great singers those kids were. Something else also happened that week that was to be a benchmark in my life, even though I didn't know it then.

My cousin Tom Sartin was living in Dallas at the time, and I called him when I got into town. He invited me to dinner at his apartment. I met his girlfriend, Ann, and we all had a very enjoyable evening. Tom took me back to the Statler Hilton in his brand-new 1965 midnight-blue Chevrolet Impala with rolled and pleated blue-and-white bucket seats. One of the prettiest cars I'd ever seen.

Tom dropped me off and he said he'd see me sometime later in the week. I walked into the hotel, got in the elevator, and went to my room.

The next morning, the desk clerk called to say that there was an envelope for me at the front desk. I went downstairs and picked it up. Inside were car keys and directions to a parking place in the Statler Hilton garage. I followed the directions and there it was: the midnight-blue 1965 Chevrolet Impala with the rolled and pleated blue-and-white bucket seats, with a $20 bill clipped to the sun visor.

Tom rode the bus to work for three days so I could use his new car. Since then, he has been like the fourth Gatlin Brother, and, on more occasions than I can possibly count, he has come to my rescue. He drove the bus when we needed a bus driver. He moved every Gatlin brother into and out of every house we ever owned. He has handled our financial and corporate affairs. He has, in short, been there for us no matter what.

Tom Sartin is trustworthy, loyal, and totally dedicated. But, believe me, it's more than an employer–employee relationship. It is a bond that is spiritual, and I thank God right here and now for Tom Sartin, a.k.a. "T. C.," and his wife, Ann, a.k.a. "Tekla." (She hates that name, but I call her Tekla anyway and she calls me Alfred.) They are very special people.

When I returned to school for my junior year, I found a big surprise waiting for me. Bradley Mills, who was the head varsity football coach, had taken over as the offense coach too. Coach Melvin Robertson was demoted to just being secondary coach, and Bud Aubuschon and Bill Herron were the line coaches.

Coach Mills did things differently. He changed offensive strategy—going from an option offense to a pass offense—and, surprisingly, he demoted me to third-string quarterback, behind my old friend and neighbor, Richard Whittenburg.

The new offense was supposed to score points almost at will, and much was expected of the Odessa Broncos—affectionately known as "The Jolly Red Giants" (derived from the tagline in those famous television commercials—"Ho, ho, ho, Green Giant"—you get the picture). But even with a great bunch of guys on the team—David Cooper, Tommy Fox, Ray Goddard, Bubba Moore, Art Overturf, Larry Priddy, Skippy Spruill, and Milton Thompson—we had trouble living up to all the hype.

We lost our first two games, to Lubbock High and to Amarillo High. After the second defeat, I was named the first-string quarterback.

One of the highlights of the year was when we beat Abilene High in Abilene, the first Odessa High team to do so in many years. All of my loyalty to the Abilene Eagles had vanished years before, and I played harder that night than I had ever played. It was a great feeling to beat a team that I had supported for so long.

The mighty San Angelo Bobcats came to Odessa toward the end of the season. They were huge, they were fast, and they had beaten us 34-0 the year before. (We didn't get a first down the whole game!) They had great players on that team—Terry Collins, Jerry Drones, Gary Mullins (an old friend), Harold Smith, Franky Stringer, and a real speedster, Julio Guerrero.

It was a great game. The good news is, we won, 14-12. The bad news is, I broke my left foot on the third play of the second half. I ran a little down-the-line option—Red 55, as we called it—and decided to keep the ball instead of pitching it back to our right halfback, Chuck Clark. I turned up inside and when I was tackled, somebody landed on my foot the wrong way.

It really hurt, but I figured I had just bruised it, so I kept playing.

X rays the next day confirmed my worst fear: the foot was broken about midway on the third metatarsus. The specialist said, "Larry, I don't think you're gonna be able to walk on that foot for three or four weeks."

I said, "If I had to walk, what could you do to help me?"

"Well," he said, "we could build a brace of some kind and tape it real tight and you could try it, but I cannot be responsible for any further injury or complication."

"I'll take care of that," I said.

When Dad got home from work, I explained everything and he said, "Let's talk to Doc Rhea [our trainer] and Dr. Bob Wright [our team doctor]."

Both men agreed that using the foot would not do any more damage, since the bones were already beginning to ossify and a brace and tape would keep them from moving much. Dad said OK, and we told the foot doctor to give me the custom-fitted brace.

I did not practice at all that week, but rode an exercise bike to stay in some kind of game condition. We had the final game on Friday against Permian High, and I wasn't going to miss it. If we could win, we would win the district championship for the first time since 1948, the year I was born.

On Friday night, Doc Wright pulled out the biggest syringe I had ever seen and gave me a shot to help ease the pain. He did the same thing to me at half time. I wore a size 11 shoe on my left foot and a big brace and a size 8 shoe on my right one. I looked like Bozo the Clown.

The foot felt a little better, and I started the game, broken foot and all. Ray Goddard scored on "Red 24" from about 50 yards, and I scored on a "34Q"—belly option to the right. We won the game, 13-0. Champions of District 24A—it makes my heart beat fast to this day.

• • •

It's hard to talk about my junior and senior years in high school and not talk about Skippy Spruill. I knew Skippy in junior high. He was one grade ahead of me at Hood. He played football and baseball and was a good ole boy—a funny, rough-and-tumble kind of guy, not much different from most of the guys I knew at that time.

It was Skippy who was responsible for my first "drunk." Actually, that's not quite true. I am the only one responsible for what happened that night and all the other times after that.

I was hangin' out at Nikki's Drive-In on Friday night in December 1964 with some of my buddies.

Two earth-shattering, monumental, life-changing events occurred that December night in 1964. I met Jack Daniels and I met Janis Moss.

Skippy and I were not real close during our football season. He was an All-American and I wasn't even All-Block, even though I was a two-way starter. I was a junior and Skippy was a senior, and he had his "gang" that he ran around with and I had mine.

All of that changed that night at Nikki's. At around 7:00, I was just hangin' with some friends, Mike Moore and Danny Harris, when Skippy came over and grabbed me by the shoulder. "Hey, Gat, come here."

I did.

"Me and Taylor and Ray are gonna get drunk over at Taylor's house. You wanna go?"

Folks, I made the biggest mistake of my life. I said, "Yeah, I wanna go, Skip."

I wish I had had the strength to resist. I made the wrong call.

So Skippy and the rest of the gang got in someone's car and took off for Pinkies, the local liquor store, to pick up the juice, while I cruised around Nikki's enjoying my new exalted status. I was soon to be one of Skippy Spruill's drinkin' buddies—pretty big doin's in Odessa, Texas.

I was just walking around, talking to some kids I knew from Odessa High, when all at once I saw a truly beautiful girl sitting in a car with another girl. She had dark hair and a beautiful face, and I couldn't keep from staring at her. Well, I've never been shy, so I walked over and said, "Don't I know you?"

"I'm Janis Moss," she replied. "You've sung at our church before."

"Oh, yeah," I said. "You're the tennis player. David Moss is your brother."

"That's right."

There are only a handful of earth-shattering, life-changing moments in our lives, and all the others are just smaller moments that play into and out of the big ones. (I'm not sure that is true, but it sounds heavy, so I'm leaving it in.) It is amazing to me that two of the most important moments of my allotted handful of "big ones" came within minutes of each other. Number one: I decided to get drunk. Number two: I met Janis Gail Moss.

I don't remember all the details of that first meeting, but I do remember sitting in the car with this lovely creature, laughing, talking, and just having a wonderful time. I think I fell in love with her that very night—no kidding. She was wonderful—pretty as a picture, a good Christian girl, great sense of humor, the whole package. There was one slight drawback: she was an older woman.

Janis was a freshman at our local junior college. She was a cheerleader, Miss Odessa College—I mean, she was big stuff—and I was just a lowly junior in high school. I gave myself little or no chance of furthering this relationship. Add to that the fact that, as I said earlier, I was on a very short leash, with my father holding the other end.

I couldn't go out on Friday night like everybody else. I was gone most weekends, singing with The Gatlin Quartet. This deal did not look very promising, but I gave it my best shot anyway. After about thirty minutes of chitchat, laughin', and using my "A material," I went for the kill and gave her my sweetest smile and my best closer, the only one I could think of under the circumstances.

"Well, Janis"—I remember this part very clearly—"if it's OK with you, someday I'll just forget that I'm a lowly junior in high school and I'll pretend that I'm an All-American football star with a nice car and a few dollars in my pocket, and I'll give you a call."

She smiled and said, "OK."

I got out of the car and told her good-bye and walked over to where Skippy and the boys were parked under the little canopy at Nikki's. They had the "juice," and we were gone.

Two of the most important, pivotal moments in my life—both in a matter of minutes. Amazing.

David Taylor lived in a little white house next door to KOSA-TV around Fourteenth Street. When we got there, I called Mom and told her I was going to spend the night with someone, don't remember who. She said, "OK." I still do not know where Dad was. I would never have tried this brave ploy if he had been in town. I was nervous and excited all at the same time.

As soon as I hung up the phone, we commenced our project for the evening: getting Gatlin drunk. I ran into some problems right away. None of the "juice" tasted good. What a letdown. I was stunned and very disappointed. I'd been told this stuff was great. I mean, all I'd heard the past couple of days was how good Bacardi and Coke, vodka and orange juice, and sloe gin and beer were.

I knew what beer tasted like. On rare occasions, when I was a little boy, Dad would let me have a sip—and I do mean a sip—of beer when he and some friends got together at our house. This only happened three or four times that I can remember, and, believe me, it was not enough beer to acquire a taste for it. I've never seen my father abuse alcohol. So understand that these rare beer drinking sessions were not drinking parties where I was allowed to participate. Only a couple of sips, that's all.

Like I said, I knew that beer was bitter and not something that I liked. But I was sure that one of those exotic potions in the beautiful bottles with the colored labels was going to be really good and that I could drink enough of it to get the desired effect: to get drunk like Skippy and Ray and the other guys. I wanted to see what all the hoopla was about.

After beer, we tried rum and Coke, vodka and orange juice, sloe gin and cold beer—ugh, it was awful. (As I tell people in my "recovery talk," it tasted like horse tinkle with the foam blown off.)

The bad news was, I couldn't get drunk. Finally, someone hit on a great idea. Let's try gin and Dr Pepper. You're probably thinking that sounds horrible. Well, it was, but I was desperate. I had to get drunk. I was honor bound and dead set on doing it. So, I forced this awful concoction down—a big glass of it.

Well, the first glass had the desired effect. I was drunk. Not fall-down drunk yet, but drunk nonetheless. So, what did I do? I drank another big glass of the same stuff. My Granny Doan always said about castor oil, "If a little bit'll do a little bit of good, a whole lot'll do a whole lot of good." In keeping with Granny's directions and in absolute accordance with my Type A, compulsive, obsessive, pedal-to-the-metal mentality, I drank a second glass, then a third, and before I could even think about drinking a fourth, I was fall-down drunk for sure. I got very silly.

At that very moment there was a knock at the front door, and right away I thought it was Dad. So I crawled under a rug and tried to hide, while Skippy and the other boys laughed their heads off and continued to have a jolly time. What I didn't realize was that nobody was laughing with me. They were laughing at me. I was not one of their gang. I was a sixteen-year-old boy who had been deceived by the older guys, deceived by Madison Avenue, and, more importantly, deceived by my own overwhelming desire to be one of the group. Peer pressure, Madison Avenue, and my own lack of self-worth made for a volatile combination when mixed with Gordon's gin and Dr Pepper.

I was no longer little Larry Gatlin, the Assembly of God church boy and gospel singer who couldn't go to the homecoming dances or to the Ector Theatre or to Nikki's with the rest of the guys. I was Larry Gatlin, Skippy Spruill's "pet" and drunker than Cooter Brown, rolling around on the floor, hiding under a rug, and laughing, not caring or worrying about anything. At that moment, I did not care about Dad or God or church or anything else. I had found a way out of my little Pentecostal prison. I was off the leash and I loved it—for a little while.

I stumbled and fumbled around, having a great time, laughing and screaming and acting like a fool, when all at once, the laughing stopped. I got violently sick. (I will spare you the gory details.)

After a few minutes (seemed like days) on my knees in front of the toilet, I rose to my feet and laid down on a bed. The room was spinning like a top.

Skippy came in about that time and looked down at me. I'll never forget it. "Gatlin," he said, "you look just like my mother."

With that, he kissed me on the forehead and passed out on top of me. Skippy was out cold, and I was about to be smothered to death. Somehow I got out from under him and made it to the living room to lay on the couch. I don't remember anything else—the first of many alcoholic blackouts.

I want to stop right here and clear the air about one thing. Skippy, old friend, it wasn't your fault. Dad, it wasn't your fault. Jack Daniels, Jim Beam, Adolf Coors, Mr. Gordon—not your fault. Madison Avenue—not your fault.

Larry Gatlin was and is responsible for the events of that night and many others like it and worse. But to sit here and point fingers and try to assign blame, well, it ain't gonna do any good. It was what it was and that's that.

I don't remember how I got home. I do remember waking up the next morning in my own bed, sicker than a dog. Oh, what a headache, what a stomach ache, and what a hangover.

Saturday morning was cleanup time at the Gatlin house. It was alley cleanup day. That's right, the alley. We were the only house in Odessa, Texas, with an alley as clean as our front yard. We chopped weeds. We planted flowers, and by the end of the day the trash can area in the alley behind the Gatlin house was Marine Corps shipshape. Can you imagine being within ten yards of a smelly trash can in my condition? One good whiff of that little unit and I was history.

Dad saw that I was really sick and he was very sweet. "Go back in the house, Son," he said. "We'll do it next week."

I went back to bed and slept until later that afternoon. We all acted like I just had the stomach flu. I don't know if Dad knew what the deal was or not. If he did, he never mentioned it. I'm fairly certain that the Dr Pepper smell could not have masked the aroma left by Mr. Gordon's finest.

Well, that's it. My first drunk. Not a very glorious picture.

A few days after that momentous night at Nikki's and David Taylor's house, my friend David Webb came over to my house one afternoon. I remember that it was my mother's birthday or my parents' anniversary—December 21 and 22, respectively. David and I were good friends (still are, even though we don't see much of each other), and it wasn't unusual for him to drop by. Yet something in his face told me he was up to something. We talked for a few minutes and then he spilled the beans.

"I know somebody who is just crazy about you, Gat."

"Who's that, Kebbie De Webbies (David's nickname)?"

"Janis Moss," he replied. "She told me at church the other day that she thought you were really cute. Can you believe that?"

Well, I couldn't believe it, but I decided to believe it anyway.

"Are you messin' with me, David Webb, or this is on the level?"

"It's on the level, my friend," he said. And the rest, as they say, is history.

I called Janis that very minute, and we talked for a while on the phone. I told her that I had not become an All-American and famous football player in the five or six days since I had seen her, but if she could somehow stand the heat from her girlfriends about going out with a junior in high school, I'd love to call her in a few days. I explained that we were leaving the next day to spend Christmas in Olney with Papa and Granny Doan, but that I would like to see her upon my return. She said, "OK."

The next four or five days were very, very long. I always enjoyed going to my Granny and Papa's house, but this time I was in love. I wanted to get back to Odessa.

I called Janis the minute I returned, and we made some plans. I really do not remember where we went. I do remember that I borrowed Mom's 1962 tan Cadillac. I called home sometime in the middle of the date, and Mom told me she needed her car, so I took Janis to my house and we traded cars with Mom—her Cadillac for my gray Morris Minor. Janis got a fairly good glimpse of what the next thirty years would be like on that very first date—riches to rags and riches to rags, Cadillacs to Morris Minors—the story of our future together that first night.

A little kiss goodnight was appropriate. Nothing sloppy and wet or terribly passionate, just a little goodnight, closed mouth, Pentecostal versus Baptist, first-date kiss. I drove home in my Morris Minor absolutely, 100 percent, head-over-heels in love with Janis Gail Moss.

I don't remember our second date. But I do remember our third date. I borrowed Mom's Cadillac again, and Janis and I went to Midland (about twenty miles from Odessa) to see the hottest movie of the year, *Goldfinger*, with Sean Connery as James Bond, 007. We had a great time. Janis looked beautiful. Afterward, we parked on the street next to Janis's house and talked and kissed, and talked and kissed some more. She told me all about being engaged to another guy for a while and that she finally realized he was not the one for her.

I said, "No, he was not the guy for you. I am. I love you, and I want you to marry me."

That was not what Janis was expecting, I'm sure, so she said, "No."

I decided I would just have to kiss her a little better. So I did and about fifteen minutes later I asked her again and she said, "Yes." (I knew she would.)

Janis's version of the entire affair—let me rephrase that, the entire event—is a little bit different than mine, but that's how I remember it, and, as they say, that's my story, and I'm sticking to it.

My senior year was great and awful. Awful because our football team was 2-8, and great because my buddies across town at Permian won the first of many state championships. Awful because coach Melvin Robertson was gone; but great because he was now the defensive backfield coach at the University of Houston. Awful because we had a new head coach: Bob Smith—not his real name. It was my goal to win a state championship in football and try to become the All-American football star that I had promised Janis I would be. You always like going out a winner your senior year, and, besides, I was hoping to attract the attention of college recruiters and perhaps earn a scholarship from one of the big universities. So much for Plan A. The season was an absolute nightmare.

My last high school game was against Permian—we played a great first half, deadlocked 0-0, but they beat us, 35-8.

Something really funny and something really tragic happened in that game. I ran a power sweep to the left and was tackled after a 4- or 5-yard gain. While I was lying on the ground, my old buddy Ricky White jumped on top of me about three seconds after the whistle.

"Ricky," I screamed, "you're beatin' the you-know-what out of us. Do you think you gotta kill me too?"

Ricky laughed and said, "Gat, I saw you lyin' there and I just couldn't help myself. I had to drill you." We both laughed, but he still got a 15-yard penalty for unnecessary roughness. Of course, it didn't matter. They still won. It really was funny, and I have a smile on my face just remembering it.

The tragic thing that happened involved me and our head coach, Bob Smith. Don't get me wrong; Coach Smith (who replaced Bradley Mills) was a good ole boy, but he had some peculiar ways of trying to connect with his players.

As I was walking off the field after my final high school football game, Ricky White—preacher's kid, the same guy who had speared me in the back forty-five minutes earlier—ran halfway across the field to invite me to say the Lord's Prayer with my old buddies, the new District Champion Permian Panthers.

Well, the guys and I gathered around each other, knelt down, and said the Lord's Prayer. When we were finished, we shook hands and ran off the field.

Imagine my surprise, a few days later, when Coach Smith called me a traitor in front of my teammates as we watched the Permian game film. Larry Wayne Gatlin, eighteen years old, saying the Lord's Prayer on the 50-yard line of W. T. Barrett Stadium in Odessa, Texas, December 1965, accused of being a traitor? I couldn't believe it.

My teammates knew what he said was not true. They had seen me play with a broken foot and cracked ribs, and they knew I gave it my all every time I played. Too bad a grown man couldn't see that.

A few days later, Coach Smith resigned, just before getting fired, and I never saw him again.

(Coach, I hope you've mellowed a little bit. We were just eighteen-year-old boys, Coach, not robots. You were too hard on us, old friend, and it was obvious to all of us that you had a demon loose inside of you. I'm sure you are a good man, but the demon was all we ever saw. As I look back, I remember our first day of spring training in 1965. I remember the smell of alcohol, a smell with which I am now all too familiar. The demon was loose. Like I say, I hope you have exorcised the demon. I am very grateful to God that I have, one day at a time, prayed the booze demon out of my life. If you have not, repeat after me—"Our Father, who art in heaven, hallowed be thy name . . .")

•   •   •

There were some real bright spots in my senior year. As disappointing as my senior football year was, a miracle happened one morning in Miss Georgia's typing class. Not the first in my life, but surely one of the most important. Let me set the scene.

Before Coach Robertson left Odessa in 1964, he promised that no matter what happened, I would get a full scholarship to the University of Houston when I graduated from Odessa High. At that time, I was not too fired up about the U of H. I really wanted to go to the University of Texas, SMU, or the University of Arkansas. But none of these schools wanted me.

So what in the world does all of this have to do with Miss Georgia Stephen's typing class? For some reason, still unknown to me, Miss Stephen left the room on this fateful day in December, while my classmates and I were clanking away on old typewriters with no letters on them. I do not remember her *ever* leaving the room during class before. But that day, miraculously, she did.

While she was gone, and while I was banging away at the terrifying speed of about eighteen to twenty words per minute, I glanced out the window. There was Coach Robertson. He got out of his car, closed the door, and walked toward the west wing of Odessa High. I had not seen him in more than six months, and to say I was excited would be an understatement. Without thinking, I jumped up from the desk and ran out of the classroom (a real no-no).

Students were normally expelled from school for several days for being in the hallway without a pass. I ran outside anyway and practically jumped in Coach Robertson's arms.

"Hey, Gat. How you doin'?" he asked.

"I'm doing great now, Coach. I've really missed you. How you doin'?"

"I'm great, Gat. I'm really doin' great. I love Houston and you will too. We're gonna have a great team in a couple of years. Do you wanna come down there?"

Since I had had no other offer of a scholarship to a major university, I said, "I sure do, Coach."

"Well, Gat," he said, "you just hurry up and graduate and the scholarship is yours."

Basically, what he was doing was handing me a $20,000 grant-in-aid to the University of Houston—$20,000 that Mom and Dad didn't have. Little did I know then he was also being used by God to put Larry Wayne Gatlin in exactly the right place, at exactly the right time, to walk through exactly the right door, that the one and only all-powerful, all-knowing, all-loving, and all-caring God would provide for a 5-foot-8, too short, too light, and too slow gamer like me. Five short years in the future, that exactly right door would lead me to Vegas, Nashville, and the world.

Anyway, back to Miss Georgia Stephen's typing class.

I said good-bye to Coach Robertson and hurried back into the classroom. I had not been in my seat twenty seconds when Miss Stephen returned to the room. I thus escaped a possible expulsion from school. (She wouldn't have done that. She was a good old girl. I had a C or D average and no prospects of anything any better, and I had no earthly shot at thirty-five words per minute with no mistakes, which is what it took to make an A.)

None of that mattered. I was on top of the world. I had seen Coach Robertson, my mentor, my friend. He had assured me that after weeks of agonizing over the football situation, college football and, more importantly, a free college education, were in my future. I was floating. I was full of adrenaline. I was jazzed.

With about five minutes left in class, Miss Stephen suddenly got our attention when she said, "Turn to page so-and-so and begin. Now!"

It was a speed test. Usually, my reaction would have been, "Oh, God, help!" But not this time. This time I felt invincible. I mean, I was a future University of Houston Cougar football player. Bring on those keys with no letters.

Ding! The bell on Miss Stephen's desk rang and I began flyin'.

(I once heard a sportscaster ask Michael Jordan, "Michael, can you really fly?" Michael flashed that world-class smile, winked, and said softly, "For a little while.")

For a little while, I flew too. I was unstoppable. I was "in the zone." My brain and my fingers were connected by some mysterious thread, and those little digits of mine—which were, in truth, too short to grip a football tightly enough to throw it very far—moved at warp speed. Click, click, click, click, click, click. Ding! Return the carriage. Click, click, click, click, click, click. Ding! Return the carriage. It was no effort, no conscious movement, just purity of purpose and perfect form. For one minute—sixty whole seconds—I was unbeatable on those keys with no letters.

Then it was back to reality. Ding! The bell on Miss Stephen's desk went off. She instructed us all to stop. Before I even looked down at my paper, I knew the verdict: I had passed. I broke the speed barrier that day with a record thirty-five words per minute. No mistakes. Everything in exactly the right place, at exactly the right time, and exactly the right number of words, typed by exactly the right ten flyin' digits.

"Good job, Larry Wayne," Miss Stephen said, surprised. "What got into you?"

"It's a long story, Miss Stephen. Trust me—you don't want to know."

The bell rang, class ended, and it was time to go to lunch, to Houston, to Vegas, to Nashville, and to the world.

Many years later, famed writer/novelist Truman Capote was one of Johnny Carson's guests on *The Tonight Show*. I remember Johnny asked, "Truman, what do you think of Norman Mailer's writing?"

Capote pulled himself up to his full height of 5-foot-3 and said in his famous falsetto voice, "John, Norman doesn't write. He types."

Move over Norman Mailer; I can type too. The jury is still out, I guess, on the writing part, Mr. Capote, wherever you are. But if Johnny Carson or anyone else ever asks ole Truman what he thinks of Larry Gatlin's writing, he can say, "Well, John, I don't know if Larry Gatlin writes, but he *sure* does type."

CHAPTER 6

*Sideburns and pinstripes and
a beautiful sister, La Donna.*

THE BALDWIN HOUSE AND THE U OF H

After graduating from high school in 1966, the University of Houston was not my only option. I was offered two—count 'em, two—other scholarships: New Mexico State University, in beautiful downtown Las Cruces; and San Angelo State University, in beautiful downtown San Angelo, Texas. With no offense intended toward either town, I jumped at the University of Houston deal.

In the fall I was ready to report to the University of Houston. Steve and Rudy and La Donna and I sang together one last time at the evening service at the Oak Cliff Assembly of God in Dallas.

I must confess that I was a bit preoccupied. Immediately following the service, I was to board a plane for Houston and enter a brand-new world—the world of major college football. Following the church service, Mom and Dad drove me to Love Field and we said our good-byes.

When I arrived at Baldwin House (the athletic dorm at U of H, commonly referred to as the "Animal Farm"), my sense of excitement soon turned to one of absolute disillusionment. Coach Bobby Baldwin assigned me to a room with a junior football player named Robbie Williams. Robbie was an OK guy, but he was a neat freak, and it did not take him long to ask Coach Baldwin to get me out of his room.

The word spread like a Texas prairie fire in a windstorm: "That Gatlin kid is here."

I was the very last member of the freshman team to arrive in August of 1966, and, since I had done a lot of braggin' the previous April on the occasion of my recruiting visits to U of H, the boys were ready for me. They intended to give me a warm welcome . . . and they did. I had not even unpacked my suitcases when the knock came at the door. What I'm about to describe to you is the most humiliating and totally animalistic behavior to which I have ever been exposed.

In 1966 freshman were not eligible for varsity competition. We had our own freshman squad and coaches and were not really a part of the team. The upperclassmen treated us like slaves. They beat us with coat hangers and they played "Cuckoo" with us. This was an infantile game wherein one freshmen is blindfolded and handed a rolled up newspaper. The varsity boys would then go, "One o'clock, two o'clock, three o'clock . . . cuckoo." At that point a lucky stiff under a desk had to stick his head out and holler, "Cuckoo," and the blindfolded stiff had to try to hit the cuckoo in the head with the folded up *Houston Post*. I ask you, have you ever heard of anything so stupid in your life?

Oh, yes, one more thing about Cuckoo. If the blindfolded guy missed the cuckoo's head, he got five swats across his butt with a coat hanger. Same deal for the cuckoo. If he got hit by the blind-folded one, he got five swats. My backside had whelps on it for three weeks. (I actually bled all over my underwear and bed clothes for the first two weeks in college.) Needless to say, this was not how I had envisioned the college football experience.

The coaches just looked the other way and pretended nothing was happening. Don't get me wrong—I developed some lasting friendships with the coaching staff: Coach Yeoman and his family, and coach Bobby Baldwin and his family, and Coach Brown, Coach Hurt, Coach Willingham, Coach Arenas, and Tom Wilson, our trainer. But I will say unequivocally that the first two weeks at U of H were the most humiliating and painful weeks of my life. And nobody in charge seemed to care one bit that we were being beaten with coat hangers every night.

Football practice was torture. We worked out at 10:00 in the morning and 3:30 in the afternoon. It was always over 90 degrees. And that was just the temperature. Humidity levels usually soared above 95 percent. We worked, I mean worked. The freshmen ran offense against our first team defense and defense against our first team offense, and we ran sprints and did drills and we got half an orange and one small cup of "Cougar pee," a horrible tasting drink on the order of Gatorade, and that was it. I cannot believe that someone didn't die out there.

•　•　•

When I was a kid, Reverend Joe Neely was the pastor of the Garden's Assembly of God Church in Midland. Steve, Rudy, La Donna, and I sang at his church on a few occasions, but I didn't know him or his family very well when I was in Odessa. Well, somehow, he found out that I was attending U of H, and he made it a priority to get me to come to his new church in Pasadena, Texas, Calvary Chapel Assembly of God. He called early one Sunday morning when I was about half hungover and insisted that he pick me up and bring me to church. He had talked to my mother and gotten the phone number, and she had said I would probably love to sing a solo. In my condition, I was in no shape to get out of bed, much less sing, but he insisted. Thank God he did, and thank God for this wonderful man and his family.

For the next four years, Joe Neely and his wife, Chauncy, and their sons, James and Louis, and their daughters, Linda and Lucy, treated me like one of the family. They fed me, clothed me, looked after me when I was sick, and in general made me one of their own. In addition to that, I was able to sit under the ministry of one of the best teachers and preachers on earth. I learned much from Reverend Joe Neely.

Oh, yeah, something else. I really missed Janis. She was six hundred miles away in Canyon, at West Texas State University, and I only saw her three or four times the *entire* year. Long-distance love is horrible. I had no money, no car, and almost no fun my entire freshman year.

I'm not going to give you a blow-by-blow description of my entire college experience, but I would like to tell you a few high points. We had some great teams and I saw some wonderful football games, all from the sidelines. But in my sophomore and junior years, things got a little better. I soon realized that I wasn't going to get to play, no matter how hard I tried. But I persisted and did my job as best I could every day.

The simple fact was that I wasn't good enough. The problem was, I didn't know it. I only got two chances to play in three years. I scored the 92nd point in our victory over Tulsa, and I got the ball to the 1-yard line against Idaho in a game we won 77–3. I played thirteen total minutes in three years. Not much of a career, huh?

Except for the fact that going to college and making passing grades kept me out of the Vietnam War, my college experience was a total waste with the exception of three or four really good classes.

The food at the Baldwin House was, for the most part, inedible. I learned early on that the cheese plate at the old Roxy Bar, not far from campus, was better than dorm food. For one dollar, I could get a platter of cheese with some smoked sausage, crackers, and a pitcher of beer. Voila! An alcoholic is born.

I really believe I was an alcoholic from the first time I got drunk with Skippy Spruill. I loved the feeling, even though the booze made me sick. I will say this: my trips to the Roxy Bar—three or four nights a week for the one-dollar cheese plate, the smoked sausage, and the pitcher of beer—certainly solidified my standing in the alcoholic community. While I was at the U of H, I tried a few other little things that would later play a big role in my life, including marijuana. I never was a big dope smoker. It slowed me down too much, and I am not a slow-down kind of guy. Speed, Dexadrine, amphetamines were OK too. Not all of my teammates took speed, but we knew who did, and on occasion, when an "all-night, Dear God, I must make an A on this test to stay out of Vietnam" study session was called for, I would go to one or another of my "pharmaceutically enlightened" teammates and beg, borrow, or steal a couple of little white pills with the crosses cut through them. We just called them "white crosses" (a bit ironic in the imagery, I guess).

Well, two white crosses and a cup of coffee, and, boy, I was off to the races. I don't know how much studying I did, but I stayed out of Vietnam.

One of the things that made my Houston experience easier to take was my participation in a little gospel quartet, The Royals. We were really pretty darn good. Harrold Johnson sang bass. His wife, Betty, sang alto. Tommy Howe sang baritone, and I sang lead. Vince Obar played great piano, and Steve Warren, one of the most talented guys I've ever known, played bass. (Steve is now Wayne Newton's keyboard player and sings the britches off of "Amazing Grace" every night during Wayne's shows.)

We practiced a couple of times a week and sang regularly on Sunday mornings and evenings in the Houston area. We never did make any money, but we did own a purple bus and some gaudy, awful-looking orange suits, and we had a lot of fun singing about the Lord, Jesus Christ. I believe that being with The Royals helped me hold onto who I really was deep down inside. The real battle for Larry Gatlin's heart and soul was now joined. Actually, my heart and soul were OK. It was my mind that was starting to play tricks on me.

I visited Mom, Dad, Steve, Rudy, and La Donna as often as I could—usually on Christmas and Easter and at times during the summer. I missed singing with my brothers and sister, and I also missed Janis. When she graduated and got her teaching certificate, she landed a position at Stuchberry Elementary in Pasadena, Texas, so that we could be together until we could get married.

I DO! . . . And I would do it all over again.

Janis and I got married on August 9, 1969, at Bethel Assembly of God Church in Odessa. Brother Vondell Drinkard performed the ceremony. I sang "The Twelfth of Never," and everything went off without a hitch. Almost. Janis caught her veil on the rock work on a planter in the back of the church just as the processional started. And Forrest Moss, Janis's father, had broken his foot a couple of weeks earlier and had to use crutches to walk his daughter down the aisle.

We decided we would honeymoon the first night in Odessa. There is no other place around there suitable for a honeymoon, and I'd waited five years for "the moment" and was not about to drive to Dallas or El Paso on my wedding night. So we consummated this marriage in the honeymoon suite of the Inn of the Golden West. We were both nervous and scared stiff and neither of us enjoyed the deal as much as we thought we would.

That's the bad news. The good news is, after twenty-seven years of marriage we enjoy each other now, more than ever. Not just the lovemaking, which we believe is God's special gift to us, but in countless other things we share. Marriage is more than sex. Marriage is giving and taking, good and bad, laughter and tears, joy and sorrow. Janis and I encourage couples to enter into the marriage relationship with prayer and in keeping with God's ordinances. In other words, try it God's way.

With my partner in life now at my side and my days at U of H coming to a close, what I had waited for my whole life—from my earliest "performances" entertaining the neighbors to singing all over the country at churches, nursing homes, and singing conventions with Steve, Rudy, and La Donna—was about to take place. It would be the opportunity of a lifetime.

PART TWO

LAS VEGAS
AND NASHVILLE

L. G. in Reno in the 1970s

CHAPTER 7

The Imperials and The King and me

THE IMPERIALS, ELVIS, AND JIMMY DEAN

One evening a few years ago, Janis and I attended a state dinner at the White House honoring President Muhammad Hosni Mubarak of Egypt. It was truly a grand evening.

On that occasion, I walked over to a man I really did not know and introduced myself: "Mr. Brinker, I've waited for a long time to meet you. I'm Larry Gatlin."

Mr. Brinker was Norman Brinker, the well-known restaurant tycoon and chief operating officer of the Steak & Ale, Bennigan's, and Chili's restaurant chains. He and his wife, Nancy, are wonderful people who give generously of themselves to worthy causes all over the world.

"Mr. Brinker," I said, "I used to work for you."

"You did?" he asked in amazement.

"Yes, sir. I sang in the lounge at the Steak & Ale on Gulf Freeway in Houston for about two months until I realized that the waiters were making $100 a night while I was making $20." He laughed as I told him the rest of the story.

Janis was teaching second grade at Stutchberry Elementary School in nearby Pasadena, Texas, and I was going to law school at U of H. We had only been married a little over a year, and we were broke. I got a job at Steak & Ale, singing in the bar, and also waited on tables there while going to school. I only knew four chords and six songs, so I learned very early to kibitz my way through the forty-five-minute set by talking to the patrons and telling jokes and acting funny. Obviously, four chords and six songs do not a lounge singer make. (No one ever requested one of the six songs I knew.)

One night an old boy sitting at the bar drinking vodka hollered out, "Sing 'El Paso.'"

I said, "Sir, it's ten minutes long and I do not know all of it."

He shut up and had another vodka, and about ten minutes later he shouted again, "Sing 'El Paso.'"

I said as politely as I could, "Sir, I do not know 'El Paso.'"

He shouted, "Well, sing the Ninth Symphony.'"

I hit a chord and sang "Freude, schoner Gotterfunken, Tochter-aus Elysium." It was a beautiful rendition of Beethoven's master-piece, right there in the bar of the Steak & Ale on the Gulf Freeway. When I finished the solo, the old boy at the bar applauded wildly, paid his check, and vanished into the night. The bar patrons exploded into laughter.

Norman loved the story, and we had a wonderful visit right there in the Red Room of the White House over canapés and champagne. (I had 7Up, thank you very much.) I then related to Norman and Nancy exactly how I finally got to Nashville.

I was waiting tables at Steak & Ale and Janis was teaching third grade. Jackie Carpenter, a waitress at the restaurant, had introduced me to her husband, Ronnie, and I soon began spending more time with him slaving over a hot putter than I was reading *Prosser on Torts* (a very boring law book) or *Sybock v. Wilson* (a very confusing case). I was also singing on weekends with The Royals.

Well, I got a call from Harrold Johnson, and he mentioned that The Goss Brothers were in town for a few days and wanted to get together. I told him that I needed to get together with Lari Goss because he was working on a lead sheet of a wedding song I had written for David Moss's (Janis's brother's) wedding. Harrold told me that Lari was staying with a friend of ours named Ruby Campbell. So I called Ruby and she told me to come on over. Lari and I talked for a while about songs and people and happenings in gospel music and then we worked on the lead sheet for "His Masterpiece Love," the wedding song.

After we finished, Ruby said, "Larry, did you know that Roger Wiles is leaving The Imperials and that they are looking for a baritone singer?"

That question—"Larry, did you know . . ."—set off a chain of events that has brought me to where I am now. "Really," I said. "Where are they now, do you know, Ruby?"

"They are in Vegas at the International Hotel [later changed to the Hilton] with Elvis, I think, at least they were a few days ago," she replied. Vegas? Elvis? Now I was really listening.

"Ruby, I've gotta go call them about that job. Thanks for telling me." I got up and started to leave, then said, "Lari, I'll see you later. Thank you for helping me with the song. I gotta go."

Bam! I was in the car and back to our little apartment in three minutes flat. It was only three blocks from Ruby's place. I immediately dialed information (1-702-555-1212). The operator (and it was a live voice then) answered on the first ring. She gave me the number.

I wrote it down, hung up, and called the hotel. I got another operator.

"The International Hotel, Las Vegas. May I help you?"

I remained calm. "Yes, uh, Mr. Jim Murray's room. Please."

Jim Murray is an old friend of mine and one of the best tenors in gospel music history.

"I'm connecting you, one moment please," the tiny voice on the other end said.

The operator rang the room, and in my mind I started thinking of what I was going to say. Someone answered the phone. "Hello." "Hello," I said. "Hello, Jim?"

"Yes."

"Jim, this is Larry Gatlin; how are you?"

Jim was cordial and friendly. "I'm fine, Larry, how are you?"

I paused, then said, "I'm fine." I paused again and then blurted out my whole reason for calling. "Jim, I want to audition for the job."

The whole conversation went downhill from there. "We don't need anybody right this minute. Joe [the piano player] is singing the baritone part. All we're doing is 'Ooh-aah–caught in a trap' and 'Ooh-aah–in the ghetto' and 'Ooh-aah–you ain't never caught a rabbit' and 'Ooh-aah–you ain't no friend of mine.' So we don't really need anybody for three or four weeks."

I tried not to sound disappointed. "I understand."

"We'll call you if we need somebody."

Jim was in Vegas in a plush hotel room. I was still in our little apartment and had to work the Steak & Ale. I figured that I would never hear from Jim or The Imperials again. I mean, after all, they were in Vegas with Elvis, and they were the top gospel vocal group in the world. I was a waiter at Steak & Ale on the Gulf Freeway in Houston. What chance did I have?

As I remember, it was about 4:00 in the afternoon. I had been to class that morning (that may not be the truth, I may have played golf with Ronnie—don't remember). The waiters had to check in by 4:30 and do the usual prep work—refill the salt and pepper shakers, fill the water pitchers, clean the tables—real glamorous stuff for a future country music and Broadway star, don't you think?

Anyway, I went into our bedroom and put on my waiter's outfit. It consisted of a plain white shirt with big, puffy sleeves and an enormous collar that made the "Flying Nun's" look small; a cute little burgundy dickie ascot; black knee britches (that's right, black knee britches); and long black nylon socks and black rubber-soled shoes that looked like boats. (We called 'em "wide oval twisters.") The whole get-up was ugly—with a capital U. (Norman Brinker, I do appreciate your friendship, and I have the utmost respect for you, but I just cannot forgive you for making us wear those black knee britches.)

So, with a broken but hopeful heart (maybe one of the secrets to life is a broken but hopeful heart), I drove the five miles up the Gulf Freeway from our apartment to the Steak & Ale, punched the time clock, and began filling the salt and pepper shakers for the five tables I was to work that Friday night in January 1971.

I must confess, it was all I could do to take orders and serve food and make change for the paying customers. My mind was in Las Vegas with Jim Murray and Terry Blackwood and Armond Morales and Joe Moscheo and, of course, Elvis! My body, however, was being dragged around by the West Texas work ethic that my dad had instilled in me as a young boy.

"Show up for work, clock in, and do eight hours work for eight hours of pay," he used to say. So I did. I showed up, checked in, and did my job. I was on the verge of a very emotional experience, if not a nervous breakdown.

So close. I was so close to realizing a dream that I'd had for years: singing for my Lord and Savior Jesus Christ and becoming a gospel singer with The Imperials. I was so excited I couldn't concentrate. That's all that was on my mind. That and meeting Elvis, of course. Then reality smacked in the face, like a ton of bricks.

"Uh, waiter, could you check on our order, please. We've got a ballgame to go to and we ordered over thirty minutes ago."

So much for me and my big dreams. I turned to the woman and her husband and said, "Yes, ma'am, I'll go check. I'm sure your order is coming right out."

I smiled and walked away but underneath I was seething. I really wanted to say, "Get it yourself, ma'am," but I didn't. After all, they weren't the ones in a foul mood. They weren't the ones waiting for The Imperials to call. They weren't the ones with big dreams of being a gospel singer. So there was no point making a scene, even if those black knee britches were ugly.

I picked up their order and returned to the table and did the usual smile-and-look-happy routine as I set their meals in front of them. I said one thing, when I really meant another. "Here you are: filet, medium-well, baked potato, and corn on the cob, just as you ordered." (Translation: "I hope you choke on it, lady, and I hope your team gets its butt beat.")

I sauntered over to her husband as he eagerly looked at the plate of food I placed before him.

"And here you are, sir, the Kensington Club, medium-rare, with an order of mushrooms and onions sautéed." (Translation: "I'm glad it's you who has to sleep with that ole bag tonight. She is major league ugly!")

I smiled and said the usual, "Enjoy your meals and just holler if you need anything. I'll be checking back with you in a few minutes."

I flashed another big smile. "Enjoy." Then I turned and walked away.

At that moment, someone from the kitchen called my name.

"Hey, Gatlin, you got a phone call. It's Elvis."

I had told the other waiters about The Imperials deal, and they had been razzing me about it all evening. So when someone said I had a call, I thought it was a joke. I walked over to the phone and answered.

"Larry," the voice on the other end said, "it's Armond Morales." (I thought, *Yes, there is a God.*)

"Hi, Armond, how are you?" I asked, followed by a bunch of small talk. Then he cut to the chase.

"When can you be in Vegas?" The most beautiful six words I had ever heard: "When can you be in Vegas?" (The second most beautiful really. "Yes, Larry, I will marry you," being the first.)

"Armond, I'll be in Vegas tomorrow."

"We'll see you then."

I couldn't believe it. My life had changed from "I hope you enjoy your meals" (and choke on them) to "I'll be in Vegas tomorrow," all in a matter of minutes. (Maybe another one of the secrets of life is that things change quickly and for the better "to him that believeth," even if he only believeth a little bit and is scared stiff.)

I hung up the phone and told my buddies. "Boys, I'm going to Vegas to sing with Elvis."

I wanted to rip off that "Flying Nun" shirt and those Little Lord Fauntleroy britches and leave right then for our apartment, but I didn't. I finished my job, checked out my cash bag and tips, and accepted everyone's congratulations before I clocked out.

Janis and I hardly had enough money for groceries, much less airfare to Vegas, so before I left I asked our assistant manager, Stu Wagner, if I could borrow the money from him. Stu was a kind and generous soul and he loaned me the money.

When I walked through the door of our apartment, I broke the news to Janis. "Janis, honey, Armond called me at work. I'm going to Vegas in the morning. I'm going to be an Imperial."

Janis was thrilled for me. Janis Gail Moss Gatlin is, without a doubt, the most unselfish person I have ever known. She knew how important and wonderful that moment was for me. Whatever her doubts or misgivings, or whatever her likes or dislikes, she has always been happy for me when life has dealt me a good hand. She might not have liked the game I was playing at the time, but she was happy for me when I was dealt good cards.

The next morning she waved good-bye, and I boarded the plane at Houston Hobby Airport for Vegas. The Imperials were staying at a little motel, The Bali Hi, about three blocks from the International Hotel. It was a dump with kitchenettes and a tennis court. Only in Vegas—a dump with kitchenettes and a tennis court.

Terry Blackwood, the lead singer for The Imperials, and Jim Murray were playing tennis when I got there. So was Joe Moscheo, The Imperials piano player, who doubled as their baritone singer. I didn't know Joe but I knew the other guys. After the tennis match we all gathered in Joe's room, and they told me the deal. I was not going to get to sing with Elvis after all. They did not need me to do the backup singing of "Ooh-aah–in the ghetto" and "Ooh-aah–you ain't caught a rabbit" and "Ooh-aah–you ain't no friend of mine."

What they needed was someone to do the backup singing of "Ooh-aah–big John–big John–big bad John" for Jimmy Dean.

Right in the middle of this month-long gig with Elvis Presley at the International Hotel they were planning to take four days off and do five shows with Jimmy Dean at the Circle Star Theatre in Phoenix. So for the next week they taught me "The Jimmy Dean Show."

During the day, we would rehearse for a couple of hours and play tennis, and then at night I would go with them to the International and watch Elvis.

I have to admit, watching Elvis Presley live, at the top of his career was magical. He was handsome and in great shape, and he enjoyed doing the shows. I had never been a huge Elvis fan. (Don't get me wrong. I liked him, and I liked some of his records and appreciated the fact that he had literally changed the direction of American music, if not single-handedly, at least single-pelvically.) I had grown up with a fellow in West Texas and done shows with a man I have written about earlier who, to this day, I believe was the greatest pop or rock 'n' roll singer ever—Roy Orbison. As great as Elvis was and as much as he did for American music, he always came in second to my friend Roy.

Having said all that, let me add this: without a doubt, the most exciting seventy-five minutes I have ever seen on a stage was at the International Hotel showroom in January of 1971 when the Joe Guercio Orchestra and Elvis's band—guitarists James Burton, John Wilkinson, and Charlie Hodge; bassist Jerry Scheff; keyboard player Glen D. Hardin; and drummer Ronnie Tutt—kicked the show off with the "Theme from 2001: A Space Odyssey." Ronnie did an incredible drum solo, and James did a hot guitar riff, and the band was doing its thing—hot and tight and blazin' as the spotlights circled the stage like searchlights at Alcatraz scanning the yard for an escaped prisoner—until The Man, "The King" himself, walked out on the stage.

Elvis ambled onto the stage amid the glow of the spotlights and a million flashbulbs. I was stage left, behind the curtain, taking it all in—every note, every move, every curled-lip smile, every nuance, and every gesture. I was "The Kid" and he was "The King." He was fabulous. He was full of energy and he sang his rear end off. He wasn't Roy Orbison, but he had the whole package—a great band, great backup singers, great moves. It was pure Elvis. I'll never forget it.

I watched both shows—eight o'clock and midnight—and afterward I was invited to the star suite at the International Hotel with The Imperials and the rest of Elvis's entourage. The "troop" gathered there three or four times a week for "breakfast." There was a spread of food the likes of which I had never seen—steaks, scrambled eggs, potatoes, beans. I expected Henry VIII to walk through the door at any moment.

When Elvis walked out of the bedroom into the big living room of the suite, "The Dance" began. Even to a wet-behind-the-ears, twenty-two-year-old, naive, and terribly excited kid from West Texas, it was bizarre. "The Dance" was an almost but not quite choreographed ten-minute reprise of the evening's performance and segue back to reality, such as it was, from karate to kudos ("You're the greatest, Elvis") to breakfast, then the pairing up and disappearing act.

I know many of you are scratching your head and asking, "What is Gatlin talking about?" Stay with me.

Elvis made his entrance, into our presence, into the living room. The band was no longer the band. The entourage was no longer the entourage. The bodyguards were no longer the bodyguards. I was no longer The Kid trying out for The Imperials. We all became—on cue, as if spoken into existence by some DeMille-like decree of "action"—the audience.

"Great show, Elvis," one of them said. "Man, you were terrific. You sang your butt off." Everyone followed, like fans waiting to see their favorite star. The result was more kudos, more back slaps, more kisses and hugs (I saw a couple of people actually jump up and down). I joined in (although I did not hug and kiss him). But I got caught up in The Dance like everyone else. I was laughing and moving in rhythm to the cadence of the nonspecific, unplanned, but compulsory exercise. Elvis was in the middle of this circle and, with his Pied Piper-like command of every person in the big room, directed us, moved us, and played us like a puppeteer.

"Come get me, Red," he hollered, and Red West jumped out of the crowd from behind Elvis. They went through a forty-five second karate demonstration to "oohs and aahs" and "Get him, Elvis" from the adoring onlookers. It was a dream. It was surreal. No, it was The Dance, Larry.

After the karate deal, everybody clapped and laughed, and Elvis kidded Red a little bit and said something to the onlookers. The Dance began to wind down. The people on the outside edges of the circle began to gravitate toward the sagging table of food or toward the corner of the room for a smoke or one-on-one conversations. It was really strange. The wind-down took about two or three minutes, and then all at once, Elvis Aron Presley, The King, and Larry Wayne Gatlin, The Kid, were standing alone, together in the middle of the Star Suite of the International Hotel in Las Vegas, Nevada.

"Elvis, you were great tonight. I appreciate your letting me tag along," I said nervously.

That's what happened. Maybe some of the dialogue is fuzzy after twenty-five years, but the feel of that evening is as vivid as this morning's cup of coffee with Janis at our kitchen table.

Elvis went to the table and heaped food onto a plate (the biggest beefsteak tomatoes I've ever seen), then came over to where I was sitting and sat down. (I remember thinking, *Dear God, don't let me say something real stupid.*) He was a different person now that The Dance was over. He was, for the next fifteen minutes, not The King, not Elvis the Pelvis. He was an ordinary man, very smart, very friendly, and totally honest and straightforward. We talked about mutual friends—The Blackwood Brothers, James and R. W., and The Statesmen.

Everyone knows that Elvis was a big gospel quartet fan. He had grown up in Memphis listening to The Blackwood Brothers, and he credited Jim "Big Chief" Wetherington, The Statesmen's bass singer, with teaching him how to stand while he was singing and how to shake his leg to the tempo of the music.

We talked about God and guns and music, and then he talked about "the third eye." He pointed to the center of his forehead and went into a very deep and sometimes rambling explanation of his beliefs about spirituality and God and the universe in general. For a West Texas kid, this was heavy stuff!

The moment took on a life of its own, and I was swept away in its tide. Looking back, I understand more clearly what happened that night. The members of the "dance troop" were simply overwhelmed by the choreographer, Elvis. For a few minutes, we unwittingly gave him control of our minds, bodies, and souls. His presence so dominated the room and the situation that we became his subjects.

Not his friends, employees, or even his family. We were his loyal subjects. After all, he was The King.

If you find this hard to believe, just stop and think for a minute. Isn't that exactly what he did to the young people of America in the fifties? En masse they became subjects of The King. They rocked when he said "rock." They rolled when he said "roll." And they all wept, unashamedly, when The Dance became a funeral march in Memphis in 1979 following his tragic death.

That night in Vegas, I returned to my room at The Bali Hi. I'm not sure how much I slept. Let's face it, from being a waiter at the Steak & Ale in Houston to being at the Star Suite in Vegas with Elvis, all in a matter of twenty-four hours, was too amazing to believe.

The next day, The Imperials had another rehearsal and they taught me "The Jimmy Dean Show." Three days later, we flew to Phoenix for the four-day engagement at the Circle Star Theatre. At the hotel, the boys told me to meet them in Mr. Dean's room so we could all get acquainted and see when we could do a rehearsal.

A few minutes later, we all assembled in Jimmy Dean's hotel room, and after the boys and Jimmy got through hugging and shaking hands and laughing and cutting up, Joe Moscheo said, "Jimmy, this is Larry Gatlin. He's our new baritone singer."

Jimmy shook my hand. "Well, hello, Larry Gatlin. Where you from, kid?" (It seemed everyone called me "kid"—even Elvis. By now, I was used to it.)

"Odessa, Texas, Mr. Dean," I replied.

He laughed. "Odessa, Texas, is where the Greyhound bus stops and the dog gets off to take a leak."

We all laughed, and I said, "Well, Mr. Dean, Plainview, Texas, ain't exactly the cultural center of the universe either." (Jimmy's from Plainview.)

He laughed long and hard and said something like, "You're OK with me, kid," and we got on with the business at hand: the rehearsal.

The Circle Star Theatre was only a hundred yards from the back of the hotel so we all walked over together. At the theater, I met Buster Bonoff, the famous promoter.

The rehearsal with The Imperials and Jimmy Dean went well, and we all went back to the hotel for lunch and a nap before the show.

Opening night was more than I could have possibly imagined: Full house, great orchestra, wonderful theater in the round (I'd never done that before), and, of course, Jimmy Dean, The Imperials, and me—The Kid. It was a dream come true. The show was fabulous; I was in heaven. We all went to dinner at Lullabelles after the show, and nobody got to bed before 1 A.M. Imagine, my surprise when the phone rang at 7:45 that same morning.

"Kid, be in the lobby in fifteen minutes. We're gonna play golf."

"Who is this?" I asked groggily.

"It's Jimmy Dean, kid. Get up and get your butt to the lobby in fifteen minutes. We're gonna play golf."

"Yes, sir, Mr. Dean," I said. There was a short pause on the line.

"Call me, Jimmy, Larry, and welcome to our little gang."

I was showered, shaved, and in the lobby in under ten minutes, and we all went to play golf.

When we got back to the hotel, Buster Bonoff was there for a meeting with Jimmy. It seems that someone had called in a death threat on Jimmy. I don't remember all the details, but Jimmy and the rest of us decided we would do the show anyway. Guards were all over the building.

On stage that night we were all a bit nervous, but we proceeded as usual. Every night, there was a point in the show where Jimmy sang a little duet with each us, while standing on a large revolving stage. When he got to me that night, I whispered under my breath, "Keep it moving, cowboy. I don't want to die on my second night in the big time, and it's harder to hit a moving target."

Well, Jimmy and I started laughing and the audience did the same, but we got through the song and the performance without any harm coming to him.

Well, lo and behold, it *was* too good to be true. Joe Moscheo called me in my room on the last day of the Dean gig in Phoenix and said he wanted to talk to me. I knew this was a tryout, but I also knew the group sounded great with me as the baritone and that I added a little personality to the group. Evidently, I added too much personality. The Imperials were fairly conservative. They stood still and sang. I moved around and sang.

"Larry," Joe said over pancakes, "you've done a real good job, but we're just not sure you're the right guy."

Joe's words hit me hard. It was over. Back to Houston, law school, and the "Flying Nun" shirt and black knee britches. "Dear God, please tell me this is not happening," I said to myself over pancakes that now tasted like mud.

Joe patted me on the shoulder. "We have a couple more guys we've promised to audition. So go back to Houston, and we'll call you

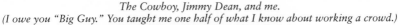

The Cowboy, Jimmy Dean, and me.
(I owe you "Big Guy." You taught me one half of what I know about working a crowd.)

71

after we've auditioned the other guys." In other words: "Don't call us, we'll call you."

"OK, Joe, that's good," I said, putting on a brave face. "I'll just pray for God's will, and if you need me, I'll be in Houston."

What I wanted to say was—"You stupid jerk. The Imperials sound great with me singing baritone, and I liven up this little group and no one can outsing me. So hire me now, and let's get back to Vegas and Elvis"—but I didn't.

I've had some long airplane flights in my time—Los Angeles to London to Paris; Nairobi to New York to Honolulu—but not one of them was as long and lonely and unbelievably sad as that Phoenix to Houston flight in January of 1971. I was crushed. I was afraid. I was humiliated. I had visions of those ugly black knee britches. And, worst of all, I was not an Imperial.

Many years later, my friend Jack Boland would tell me, "Larry, know this one thing for sure. Sooner or later God will get your undivided attention."

Well, although I didn't know Jack Boland then, and although I had not yet heard this gnomic saying about God getting my undivided attention, God now had it. I didn't eat much. I didn't sleep much. I didn't talk much (hard to believe, huh?). I didn't play golf much (and, if you know me, that is really hard to believe). I didn't go to law school much. I didn't do anything much—except pray.

The only thing I *really* ever wanted to be was a gospel singer. Oh, I'd thought about a baseball career like half the other boys in America, and I'd had dreams of trying big murder cases as the next Perry Mason or F. Lee Bailey. But in my heart of hearts, the one thing I really wanted to be was a gospel singer.

"God, I'll do anything," I prayed then. "Father, not my will but Thine be done." Then I prayed some more. "You said that I could ask for anything in Your name, Lord, and it would be accomplished. Well, Lord, I'm asking in Your name, please let me have this job with The Imperials."

Then I closed, "Nevertheless, not my will but Thine be done."

I moped around our little apartment, and I prayed. Mopin' and prayin', mopin' and prayin' for two weeks—that's all I did. Then the phone rang.

"Larry, it's Joe Moscheo." My heart started racing. It was really him.

"Hi, Joe."

Joe was always a man of few words, so he got right to the point. "Could you come back to Vegas and do 'The Jimmy Dean Show' for a month at the Landmark? We'll pay you $175 a week. We start on Thursday."

My heart was beating so fast I could feel it in my throat.

"Sure, Joe, I'll be there tomorrow."

I hung up the phone and starting screaming and jumping up and down. "I'm an Imperial," I shouted. "I'm an Imperial."

Right away, I called Janis at school and told her the good news. She didn't start screaming and jumping up and down (inappropriate behavior for a school teacher), but she was happy for me and for us. Our prayers were answered.

That January, I walked into the main showroom at The Landmark Hotel, feeling like a new man. Part of me still couldn't believe I was in Vegas again. I wanted to pinch myself; it all seemed like a dream.

As I walked through the showroom, I passed a group of people seated in the audience. Some of the orchestra members were already on stage. Dottie West was getting ready to start her rehearsal. I was not a big country music fan, so while I'd heard of Dottie, I did not know any of her songs or what she looked like.

I walked toward the group of people waiting offstage, and right away this beautiful, petite redhead with bright blue eyes and an illuminating smile walked up to me. "Hi, I'm Dottie," she said, shaking my hand.

"Hi, I'm Larry Gatlin. I sing with The Imperials."

Dottie quickly sized me up. "Well, you may be Larry Gatlin, but you look like Mickey Newbury. Doesn't he look like Mickey," she asked Jimmy Johnson, her bass player.

Jimmy nodded. "They could be twins."

Well, I didn't know who Mickey Newbury was either, but I would sure find out.

I liked Dottie at once. The rehearsal was great. She had a good band—Snuffy Miller on the drums, Jimmy Johnson on bass, Willie Rainsford on piano, and her husband, Bill West, on pedal steel guitar.

The gig at The Landmark was for a whole month—seven days a week, two shows each night at eight o'clock and midnight. Jimmy would open the show, and we'd sing backup for four or five songs before he'd do some comedy bits and a couple of solos. Then he would introduce Dottie and she would do her nearly thirty-minute show. After that, Jimmy would come back out and introduce us, The Imperials. We sang Bill Gaither's great song, "He Touched Me," and then Jimmy would close the show with "Big John." It was a great show. I learned a lot. I watched almost every night from the wings.

Years later in interviews, I would make the statement that I learned about songwriting from Dottie West, Kris Kristofferson, Willie Nelson, Mickey Newbury, Roger Miller, and Johnny Cash. Let me go on record, again, by saying that most of what I know about communicating with an audience, I learned from Jimmy Dean. He was my very first teacher. Actually, come to think of it, my old gospel buddies, James Blackwood and Jake Hess and Hovie Lister were my very first teachers. I learned from them too.

But this was different. This was not a gospel concert or a church service. This was Vegas. This was a nightclub where people had paid big bucks to be entertained, and the old cowboy, Jimmy Dean, was a master. Jimmy would be the first to admit that he was not the world's greatest singer (he was a good singer, but not a great one), but he was (and still is) a great entertainer. His instincts, his timing, his basic knowledge of people and of what would work and what would not were the best I've seen. He sang, he told jokes, he picked on people in the audience, he poked fun at the band and politicians, and he had a great time. He was as natural as natural could be and the people loved him. I never saw him do a bad show.

Three things happened during The Landmark gig that will forever be etched in memory and that ultimately changed the course of my life.

Elvis had something to do with the first. He had closed his month-long gig on Wednesday at the International Hotel, and we opened the next night at The Landmark. Elvis and his "group," the Memphis Mafia, had decided to stay in Vegas for a couple of days and just hang out.

The following week, on a Monday or Tuesday night, Elvis wanted to go to Los Angeles, so he and the Memphis Mafia jumped in cars and drove to the airport where Elvis's private plane was waiting. The pilot taxied out toward the runaway and was preparing to take off when Elvis suddenly said, "Hey, let's go see The Imperials and Jimmy Dean."

Someone relayed the message to the pilot, and the big jet came to a screeching halt. Elvis and the gang jumped into some black stretch limos that appeared out of nowhere and off they sped toward The Landmark, six miles away.

When Elvis and his entourage made their entrance in the middle of Jimmy's second or third song, it was pandemonium. Of course, Jimmy stopped the show and introduced The King, and people all around him started screaming and hollering and trying to get to him. He shouted, "Please, folks, I just came to see Jimmy Dean and The Imperials. It's his show and I'd love to just be a part of the audience." (I'm paraphrasing here, but that's close.)

The King had spoken and things settled down. Jimmy did another great show. Dottie sang great and The Imperials sang "He Touched Me" like it had never been sung before. I did the solo on the second verse: "Since I met this blessed Savior. / Since He cleansed and made me whole, / I will never cease to praise Him. / I'll shout it while eternity rolls." Then we changed keys, and Jim Murray came in with one of the all-time great tenor voices and sang, "He touched me, oh, He touched me. / And oh the joy that floods my soul. / Something happened and now I know. / He touched me and made me whole."

Ladies and gentlemen, boys and girls, the audience—led by Elvis and the Memphis Mafia—raised the roof. They stood up and applauded and screamed. If we hadn't been in a Vegas nightclub, you'd swear a Pentecostal revival had just broken out. Jimmy came back out on the stage to do "Big John." When he finished, Elvis and the Memphis Mafia and the audience raised the roof again.

Red and Sonny West hurried Elvis backstage. He had a cane and a huge black flashlight, and he looked like some kind of god—tanned faced, slicked-back jet-black hair, a black suit, and a cape of some kind. It was Elvis. The King of Rock 'n' Roll and Batman all rolled into one.

Elvis was very gracious and patient with all of us—his royal subjects—as the hotel photographer took pictures. As Elvis tried to leave, he looked at me and said, "You sing good, kid. Keep it up."

Well, I wouldn't say I heard thunder roll or saw lightning flash, but I was definitely elevated to a higher plane. Elvis *liked* my singing.

Elvis and his entourage went back to the airport, hopped on the plane, and flew to Los Angeles. That was the last time I saw him up close or talked to him in person.

Four years later in April of 1975, Elvis did a concert at Murphy Center at Middle Tennessee State University in Murfreesboro, and Janis and I went. I had bought Elvis a beautiful turquoise bracelet, and Felton Jarvis, his producer and my great friend, delivered it to him backstage. Elvis had just recorded "Help Me" on his latest album.

That night at the show, he said, in that mumbling, rolling voice of his, "Larry Gatlin has written a great song called 'Help Me,' and we'd like to do it for Larry. He's here tonight. Stand up, Larry."

Janis and I were behind Elvis, about forty rows up it seemed, in the cheap seats, but I had my binoculars focused on him. "Stand up, Larry," he said. Yeah, right. There were only twenty thousand people in the place, many of whom had not sat down for two hours. So Larry didn't get much of a chance to be spotlighted in this crowd.

As God is my witness, an eighteen-year-old kid, with long dirty lookin' shaggy hair, stood up in the front row and waved to Elvis, and The King had the spotlight put on him.

"Ladies and gentlemen, Larry Gatlin." Then he added, "Great song, Larry, and thanks for this beautiful bracelet," which he showed the crowd.

Well, shaggy head took my bow and waved to the crowd, and then Elvis Presley sang a beautiful version of my song "Help Me" to twenty thousand adoring fans in Murphy Center. That was the last time I ever saw him.

The people loved it, I loved it, the shaggy-headed kid loved it, and, most important to me, Elvis sang it like he loved it. In a whisper I remember saying to myself, "You sing good, kid; keep it up." No thunder, no lightning—but once again I was elevated to a higher plane by this magical, mystical figure, Elvis Presley.

The second big event in Vegas started out at a blackjack table. I was sitting at "center field" playing "24" when Jimmy Dean came up to the table and sat down at third base. He asked, as I recall, for a $10,000 marker, and the pit boss, Walter Rabital, promptly got it for him. Jimmy signed it, and the dealer gave him the chips. We played for a while, and Jimmy had a couple of scotches. We played a little more. Before I knew what was happening, my friend Jimmy Dean had lost ten thousand bucks.

Jimmy was not drunk but he was feeling frisky, and he wanted to keep playing. "Walter?" he hollered. "Somebody go get Walter Rabital." He just kept hollering, "Get me Walter Rabital."

Walter Rabital, it turns out, had gone home, and the new pit boss would not give Jimmy any more money.

"Call him at home," Jimmy hollered. "I want some more money."

"Mr. Dean," I said, "why don't we call it a night. You've lost $10,000. Let's get 'em tomorrow."

Jimmy looked at me and said, "I'll lose another $10,000 if I want to, kid, because I've got it to lose."

Then I said, "Well, sir, you're gonna have to whoop my butt right here and now, because I ain't gonna let you lose any more money."

There was dead silence at the table.

"You got balls, Gatlin," he said. "Let's go home."

He put his arm around my shoulder, and we walked out of the casino, out the back door, and to his suite. He fumbled in his pocket and got the key. I unlocked the door and we went inside.

He said, "I gotta pee, kid."

He sort of leaned up against the wall of the bathroom and did his business. Right in the middle of his urinary moment, Jimmy said, "Gatlin, you know you're not gonna get the job, don't you?"

Bam! Crash! Boom! The bomb had been dropped.

"But Jimmy, I already have the job. Joe and I have talked about my salary and moving to Nashville and everything."

"Well," he said, "I don't care what you've talked about, you ain't gonna get the job." I was stunned.

"Why not, Jimmy? We sound great together."

"You stand funny. You move funny. You're not a real quartet guy. They know that you're gonna be a star, and they don't want to have to go through the trouble of hiring another guy in a couple of years when you go out on your own. Besides, they have a guy they like better, and he'll do it their way."

I couldn't talk. There was a Texas-sized lump in my throat. So I didn't say anything.

I turned to leave. "Hey, Larry."

"Yes, sir," I said as I turned back toward him.

"They're right, you know."

"What?" I asked.

"You don't fit in. You sound great, but you don't fit in. They're right about something else."

"What's that, sir?"

"You *are* gonna to be a star," he said. "Now get outta here. I'm goin' to sleep."

"Yes, sir," I said. "Call me if you need me."

That was it. I closed the door and walked out of the hotel and back down the street to The Bali Hi. I'm not sure, but I think I cried. If I didn't I should have. My world had suddenly become a terribly confusing place.

The third thing that happened in Vegas of great importance happened in Dottie's dressing room. She was getting her hair done for the show when I knocked on her door.

"Come in," she hollered from the back room.

"Dottie, it's L. G.," I said as I walked in. "May I borrow your guitar for a few minutes, please?"

"Why sure, Larry," she hollered. "Help yourself."

I sat down on the couch and picked up the Ovation guitar that Glen Campbell had given Dottie as a present for appearing on his television show a few weeks before, and I started playing and singing the lyrics to a song I had in my head.

"Why, tell me why, did I treat her like I did. / Like the boy who robbed the cookie jar, I ran away and hid. / I don't know why; it's just me." (Not exactly "I've Done Enough Dyin' Today" or "All the Gold in California.")

Dottie heard me and looked up. "You're making that up, aren't you?" came the question from the back room.

"Yes, ma'am," I said. "I am."

"Well, it's good," she said as her hairdresser finished putting her hair in ringlets. "You need to finish it. You look so much like Mickey Newbury, you've got to be able to write songs."

Thank God for my resemblance to Mickey Newbury or I might never have caught Dottie's attention.

By this time, the Landmark gig was almost over. I think we had three or four days to go—by now it was near the end of February. Greg Gordon, the guy The Imperials had wanted from the git go, had dutifully flunked his draft physical, which meant he didn't have to go to Vietnam, which meant he could go to Topeka and Tuscaloosa—wherever—with The Imperials. No one from the group ever told me that I was not going to get the job. I guess Jimmy might have told Joe that he had let me know a couple of nights earlier. So everybody assumed that since I already knew what the deal was, there was no use discussing it.

The appearance of Greg Gordon in Vegas pretty much removed any remaining doubt in my mind. It was a very awkward three or four days. Dottie, sweet Dottie, came to my rescue that night in her dressing room.

"Larry," she said, "I've got a publishing company in Nashville, and I'm always looking for songwriters. I think you are one. Go home and write some songs and send them to me. I'll try to help you if I can."

Although I was dying inside that I was no longer an Imperial, God allowed this very sweet lady to cross my path at the exactly the right moment. (God has a way of doin' things like that.) There was a much bigger plan for me than singing baritone for The Imperials. A whole world was out there waiting for Larry Gatlin songs and Larry Gatlin records and Gatlin Brothers concerts and albums and TV shows.

That night in 1971 in Dottie's dressing room at The Landmark in Vegas, I could not have imagined all of those things because my heart was broken. But God's heart was not broken. His heart was inclined toward me, and He knew what great things were in store. He used Dorothy Marie Marsh West to bring them about. I'll always be grateful for her kindness and compassion in that dressing room. It was the start of great things to come.

When the gig was over, I said good-bye to everyone and loaded my suitcase onto Dottie's bus. Bill West, Dottie's husband, had offered me a ride as far as Oklahoma City. I was broke and the bus ride saved me some money. I flew from Oklahoma City to Houston, and Janis picked me up.

I wrote eight songs in the next week or so, and one day Janis borrowed her school's small Wollensak reel-to-reel tape recorder and I recorded them. I immediately sent them to the address Dottie had given me, and Janis and I both prayed and waited. We waited and prayed and prayed and waited some more, then one day we got a phone call, one that would lead us to the Promised Land—Nashville, Tennessee.

CHAPTER 8

Big hair! Larry Wayne and Go Go Dottie

$\mathscr{A}$T THE RIGHT PLACE, AT THE RIGHT TIME

Over the next twenty years or so, I would hear the five words—"Hello, Larry, this is Dottie"—hundreds of times, but they would never sound as sweet as they did one night in May of 1971. I had not heard anything from Dottie West about the songs I had sent and had pretty much given up hope of a songwriting career in Nashville, so I was surprised to hear her voice.

"When can you come to Nashville, Larry," she said, "so we can talk about your songs and your career?" My heart leaped for joy.

"I'll come over whenever you want me to."

"How about tomorrow," she said. It was just like her. No time like the present. Let's do it now.

"OK, Dottie, I'll be there."

"Don't you worry about a thing, Larry. I'll have a prepaid ticket for you at the airport tomorrow, and we'll put you up in Nashville."

Dottie's husband, Bill, picked me up at the airport the next day and took me to their house on Shy's Hill Road. I stayed with them for a week and went on the road with them a couple of times, and we sang and wrote songs. Dottie convinced me I had a great future as a singer and songwriter, and she promised she would help me.

Dottie wanted me to move to Nashville permanently and said she'd pay me $100 a week as a staff writer for her company, First Generation Music. After a few days, I flew home to Houston to talk this deal over with Janis.

"Honey, what do you think?"

"Larry, I can teach school and you can wait tables, if you have to," she said. "We can make it. You are never going to be happy if you don't try this."

I quit law school and broke the news to my family. I promised Steve and Rudy and La Donna right then that once I made it in Nashville, I would find a way to bring them there so we could establish ourselves as a singing group again.

We said our good-byes, loaded up the car, hitched it to the back of the Ryder rental truck, and were off to Nashville.

The next day Janis and I pulled up to Dottie's house with our car in tow; she was still asleep at 6:00 P.M. Dottie was a night person; I was soon to become one too. As I look back on my twenty-one years in Nashville, it is a wonderful blur, for the most part. The blur began that night.

Dottie West welcomed us to Nashville and before we even unpacked she said, "Larry, you've got to meet Mickey. I'll call Hank and Jeannie and we'll drive over to Hank's boat."

By Mickey, Hank, and Jeannie, she meant Mickey Newbury, Hank Cochran, and Jeannie Seely. It all sounded great—almost too good to be true. I mean, I hadn't even been in town five minutes, and already Dottie wanted to introduce me to these people.

At this point Janis and I were tired—more like, exhausted. We had just driven all day, but I was excited about meeting Mickey so I said, "That's great, Dottie," and I tagged along while Janis stayed at the house and went to sleep.

Dottie and I drove to Hank Cochran's boat somewhere out in Hendersonville, and we all took a boat ride across Old Hickory Lake to the dock where Mickey and Suzie Newbury lived on their houseboat. We started this little trip from Dottie's house about 8:30 that night, and we didn't get to the Newburys' houseboat until around 6:30 the next morning. Mickey and Suzie were asleep, so we waited. What time it happened to be never was really important to Dottie. She just did whatever she wanted to do, whenever she wanted to do it.

Well, I was really tired, so I took a short nap. Around 10:00 that morning this guy sort of ambled down the bank toward our boat. It was Mickey Newbury. He brought coffee, and we all sat and drank coffee and smoked cigarettes, and then he said, "I want you all to hear something I did last night."

Right then and there, Mickey sang "An American Trilogy" for the first time. I'll never forget it. What a voice. What style. What a great piece of Americana. Here I was, a wet-behind-the ears, naive, and terribly excited twenty-three-year-old kid sitting in Hank Cochran's boat listening to one of the greatest songwriters alive, and I had only been in Nashville for sixteen hours. Mickey had written "She Even Wrote Me Up to Say Goodbye" and "Just Dropped In (to See What Condition My Condition Was In)" and "Sweet Memories."

We passed the guitar around, and Hank Cochran, another one of the great Nashville songwriters, sang a couple of songs. He was a legend, with "Make the World Go Away" and "Little Bitty Tear" and "I Fall to Pieces" to his credit.

Then Dottie, who'd had her share of hits too—"Here Comes My Baby" and "Would You Hold It Against Me?"—Dottie handed me the guitar. I sang a couple of my new songs and everybody was nice and complimentary. Mickey and I liked each other from the start.

We were both Texas boys, and over the years he would become a good friend and a great influence on my writing.

That was the first "guitar pullin'" I had ever experienced. There would be many more.

I don't remember how or when we got back to Dottie's house, but as I said, the blur had begun.

Dottie West would be responsible for many more nights of music and "guitar pullin'." She loved good songs and songwriters, and they all flocked to her—Kris Kristofferson, Willie Nelson, Roger Miller, and Red Lane. I would soon become part of this crowd—the wildest and most talented bunch of songwriters I've ever seen—and I would meet them, all because of Dottie.

Janis and I stayed with Dottie for a few days while we looked for an apartment. We also stayed with my cousin Betty Johnson and her husband, Loren, two of the greatest friends we have, until we could get on our feet. They fed us and gave us a place to call home and helped us survive for the first two months until Janis accepted a teaching job and I started getting paid by Dottie's company.

One day Dottie called me and said, "Larry, I'm gonna be gone for two weeks and when I come back, you're the bass player. You can do it, so go to work."

Dottie was so convincing, I thought I could do it too. I was never so wrong in all of my life.

One cannot learn to play "Chopsticks" on the bass in two weeks, and besides, I didn't work at it. I thought, Gatlin, you've got a great ear, and you can just slide your fingers around and peck and scratch and no one will know the difference. Wrong again.

On the first two gigs I started to learn a little bit, especially on Dottie's songs, but the third stop of the tour told the tale. We were playing at a little beer joint somewhere in North Carolina, and someone requested Lynn Anderson's "I Never Promised You a Rose Garden" (it was a number-one hit on both the pop and country charts). Well, that song has more chords in it than the Hallelujah Chorus, and it sounded like I was playing with boxing gloves on. Dottie had to call Nashville and get another bass player. I appreciated Dottie's efforts. She was trying to get me some experience and pay me some more money.

Dottie took me around to meet more of her friends in the music business. One of them was Jerry Bradley, the legendary record producer. She had given him a copy of my original tape of songs—the one that brought me to Nashville in the first place—and had him listen to it. He liked what he heard and apparently raved about it.

Prior to all of this, I had told Dottie about my brothers, Steve and Rudy, and our sister, La Donna, and how we had this little singing group, and she got very excited. I told her that without a doubt, we sang the best harmony on earth. So Dottie immediately said, "Well, let's get 'em here and hear some of it."

Steve and Rudy and La Donna were all in school at the time, but the next thing I knew they were in Nashville, and we were auditioning for Chet Atkins and Jerry Bradley at RCA Records. The two men agreed to let us sing backup on Dottie's new album. A few days later we were in Studio A at RCA with the greatest studio musicians on earth—Grady Martin, Bob Moore, Billy Sanford, and Pete Drake—in our first recording session for a major record label.

It was awesome. And it was a really beautiful album. Dottie recorded two of my songs, "You're the Other Half of Me" and "Once You Were Mine." A few weeks later Dottie took me to talk to Chet Atkins about signing The Gatlins to a record deal. He said he would like to sign me as a solo artist. Not the group—just me.

I thanked Chet for his time and his honesty, and his interest in me as a solo artist, but told him that Steve, Rudy, La Donna, and I had planned a singing career together for so long, I thought we should keep trying. He said he understood and wished us success. Chet is a gentleman, through and through.

One night in October 1971, Steve, Rudy, and La Donna were in Nashville again. We gathered around a tape recorder at Dottie's house and recorded a song I had just written, "Rain."

I played guitar and Steve, Rudy, La Donna, and I sang the britches off of it. Snuffy Miller, Dottie's drummer, tapped the keys in his pocket to keep rhythm, and we created a magic sound on that little home tape recorder that evening.

A few nights later, Kris Kristofferson came over to see Dottie. Dottie played the tape for him, and he loved it.

A few days after that, Dottie called me and said, "Kris is cutting at Monument. Let's go see him."

I raced over to Dottie's house, and we dashed back to the Monument Recording Studio. When we walked in Kris was recording a song called "The Valley of the Never Do No Good" (I think it is a Red Lane song, I'm not sure), but he immediately stopped the session when he spotted us. I couldn't believe it. He had seven studio musicians being paid to cut a record, and he just stopped the session!

Well, when Kris saw Dottie through the big glass window of the recording studio, he said in that growly, scratchy, lovable voice of his, "Hey, Dottie, you got that tape of those kids from Texas? I want Fred to hear it."

"No, it's at home, but Larry is here with me. He'll go get it."

I raced to Dottie's and back. When I returned Kris introduced me

*Grand Ole Gospel Show. Me and Kris doing "Help Me" and "Why Me."
The first time "Why Me" was ever sung publicly.*

to Fred Foster, his producer and the president and founder of Monument Records.

The room suddenly became very quiet as the studio engineer cued up the tape and played it. I sat in silence as Fred, Kris, Dottie, and a bunch of studio musicians and technicians stared into space and listened. I wasn't sure whether they liked it or not until the song was over. Kris wiped a tear from his eye, and every one of the musicians sat and marveled at the sound we had put on that tape.

Finally Fred Foster looked at me and said, "Son, you come see me Monday, and we'll get in the record business together."

I went to see Fred on Monday and signed my first recording contract, and we got in the record business together, just like he said. Dottie and Kris and Fred—what a trio. I owe them more than I can say. And that, folks, is how I and the rest of the Gatlins got started in the record business—and country music.

•   •   •

As I said earlier, when I was a boy, I was not a country music fan. I was a gospel music fan. I loved Roy Orbison and The Beatles and '50s rock 'n' roll, but country was not my bag. I'd heard of the Grand Ole Opry in Nashville, but had not listened to it on the radio and didn't know of its great performers and great traditions.

My perception of country music and the Opry changed dramatically the first time I walked into the old Ryman Auditorium in July of 1971. Dottie was doing the 9:30 spot on the Opry that night, and what I saw amazed me—a stage smaller than the one in my high school in Odessa and hundreds (seemed like thousands) of people milling around backstage, most of them doing absolutely nothing. It was hot—dear Lord, it was hot. And then Roy Acuff introduced Porter Wagoner, and a tall, handsome man in a pink suit, embroidered with wagon wheels and cacti, strode onto the tiny stage to the roar of two thousand people, and the magic started.

All these people who had been doing absolutely nothing started doing absolutely something—playing guitar, fiddles, a single snare drum (all they would allow on the Opry in 1971), a bass, a steel guitar, a dobro—and backup singers started singing. It was amazing. It was if Cecil B. DeMille had said, "OK, ladies and gentlemen, all ten thousand of you will stop milling around, doing absolutely nothing, and when I say 'action' you will, in orderly fashion, follow Mr. Heston, a.k.a. Moses, through the parted Red Sea to the other side."

Cecil B. DeMille was Opry producer Grant Turner, and the cast of thousands was the greatest band of musicians on earth—the Opry band, and Porter's band, the Wagonmasters (including George McCormick on guitar, Mack Magaha on fiddle, and Buck Trent on banjo). The Red Sea was the stage of the Grand Ole Opry, all coming together exactly at the right time, in tune, in perfect tempo. The chaos turned into perfection.

Moses, a.k.a. Porter Wagoner, sang "Wreck on the Highway" or "Mountain Dew" or something—and the place went bonkers. Cameras flashed, people screamed, babies cried, and everyone had a great time. I was now a fan of the Grand Ole Opry—it was, and is, an amazing spectacle.

Porter introduced Dottie, the bands changed places as quickly and effortlessly as football teams alternate the punting team for the defensive team, and they were off again. Different song, different band, different star—same spectacle. Amazing.

Dottie was great. What a terrific country singer she was. A little later that summer, the Gatlins got to sing with her on the Opry for the first time. The stage of the Grand Ole Opry—the names read like a "Who's Who of Country Music"—Chet Atkins, Patsy Cline, Flatt and Scruggs, Don Gibson, Jack Greene, Grandpa Jones, Minnie Pearl, Jim Reeves, Marty Robbins, Jeannie Seely, Hank Snow, The Statler Brothers, Ernest Tubb, Porter Wagoner, Kitty Wells, Tammy Wynette, and, of course, Bill Monroe, Roy Rogers, and Hank Williams. And now the Gatlin family with Dottie West. (The only bad thing was that we had bought some 100 percent wool pants with matching vests to wear on the Opry. They were very hot and unbelievably ugly. We looked like a cross between the Mamas and the Papas and polar bears. Really, really hot. Really, really ugly.)

Six short years later, in January of 1977, my wonderful friend Hal Durham, the boss at the Opry, asked us to become members of the

Grand Ole Opry. I said, "Wow, you betcha," and we were officially accepted into the Opry family as its sixty-first members.

• • •

On a cold, snowy January day in 1972, Steve and Rudy and La Donna and I went into the Monument Recording Studio and started recording songs. Fred was our producer. Our first single, as "The Gatlins," was "New York City," released in September of that year, followed by "My Mind's Gone to Memphis," "Try to Win a Friend," and "Come On In" the following year.

We were neither fish nor fowl. We were gospel-country pop-something, and while we sang great, we just didn't click on radio.

I sang some songs for Conway Twitty about this time, and I'll never forget his reaction. He said, "I can't tell if they are good songs or if you just sing 'em real good, kid." (Even Conway called me "kid.") He never did record any of them, so evidently he didn't think they were very good.

Don't get me wrong, there were a few really good songs, but The Gatlins' first recording effort at Monument didn't really hit the mother lode.

Fred Foster didn't think the group thing worked either. He told me he wanted to develop me as a solo artist. Perhaps we didn't have the right material, perhaps we were ahead of our time. Whatever the reason, Steve and Rudy and La Donna went back to Texas, much to my disappointment. They were all still in college—Steve was in his senior year at Texas Tech University; Rudy was in his junior year there, and La Donna, crowned Miss West Texas of 1972, was now a sophomore at Odessa College; they all wanted to finish their education. I stayed in Nashville and continued to learn and write and record songs for Fred.

I was very lucky because I never starved in Nashville. Some of my music had been recorded, which is more than most songwriters who have spent their lives there can say. I never had to go the route of knocking on doors or pleading for a chance to be heard. Fred Foster, fortunately, believed in me. So did Dottie and Kris and a whole lot of others.

About this time, Janis informed me that she was pregnant. Wow! I was so happy I cried. I was making $100 a week with Dottie, when something really bad and something really wonderful happened all at once. Thankfully both situations had happy endings.

The bad thing happened between me and Dottie. She and I had a terrible argument one day. I had told Jimmy Moore, a wonderfully goofy photographer in Nashville, that Dottie was really sweet and that she had been very good to me, but one of the reasons she brought me to Nashville "was to make money from my songs." I said it innocently, and I would say it today.

Dottie brought me to Nashville for three reasons: she liked me; she knew I had talent; and she wanted to make money from publishing my songs. What's wrong with that?

Well, by the time the story got back to her, I had said that the *only* reason she brought me to Nashville was to make money.

Third-hand information is usually bad information. The information Dottie got was *really* bad. She was furious. She screamed at me for an hour. I had never seen her that upset.

"You know what you've done, you ungrateful little___?"

She ranted and raved about how ungrateful I was, while I tried my best to defend myself.

"Dottie, you've got to believe me. That is not what I said."

It was no use. She would not listen. She stopped paying me the $100 per week and basically told me to get lost. So there I was with no job, a pregnant wife, and $11 in the bank. Welcome to the big time, kid.

For six months Dottie wouldn't talk to me, and with Janis pregnant and knowing we could not possibly make it on her salary alone, I accepted some part-time work. I worked as a janitor by day at WLAC-TV in Nashville (Jim and Shirley Bridges, wonderful friends of ours and across-the-hall neighbors, helped me get the job) and as a light man at night for Jack Greene and Jeannie Seely at Roger Miller's King of the Road Hotel. When I wasn't sweeping floors during the day, I wrote songs; then at night I would handle the lights for Jack and Jeannie.

In defense of Dottie, I must say this. She was going through some awful physical, financial, and marital trouble during this time, and I'm sure this played a big part in her blowup at me. She had some serious surgery, and while she was recovering, I went to see her and we made up. I assured her that the way she was told the story was not the way I had said it.

"Dottie," I pleaded, "let's not continue to be enemies. This is ridiculous."

We hugged and smiled at each other, but things were not great.

While working the lights at the King of the Road Hotel I met a guy who changed my way of looking at the world forever and influenced my songwriting like no one else. He was the wildest, wackiest, most creative guy I have ever known—Roger Miller.

Working the lights consisted of bringin' 'em up and bringin' 'em down. There was not really a lighting console at the hotel, and if there had been one, I wouldn't have known how to operate it.

Jack and Jeannie had taken me under their wing. They were doing a two-week gig at the hotel, and one night, in the middle of their show, Jack said, "Folks, our light man Larry Gatlin is the best young singer/songwriter in Nashville, and we want you to hear him. Give him a nice hand . . . Larry Gatlin."

I got up from the lighting console, such as it was, sat down on a stool on stage, and sang one of my new songs, "Everything I Know About Cheatin'." Well, the place went crazy. The late great Faron Young was sitting in the audience, and after I finished he stood up and said, "Young fellow, sing that song again. I want to hear it again."

"Mr. Young," I stammered, "I can't sing the song again. I'm just the light man."

After the laughter died down, a voice from the dark spoke these words: "I own this joint, and I want to hear it again." Enter Roger Miller.

"Sir?" I questioned. A man leaned forward in his chair into the "bleed" from the stage lights and said a bit louder, "I said I own this joint, and I want to hear it again."

I didn't argue. I sang it again, and that night after the show I met Roger Miller for the first time. We liked each other at once, and for the next fifteen years or so he would be my friend, my hero, and my teacher.

• • •

My job at the television station lasted only three months; I knew from the start it was temporary. One Friday afternoon the station manager called me into his office and fired me.

Getting fired was not much fun, but some good stuff was just around the corner. Fred Foster told me I should go see Bob Beckham, his partner at Combine Music, to try to work out a better publishing deal for Dottie and me. She didn't have anyone to work the catalog, and since she was on the road so much of the time, the songs I was writing were just lying on her desk at home. Worse, there was nobody to pitch songs, produce demos, or register the copyrights.

I talked to Bob, and he put together a very fair deal for Dottie and me. Dottie liked the offer so we signed an agreement with Combine, and it proved to be an extremely profitable venture over the years for all of us.

For the next fifteen years Bob Beckham would be my publisher. In all that time, it never occurred to me to do an audit of him. He is the most totally honest man in the music publishing business, and he is a dear, sweet friend. He's nuts, but he's a good man and a great publisher.

Around this time I wrote "Help Me." It was because of this song that another wonderful thing happened in my life—another turning point.

Every Sunday, Janis and I worshiped at the Evangel Temple in Nashville. One Sunday, the church's pastor, Reverend Jimmy Snow, asked me to sing "Help Me" in church. June Carter Cash was there that morning, and she wrote my name down on the back of a blank check and started bugging Johnny about me.

She told Johnny, "You've got to hear this boy sing."

A few weeks later I sang in church again. This time the "Man in Black" himself was with June. Johnny came up to me after the service and said, "What are you doin' tomorrow, Son?"

"Nothing," I said nervously. "I got fired Friday."

Backstage at the Palace with John and June and Janis.
John played Wiley Post that night to my Will Rogers.

Johnny smiled. "We're makin' a movie. We're going to screen it tomorrow and write the music for it. You want to write some music for the movie?"

I gulped hard. "Yes, sir, Mr. Cash, I'll be there."

The movie Johnny wanted me to help score was "The Gospel Road," a musical journey through the Holy Land, following the story of Jesus Christ from His birth to death and His resurrection.

I showed up the next day at Johnny's House of Cash Studios, and over the next two weeks we recorded the soundtrack for the movie. Johnny invited a bunch of pickers, songwriters, and all sorts of musicians to watch the movie on a blank wall, in order to get some musical ideas. He used some of the finest songwriters in the country—Kris Kristofferson, Joe South, Harold and Don Reid, and me.

Johnny asked Kris to write a song for the Last Supper scene, and he wrote, "Jesus Was a Capricorn." I wrote "The Last Supper," which Johnny sang for the soundtrack. Kris later recorded "Capricorn" as the title song for his new album.

If it wasn't for June writing my name down on that blank check and Johnny giving me that job and many others, Janis and I probably would have starved to death. Instead, Johnny paid me union scale, four sessions a day for two weeks, and I made $1,100. I couldn't play the guitar very well, but he paid me just for showing up.

Like Dottie and Kris and Fred, Johnny believed in me from the start. He showcased me as an up-and-coming artist in his show when he and June went on tour—a show that at times featured such well-known, established artists as The Carter Family, The Statler Brothers, Carl Perkins, and the Oak Ridge Boys—and on many of his network television specials. Johnny and June are two of the kindest and most generous people I have ever known. They are dear friends, and I will always be grateful to them for their support.

A couple of Sundays later, I would again be at the right place, at the right time. It was at the Evangel Temple.

Reverend Snow asked me to sing "Help Me" again. That morning Kris Kristofferson came to church with Connie Smith and was moved by my song. It was a powerful, sweet moment in that little church, and we were all uplifted by the moving of the Holy Spirit of Almighty God. I've seldom felt the anointing of God the way I felt it that morning. We all prayed and cried and rejoiced and were exceedingly blessed.

While riding in Connie's car on the way home from church that day, Kris wrote "Why Me." Connie told Reverend Snow about the song, and he asked if Kris would sing it the next Friday on "The Grand Ole Gospel Show," broadcast on WSM Radio.

Kris asked me to sing harmony, and on that fateful Friday night—on one of the most famous stages, in one of the most famous theaters, in a city famous the world over for music—Kris, Connie, and I sang "Help Me" and then gave the debut performance of a song that would become a gospel standard in a matter of a few months, "Why Me."

I will never forget that night. It was electric. There may have been a few dry eyes in the house, but not many.

A few weeks later, Kris, Rita Coolidge, Kris's girlfriend and soon-to-be-wife, and I recorded both songs for Kris's *Jesus Was a*

Capricorn album, released that year. We all knew that it was a magical recording session. Fred Foster, our producer, had picked many songs in years past to be singles—"Detroit City" by Billy Grammer, "Don't Touch Me" by Jeannie Seely (another great song written by Hank Cochran), and all of Roy Orbison's great songs on Monument. Fred was not really a musician or a singer, and he was not a hands-on producer. His immense talent is in putting the right musicians and singers together. And he knew good songs when he heard them.

Well, this time, he missed. He released three or four songs from Kris's album, and none of them did a darn thing. Then, something wonderful happened. My old friend Joe Casey, then a local promotion man for CBS Records in Atlanta, talked Jim Howell of WSB in Atlanta into playing an album cut of "Why Me" from Kris's new album. When Jim played it the switchboard at the station lit up like a Christmas tree.

An Atlanta record store owner later called Tex Davis, our zany, wonderful promotion man at Monument, and immediately ordered twenty thousand singles of "Why Me."

Tex screamed into the phone, "We ain't got twenty thousand singles of 'Why Me.' We ain't got one single of 'Why Me.' 'Why Me' ain't even a single."

"Well," the Atlanta record man said, "you better start pressin' and shippin' 'cause I've got hundreds of requests for it right now. It's a smash record, and you guys had better get on the ball."

Just over ninety days later, "Why Me" was number one on the *Billboard* country charts. It became Kris's first number-one country hit and was certified gold.

In July of 1973, after "Why Me" was a major hit, Kris called one morning to ask if I would perform with him and Rita at the upcoming convention of all of the CBS record executives and salespeople at the Fairmont Hotel in San Francisco. Fred Foster would tell me later that Kris had to fight the folks at Columbia to get me on the show. (Fred was listening to Kris's phone conversation with some bigwigs at CBS in his office.)

"Well, if Larry Gatlin doesn't go, I don't go."

Suffice it to say, I went to the convention in July of 1973. We sang a couple of songs together, then Kris had me do "Penny Annie" solo, and he and Rita sang harmony on "Sweet Becky Walker" (both from my upcoming album, *The Pilgrim*). When we did "Help Me" and "Why Me" the place exploded. Everyone clapped and stomped and whistled and threw roses at our feet.

Some people may scoff at the next statement, but it is true. The Holy Spirit of God fell again in that place, the Fairmont Hotel, on a bunch of half-drunk, half-stoned, wild and woolly record men and women, and they threw roses and they cried—Ron Alexenburg, Rick Blackburn, Fred Foster, Goddard Lieberson, and Bruce Lundvall. It was a moment for the history books—a room full of our wonderful Jewish brethren, crying like babies over a song about Jesus. Wow!

Kris cried. Rita cried. I cried. Music is still the great mover of my soul, and the Holy Spirit was then and is now, no respecter of persons. When hearts are in one accord, the Spirit will be there amongst them. That's what happened in 1973 at the Fairmont Hotel at the CBS convention in San Francisco. It can happen again.

Kris helped me more than I can say. I believed then and believe now that he has written more great songs than any other songwriter. I have not gone bonkers on you. I have heard Cole Porter, George Gershwin, Rogers and Hammerstein, and Hank Williams. But if you take a look at Kris's catalog of songs, you will see what I mean. "Bobby McGee," "For the Good Times," "Help Me Make It Through the Night," "Lovin' Her Was Easier," "One Day At a Time," "Why Me," "Nobody Wins," "Come Sundown," "Silver Tongued Devil," "Darby's Castle"—and the list goes on. Some of his greatest songs are stuck away on those old albums and were never hit singles. But they are great songs nonetheless.

After Kris married Rita, he moved to Los Angeles in pursuit of an acting career and we drifted apart, logistically, not personally. Rita kind of shielded him from all of us rowdies from the Nashville days, and I haven't seen him very much in the last few years. When we do get together, it's like old times. I love him and I know he loves me. We don't see eye-to-eye on everything, but the music in our hearts is always in tune.

When we learned that Janis was pregnant, we decided to name the baby after Kris. On November 14, 1972, our daughter, Kristin Kara Gatlin, was born in Nashville. She is the sweetest, zaniest, prettiest, most wonderful little girl in the world, and I love her very much.

Kristin is now doing some shows with me. She sings Rudy's part and sings it very well. She's prettier than Rudy and she's cheaper, and my heart just swells every time we sing together. It's great. (Keep up the good work, K. K. Maybe ole Dad will give you a raise. Just maybe.)

It was Johnny Cash who gave me the nickname "Pilgrim," which sort of stuck and later evolved into the title of my debut album for Monument Records, *The Pilgrim*. I wrote all the songs, including my first small hits: "Sweet Becky Walker" (featuring backup vocals by Kris and Rita), "Bitter They Are, Harder They Fall," and "Penny Annie." None of them were Top 10 hits (more like Top 40 and Top 50 hits), but they helped get my record career started.

I remember being so excited about doing the album that I probably wrote a hundred songs before I felt I had ten strong enough to

Kristin Kara Gatlin with her namesake Kris Kristofferson

be included. Perhaps that was a bit much, even for my first album, but I followed the good advice once given to me by my old friend Red Lane: "The difference between a bricklayer and a brick mason is like the difference between a songwriter and a song craftsman. A song craftsman is like a brick mason because every word has a place. A bricklayer builds a wall; a brick mason builds a building. A songwriter writes a song; a song craftsman creates a masterpiece."

I began playing at small nightclubs and lounges all over the country. For some of these bookings, I reunited with Steve and Rudy and La Donna. I still wanted the group thing to work for us. But most of the time I performed solo, on a single bar stool with only my guitar—no backup singers, no band, just me.

• • •

I learned more about how to write a song from Roger Miller than anyone else. I wasn't as smart as Kris (I'm still not). I couldn't write like him. I tried, but it didn't work. I wasn't a legend like Johnny Cash. I couldn't write like him either. I wasn't as moody or deep as Mickey Newbury. I couldn't write like Mickey. I tried, but it didn't work. I didn't say things like Willie. I tried but it didn't come out right. But I was clever like Roger and quick and my head was on my shoulders, just a little bit sideways. I was weird like Roger. We thought alike. We talked alike, and I think we wrote songs alike. Not exactly, mind you. (I didn't write "You Can't Rollerskate in a Buffalo Herd," but I did write "Ode to the Road.")

It was Roger who taught me to look at the world a little bit sideways. We spent many hours together passing a guitar back and forth, singing new songs. He was truly one of a kind. I miss him every day.

I want to close this chapter by telling you about three nights with Roger Miller. The single funniest thing I've ever experienced occurred a couple of blocks from the Beverly Hills Hotel at 3:00 in the morning. Roger and I were taking one of Johnny Rivers's backup singers home. We were in Roger's rented, yellow Volkswagen. Leah, Roger's wife, had kicked him out of the house and would not let him have either of the Bentleys. So he had rented a yellow VW.

We had been at The Troubadour to see Johnny Rivers and Chy

Me, Lee Greenwood, Kris Kristofferson, Roger Miller, and Harlan Howard

Coultrane perform. After the show, a girl went into a seizure and decided that she was demon possessed. (She'd seen the movie *The Exorcist* that evening.) Tommy Smothers, who was with us, got a glass of water from the kitchen and immediately started sprinkling "holy water" on the girl, trying to exorcise the demon out of her.

We were all higher than kites. We'd been smoking dope in Rivers's dressing room, and it all seemed very funny. The girl was obviously not demon possessed; she was trying to get Johnny Rivers's attention. And it worked. I know this all may sound irreverent and even sacrilegious; I do not mean for it to be. But it was so hokey and she was so stoned and we were so stoned, and with Tommy Smothers as the exorcist with the "holy water" . . . well, I guess you had to be there.

Suddenly, I heard police sirens out front, so I grabbed Roger by the arm and pulled him out the back door.

"Roger, we don't need to be here, ol' pal. Let's move."

We did. We went up to Rivers's house somewhere on Mulholland Drive for a little while but got bored pretty quick. We wanted to sing some songs and do some drugs; Rivers wanted to listen to Paul Simon records. So Roger and I got in the VW and took off for his house. (No offense intended to Johnny Rivers or Paul Simon, but Roger and I had things to do and crossing the "Bridge Over Troubled Water" for the millionth time was not of them. Boy, I wish I had written that song. Paul Simon is a song craftsman, and Johnny Rivers is a great performer.)

On the way out, one of Rivers's backup singers asked for a ride and we obliged. We started toward Coldwater Canyon, and about two blocks past the Beverly Hills Hotel at 3:00 in the morning, a coyote walked out in front of the car and stopped in the middle of Sunset Boulevard.

Roger stopped the car, put it in park, and looked at me. "That's great dope, ain't it?"

"Yes, it is," I said, "but that's really a coyote."

"No, it ain't; it's a dog."

"Roger ol' friend, I'm from Odessa, Texas, and I know a coyote when I see one."

"Well, I guess we'd better report it."

"Who's gonna believe us?"

Roger smiled. "Let's run over it and take it in."

"We do not need to be in the L.A. police station at three o'clock in the morning in our condition, with a run-over coyote."

"Good call," Roger said as he put the car back in gear and slowly drove toward Wile E. Coyote. The animal ambled off toward the Beverly Hills Hotel. (Maybe he was going to the Polo Lounge. There are wolves and coyotes there all the time—foxes too.)

Roger went into his "CBS News" mode: "Gatlin, Miller found molesting coyote. Animal husbandry charged."

It may not be funny to someone who is in his or her right mind, but to a couple of old boys who were loaded to the gills on really strong marijuana, it was a belly laugh.

We proceeded to Coldwater Canyon to take the lady home. About a block before we got to her house, we saw a German shepherd lying on its paws in a front yard. Roger steered the little yellow VW bug over toward the dog, rolled the window down and said, "Hey, you want to kiss a coyote?"

That's not exactly what he said, but on with the story.

I laughed until I was holding my face to keep from laughing. Johnny Carson is fast, no doubt about it, and he's funny, no doubt about it. But Roger Miller was the fastest, funniest man I've ever been around.

When I finally stopped laughing and we got to the lady's house, we told her good night and drove toward Roger's. Then, all of a sudden, I said, "I'm hungry.

"Well, if we had some ham, we'd have some ham and eggs—if we had some eggs," Roger said. And I started belly laughing all over again.

At the time, Roger was living in the old guest house of the Barrymore mansion. I fell asleep sometime that morning on the couch downstairs in the living room.

On another occasion, Roger said simply, "You wanna go over to Streisand's house?" He said it kinda like, "You wanna run down to Wendy's for a burger?" I nearly tore the door off getting into the car.

Jon Peters, her feller . . . boyfriend . . . whatever, opened the door when we rang the bell, and when Roger introduced me, Jon said, "Oh, Larry, what a coincidence. Barbra is in the living room trying to figure out the chords to one of your songs. She really likes it. Go on in there and help her, and Roger and I will bring some drinks. Glen's in the kitchen. We're talking about some stuff. We'll be right there."

I mumbled something and walked off toward Barbra Streisand's living room.

"Miss Streisand," I said to the lady sitting on the floor, "I'm Larry Gatlin. Jon told me you like one of my songs."

"Yes, I do," she said softly and graciously. "I really do. I have the lyrics here in my notebook somewhere, and I was looking at it just a few minutes ago, trying to figure out the melody. "

With that she thumbed through the notebook until she came to the page she was looking for. "Here it is," she said. "Help me with the melody, will you, please?"

I said, "Sure." My heart sank as I looked down at the page.

"Well, Miss Streisand."

"Barbra," she said.

"Well, Barbra, this is not one of my songs. But a good friend of mine, Red Lane, wrote it, and I do know how it goes." I took the guitar that was lying there and started playing and singing, "I'll just keep on fallin' in love, 'til I get it right." I sang a few more lines and she interrupted.

"No, that's not the one. I like that one, too, but that's not the one I'm thinking about." She took the notebook and started another search.

"Is this one yours?" she asked.

"Yes, ma'am, that one's mine." I was ecstatic. Right there in her own handwriting, one of the greatest singers of all time had written down the words, to "Try to Win a Friend."

I sang it for her. When I stopped, she said, "Please send me a tape of that song. It's beautiful."

I said, "Thank you," and about that time Jon, Roger, and Glen Campbell came into the living room, and we all had a couple of drinks. Unfortunately, I don't remember much more about the evening. I do remember that Roger, Glen, and I sat in Glen's car in Barbra Streisand's driveway until the sun came up, drinking vodka and snorting cocaine.

I remember Roger saying something like, "Glen, you are doing too much of that stuff. You've got to get a grip on your coke habit."

On our way back to Roger's house later that morning (we were in his car now), he told me, "Gatlin, if I ever get as bad as Campbell is on that stuff, I'll quit."

Well, in the not-too-distant future, Roger and I were both in bad shape from our respective cocaine use.

I want to stop right here for a minute. I promised you at the beginning of this book that I would not trash anyone. So let me explain.

A couple of years ago, before Roger died, he got himself straightened up. He married Mary Arnold, and they adopted two beautiful kids, Taylor and Adam, a girl and a boy, and moved to Santa Fe, New Mexico. I was so proud of Roger. He was doing good, until the cancer came. If Roger Miller had not gotten his life together and shared his experiences publicly, I would not have brought all this stuff up.

Same thing for Glen Campbell. With the help of God and his wife, Kim, he pulled himself out of the pit and totally rededicated his life to God. I've told this story, not to drag anyone through the mud but to make a point: "There is always hope. With God there is always hope."

Glen and Roger and I were not bad guys needing to get good. We were sick guys needing to get well, and we all got well, at different times and different places, through love and faith and the mercy of God. The three prodigals came home, and the Father forgave us and healed us, and I rejoice and give God the glory.

Barbra recorded "Try to Win a Friend" for her fabulous *Superman* album in 1977. Her executive producer, Charles Koppleman, told my publisher, Bob Beckham, the song would be included in the album if we would split the publishing royalties with her.

Bob Beckham at Combine Publishing had a firm policy: he did not split publishing royalties with anyone. If you liked the song, record it, but the writer still gets the money. That was Beckham's deal and everyone in Nashville knew it. Others played the "publishing game" with producers and artists and record companies, but Beckham would not give in. (He still got a lot of songs recorded because he had a such a great catalog—Kris, Bob Morrison, Dennis Lindy, Larry Gatlin, and scads more I can't think of.) So Beckham called me.

"Gat, Streisand has cut 'Try to Win a Friend' and wants to put it on her new album, but she wants half the publishing. Now, Son, you know how I feel about splitting the publishing, but this is not a normal circumstance. If you want to do it, I will, even though I've never done it before."

"Bob," I said, "tell 'em I'll split the publishing with her if she'll split her next movie with me."

Boy, I wish I had that to do all over again. *Superman* sold millions worldwide, and not being on that album has cost me a small fortune in royalties. Hindsight being what it is, Barbra deserved half of the publishing. She is Barbra Streisand, a legend, and legends deserve special accommodations. Having a song of mine on her album would have been one of the highlights of my life. I messed up, and I'm certainly sorry. It's not just the money. It's really not. What I would give to hear her sing, "When it's over, really over. There ain't nothin' can start it over again."

I later asked Barbra about the song at the CBS party after the Grammy Awards in New York in 1981. She said, "Larry, I really didn't sing it the way I wanted to sing it."

Well, Barbra, Charles Koppleman, your friend and former executive producer, now owns the publishing on the song since he bought Combine a few years ago. So you and Charles can split the publishing. The only thing that remains is for you to sing it the way you really want to sing it.

I have been very lucky to have some great singers record and release my songs, and I'm grateful. Of all the singers who have not released one, the name Barbra Streisand tops my wish list.

CHAPTER 9

The 1976 BMI Awards Dinner
Me, Ed Cramer, Dottie West, Bob Beckham, Frances Preston

$\mathscr{T}$HE BREAKOUT YEAR

Every artist has what they call a breakout year. Ours was 1975. That year I wrote and The Gatlins recorded "Broken Lady," our first number-one hit.

Everything started to build from the moment I embarked on my first promotional tour for Monument Records in August 1974, starting with a barbecue send-off for the music promoters and local press at Exit/In in Nashville that also promoted my second album, *Rain-Rainbow.*

Ron Bledsoe, president of Columbia Records, climbed up on stage and introduced me as that "fantastic new artist, Larry Gatlin." Then the lights came down, and they showed a short film about me, including accolades from Johnny and Kris, to get people all pumped up. For an entire hour I sang songs from the album—"Delta Dirt," "Help Me," "Let's Turn the Lights On," "Rain," and "Those Also Love."

I sang at little bars and clubs and college coffeehouses across the country. "Delta Dirt" was getting good airplay (sales topped 20,000 units in the first month), and in a very short time, it climbed up the country charts and became my first Top 15 hit.

That October I was at the National Quartet Convention in Nashville and overheard someone say Terry Blackwood's father, Doyle, was very ill and not expected to live through the night. The Imperials needed someone to fill in for Terry so he could go home to Memphis. I called Terry in Vegas and said, "Go home, Terry. I'll be on the next plane to Vegas." I filled in for him with the Jimmy Dean Show for about a week at the Desert Inn.

When I joined The Imperials, Jimmy very graciously pointed out to the audience that I already had a very promising solo career. He even let me sing "Help Me" a few times in the show.

In 1975 we recorded our third album, *Larry Gatlin with Family and Friends*. The first single from the album, which was released in 1976, was "Broken Lady," and it became the fastest-selling single of our career to that point. In just fifteen weeks the song climbed to number one on the *Record World* country singles chart.

I had finished writing "Broken Lady" in the living room of my good friend Samuel Finley Ewing, while visiting with him and his family in 1975. Most people called him Finley but I always called him Sam. He was a real prize—an original—the patriarch of the real Ewing family—not the made-up Hollywood, TV bunch with J. R. and all those degenerate, immoral, dysfunctional weirdos.

Darrell Royal, my good friend and the football coach at the University of Texas, had introduced us in 1973 in Galveston at his golf tournament benefiting the Boys Club. When Darrell told Sam Finley Ewing that his "celebrity" would be Larry Gatlin, Sam said in his own inimitable style, "Darrell, you and I are supposed to be friends. I paid $1,000 to play with a star. I ain't never heard of Larry

Gatlin. I want to play with Willie [Nelson] or Charley [Pride] or Alan Shepard. Who the h— is Larry Gatlin?"

Darrell looked at his old friend and said, "Just play with him, Finley, and shut up. He's gonna be a star, and you'll like the kid."

We hit it off at once. I picked on Sam about his ugly pink golf shoes, and he picked on me about my long hair, muttonchop sideburns, and paisley golf pants. We just messed with each other for two days straight and for the next twenty years.

I have stayed at the Ewings' house when a hotel room would have pretty much busted me. They loaned me cars from Ewing Buick, on North Dallas Tollway, when a rental car would have *certainly* busted me, and they gave me their unconditional love.

Steve and Rudy and La Donna came to Nashville to do the recording sessions with me for the album, and "Broken Lady" was the product of one of them. We knew we had something special the minute we recorded the song. It was simply one of those moments when everything fits together and everybody knows it. We knew in the "run down," or the first take, that we were making a great record.

After taking off our headphones we all started complimenting each other and smiling and laughing, except for Grady Martin, our studio guitarist. (Grady played the guitar part on Marty Robbins's hit, "El Paso"—start to finish. No overdubs, just straight through.)

Grady, one of the greatest guitarists in Nashville studio history, said, "There's something missing. Let's do one more." Then he got up and said, "I'll be right back."

Grady looked at one of the technicians as he stood up to leave and said, "Put me a rhythm guitar mike over there behind that baffle."

He walked out of the studio, and we all looked at each other.

"What the h—," someone said. "If Grady says it's missing something—it's missing something."

Steve and Rudy and La Donna and I walked back into the studio and took our places—and waited—and waited—and waited. No Grady. Finally, after about five minutes, Grady walked into the studio, carrying a mandolin. I almost laughed out loud. I thought, *surely this is a joke*, but I didn't say anything. I'd seen Bill Monroe play mandolin with his Bluegrass Boys, and I loved it. But I was not a bluegrass singer, and The Gatlins was not a bluegrass group. Still, Grady Martin was Grady Martin, and out of respect for him and the hundreds of hits he had played on, I stifled my laugh and waited.

Grady sat down, adjusted the guitar mike, and strummed the mandolin a bit.

"Count it off," he said authoritatively, and Kenny Malone, the drummer, did just that.

"One, two, three. . . " Kenny cued us.

"She's a broken lady. . . ."

Well, we all started the song again, all of us except Grady Martin. We did the chorus part up front, in four-part harmony, then I took the solo on the verse and Grady came in under me with a little tremolo mandolin part. I remember to this day the hairs standing up on the back of my neck when I heard what he was playing.

When Grady got to the chorus part again and everybody started blending, the track came alive. Everybody was rocking. Tommy Cogbill, Bobby Emmons, Kenny Malone, Bobby Wood, Reggie Young. As Kenny Malone played the backbeat on the snare, Grady started playing a little contrapuntal rhythm pattern on that darn mandolin, and all heaven broke loose.

The instant the red light went off in the studio, we all started toward the control room to listen to the playback. The idea of another take was out of the question. Most of the time a producer will say something like, "Hey, that was really great. Let's do one right behind it." Not this time. This one was perfect. It was magic.

When it was over, we congratulated each other on the track and broke for dinner. To my knowledge, we did not overdub a single note on that track. It was just right the way it was.

I was in Fort Worth doing a gig at a beer joint called The Rhinestone Cowboy when "Broken Lady" reached number one on the *Record World* country charts. Tex Davis called me at the hotel and told me the good news. "Larry Wayne, we got a number-one record, you little devil."

With the success of "Broken Lady," Janis and Kristin (now almost three) and I moved into a modest three-bedroom house in nearby

Antioch, a suburb of Nashville. It was a nice home, and we needed the room: Janis was pregnant again.

Steve, Rudy, and La Donna were not living in Nashville then. In late 1974, I heard that "The First Lady of Country Music," my friend Tammy Wynette, was looking for a new backup group. I called her right away.

"Tammy," I said, "my two brothers and my sister can really sing. Would you let them audition for you?"

"Why, Larry," she said sweetly, "I'd love to hear them."

I called Steve, Rudy, and La Donna in Texas, and they were in Nashville, sitting in Tammy's kitchen, before sundown. She hired them on the spot. They went on the road (as a group called "Young Country") and worked with Tammy for about ten months, gaining some valuable experience and making a little money. (Tim Johnson, La Donna's husband, was also part of that group.)

When I realized I was going to make some money from "Broken Lady," I decided that it was time to put our group together. I went to the kids after they returned from an engagement with Tammy and said, "I think we ought to try this deal. I'll put up $20,000 to get us started, and we'll hit the road. Whaddya think?"

It was like a scene straight from one of those Andy Hardy movies, with Mickey Rooney and Judy Garland, where they decide at the last minute to put on a big show.

Steve, like Mickey, said, "I've got the truck."

Then Rudy, not quite Judy, piped in, "I've got an amp."

And I said, "Let's do it!"

We all agreed and The Gatlin Family Quartet was back together again!

Steve, Rudy, and La Donna told Tammy of their decision, and she was very supportive and wished us well. My old high school buddy, Clayton Bowles, owned a little nightclub in Memphis with his brother Dick. I called Clayton and asked if we could start our career at Solomon Alfred's, and he said, "Come on."

We loaded up our equipment in Steve's old white pickup truck, threw a canvas tarp over the back in case it rained, and off we went to Memphis.

Clayton paid us $1,000, and we did a week there with our new band—which included my cousin Brent Johnson on drums and B. James Lowery (formerly of the Oak Ridge Boys) on guitar. Everybody loved us. Steve learned to play bass in a week (he was a lot better at it than I was), but he didn't see the audience for the first six months because he still had to look at his fingers.

After Solomon Alfred's, we landed a good gig at the Fairmont Hotel in Atlanta. Nobody showed up but the money was good—$5,000 a week. We negotiated a deal with Shorty Lavender, The Statler Brothers' agent, to buy the group's old bus, and we hit the road.

A few years earlier Johnny Cash had recommended that I sign with Marty Klein of APA, one of the top agents in the business, to represent me. APA had sent D. J. McLachlan, from its Miami office, to watch me perform, back when I was still doing my usual bar stool and acoustical guitar routine. We met at the Lion's Share Submarine Shop in downtown Miami, and after the show, D. J. came up to me. "I've just seen the best new singer/songwriter in America, and together we are going to go to the very top of this business," he said.

Over the next eighteen years D. J. would become like a brother to us, and he was right—together we did go to the top. D. J. was the missing piece to the puzzle, and with people like him and Marty and other great agents at APA—Bruce Nichols, Burt Taylor, Fred Lawrence, Danny Robinson, and Bonnie Sugarman—we went from playing small clubs and coffeehouses to bigger name clubs and fancy Vegas lounges. We started doing more TV and the records started doing better. We were on our way.

●   ●   ●

I've got to tell you about a solo gig I did before my brothers and I got back together. In the early 1970s I played the small but prestigious Boarding House in San Francisco. Bruce Nichols had lined up the gig. Many great folksingers had performed there—Joan Baez, Bob Dylan, Joni Mitchell, Judy Collins.

My opening act was an up-and-coming comedian named Steve something—Steve Michaels? Steve Mitchell? Steve Martin? That's it, Steve Martin. He was funny—arrows-through-the-head, fish in his pants, magic tricks, and balloon animals. I had never seen anything like him. Neither had anyone else.

One night, in the middle of his act, he took the entire audience outside the club, hailed a cab, picked out three or four people, and rode with them around the block while doing a "command performance." Then he picked up three or four more and did the same thing, until he had performed for the fifty or sixty people in the audience. Finally he brought them all back into the Boarding House, got them seated, went back on stage, and closed his show with a hilarious bit. Well, when I took the stage and opened with "Penny Annie," my most poignant and moving song, I was greeted with stunned silence. These people were emotionally unequipped to go warp speed from arrows-through-the-head to "she shoots away the pain, but it comes again too soon."

I didn't exactly bomb, but I was less than spectacular. Herb Caen, San Francisco newspaper columnist, was kind and gentle in his review. (I think he just felt sorry for me having to follow Steve.) I think he said I had a nice voice and some good songs, but I should open for Steve next time. Well, a few years later that happened at Harrah's Tahoe and believe me—it worked a lot better when Larry Gatlin and the Gatlin Brothers went on *first*.

Steve Martin is an amazingly funny man. In 1976 Marty Klein, our mutual friend and agent, had booked Steve as a regular on the summer-replacement TV variety show *Johnny Cash and Friends*, which also featured June Carter Cash and comedian Jim Varney, and was produced by my friend Joe Cates. It was this show, I think, that catapulted Steve into stardom. Nobody had ever seen this kind of humor, and the audiences laughed at him until their faces hurt.

•   •   •

In a short time we became a successful recording group, and sales of our records picked up measurably. Our *Larry Gatlin with Family and Friends* album was moving up the charts, peaking at number 24 on *Billboard*'s Hot Country LPs Chart (our first album to crack the Top 30), and our career was gathering steam. But all was not well.

Steve and Rudy and I were already traveling down the wrong road. We were all drinking too much and drugs had become a part of our lives. La Donna and Tim figured out early on that they did not want to travel down the same road. They were with us only six or eight months when they decided to leave the group and return to Texas to raise a family and sing gospel music.

When La Donna told me the news, it broke my heart. All I had ever wanted to do was to sing with her and my brothers. I had turned down a solo deal with RCA and with Chet Atkins so I could stay with the group, and now she was breaking it up. I was furious and hurt. As I look back, though, I was selfish and wrong to be so upset. It was always I, I, I—what I wanted, what I planned, what I dreamed. I just assumed that Steve and Rudy and La Donna wanted what I did. Steve and Rudy did. La Donna did not.

As hard as I tried to talk her out of it, La Donna and Tim packed up and moved back to Texas. Once again, Steve and Rudy and I were a trio.

For the past few years, I had sung the lead, La Donna had sung the third above, Rudy had sung the fifth below, and Steve had either sung the bass part or doubled the tenor part or doubled the low part. It was a fabulous sound.

Well, *that* sound was to be no more, so Larry, Steve, and Rudy had a big powwow on my patio and came up with a plan. I would sing lead, Rudy would sing tenor, and Steve would sing baritone. We tried it on a few songs and it worked, so we took it into the studio. "Broken Lady" was already a number-one hit and we needed a new album and a new single or the momentum could be lost.

We found that "new sound" we were looking for with our first single as a trio, "Statues Without Hearts." We recorded it in the winter of 1976, during a break from touring, along with a number of other songs. The result was *High Time*, our fourth album for Monument and my first with Steve and Rudy.

Somewhere in all of this Janis had a baby boy, Joshua Cash Gatlin. I was in the delivery room with her this time, on May 30, 1976, as

Dr. George Andrews sang "Amazing Grace" and delivered my boy. I was estastic.

I went to the nearest phone and called Johnny Cash. "John, Joshua Cash Gatlin has just discovered America."

John hollered, "June, the Pilgrim says that Joshua Cash Gatlin has just discovered America. Ain't God good?"

The new sound worked. *High Time* went on to become our fastest-selling album to date, and "Statues Without Hearts" became our second number-one hit and was nominated for a Grammy Award—we lost. I was also nominated for best male vocalist but lost to my good friend Ronnie Milsap.

After that, we turned out one hit record after another—"I Don't Wanna Cry," "Love Is Just a Game," "I Just Wish You Were Someone I Love," and "Night Time Magic." Suddenly we were a hot commodity.

We made many wonderful friends in radio and television, in and outside of Nashville. We did Dinah Shore's show many times. When Dinah and the Gatlins and Lonnie Shore and Burt Reynolds all showed up at the same place, at the same time—things usually got out of hand. It was a riot. She was truly one of the sweetest people I've ever met.

We did *The Mike Douglas Show* several times, and it was always a lot of fun. Mike is a nice man, and I like him a lot.

We also had fun doing Merv Griffin's shows. He was always crazy and funny and goofy, and, man, what a band he had—Ray Brown, Herb Ellis, Jack Shelton, Mort Lindsey, and the rest.

One "Merv" show that especially sticks in my memory was a songwriters' special. Merv's guests were Judy Collins, Roger Miller, Alan and Marilyn Bergman.

Judy sang "Both Sides Now." Then Roger did "Husbands and Wives," and the Bergmans played "The Windmills of Your Mind" theme from the motion picture *The Thomas Crown Affair*.

Finally Merv said, "Well, Mr. Gatlin, it's your turn."

So I took my guitar and sat down on a stool and sang "I've Done Enough Dyin' Today." It stopped the show. Merv oohed and aahed, and the Bergmans were very complimentary. Roger just laughed, which meant he was proud of me, and Judy Collins recorded "Dyin'" about a year later. It was a wonderful day. (If someone said to me, "Kid, you've got three minutes, so hit us with your best shot," I think I would have to sing "Dyin'." Of all the songs I've written, it's still my favorite.) Thanks, Merv. You're a nice man too.

In Nashville, of course, there was good ole Ralph Emery. From the first day I came to town, Ralph was nice to me. As far as I'm concerned, he is one of the reasons country music is as big as it is today. He, along with producers Joe Cates, Gary Smith, and Dwight Hemion, put country music on television. Joe and Gary and Dwight are probably not names you recognize, but they are three of the most important producers of country music shows. (Joe did most of Johnny Cash's specials over the years, and Gary and Dwight produced many country music specials, including our own for ABC.)

I did Ralph's popular early-morning *Ralph Emery Show* on WSMV-TV, as well his radio show on WSM many times. Ralph believed in me and liked me, and we always laughed and giggled and cut up and had a good time. Some people didn't understand him or his personality, but I always thought he was a pussycat—a really nice man. I owe him a lot.

In July of 1976 I remember watching the Democratic Convention from a hotel room in Memphis. We were working at Solomon Alfred's when Governor Jimmy Carter received the party's nomination, and within a couple of months he was President Carter. A short time later, we were invited to entertain at the White House. Our friend Jim Free from Columbia, Tennessee, was President Carter's congressional liaison and a big Gatlin Brothers fan. So when the opportunity arose, he invited us.

I previously had met President and Mrs. Carter at the premiere of Johnny Cash's movie *The Gospel Road* in Atlanta in 1973. On that occasion, Governor Carter told me I was one of his favorite singers. In fact, he told me I was his third favorite after Johnny Cash and James Talley. I didn't know much about Mr. Talley and have not heard much about him in years, but the Cash fellow I know, and I figure I'm lucky to be in third place.

There was a big White House reception in the East Room. James

Talley sang. He was very good, and I enjoyed his music. After another young singer sang two original songs, he said his favorite song was "Penny Annie" and one of his favorite songwriters was Larry Gatlin. He then sang a beautiful rendition of my song. I sang next after him.

I didn't know the young man, but he had a wonderful voice. I lost track of him, didn't remember his name, and didn't think too much about it until one night in 1991 when I saw my buddy Gary Morris as Jean Valjean in *Les Miserables*.

I do not remember how it came up, but Gary asked, "Do you remember singing in the East Room for President Carter back in 1977?"

"Yes, I do."

"Do you remember a guy singing 'Penny Annie'?" he asked.

"Yes, I do. The guy was fabulous."

"That was me."

I was floored. I had known Gary Morris for six or eight years. I had done shows with him, played golf with him, and seen him at numerous award shows. It never dawned on me that he was the East Room mystery man. After we had a good laugh about this, I went out the stage door, back to the front entrance of the theater, took my seat, and watched the show.

Gary sang like a bird. What a voice. What a great singer and a good guy. A little misunderstood sometimes perhaps, and maybe at times a bit temperamental (takes one to know one). But a nice guy at heart and one of the greatest singers I've ever heard.

Back to President Jimmy Carter. During his reelection bid in 1980, Freebie (that's what we called Jim Free because every time he got us a gig it paid no money) called us. He was frantic. "You've got to come to Muscle Shoals for a big rally. The president needs you . . ." etc., etc.

We did our two shows at the Vermont State Fair in Montpelier, got in our little Aerostar (we had a plane by now), and flew to Muscle Shoals, Alabama. When we arrived about 2:00 in the morning, Rick Hall, the one and only Rick Hall—an absolute nut and a great guy and record producer—picked us up and took us to his house. We slept about four hours before he woke us up. His wife, Linda,

Vice President Walter Mondale, me, President Jimmy Carter, and Janis

had fixed us scrambled eggs, gravy and sausage, cat head biscuits (they're as big as a cat's head), and hot coffee. We ate quickly and then Rick, with an escort from some of Alabama's finest troopers, covered the twelve miles from the house to the city park in about five minutes. (If he'd picked us up in Montpelier with that trooper escort the night before, we could have been in Muscle Shoals at 11:30 instead of 2 A.M.)

President Carter gave his little stump speech, and then it was our turn to sing. Right in the middle of "All the Gold," an uninvited choir joined in. I'm sure they were uninvited. I don't remember asking anyone in white robes and hoods. I just do not remember asking for their help on "All the Gold," but they were there all the same. The Ku Klux Klan. The Knights of Whatever. The Kings of Hate. The KKK.

I had never seen the Klan up close, and I hope I never do again. It was frightening. I was stunned. Looking back I guess I was also ashamed. On occasion I have been less than kind to people of color, to people of different religions, to people from other countries, and I will confess here and now: I am ashamed of that.

I have never worn a white robe or a hood over my face or carried a burning cross, but am I any better than those who have if I harbor prejudice in my heart? Tomorrow morning? No, this morning I will pray for guidance, enlightenment, and wisdom. I will forgive all of those who have wronged me, and I will ask to be forgiven and guided into a loving frame of mind toward *all* people, regardless of race, creed, or color. After all, what color is God?

(President Carter lost the election, and six months later I was back in the White House with my brothers, singing in the East Room for President and Mrs. Reagan—only in America, folks. Only in America.)

PHOTO COURTESY OF SONY MUSIC

*Is this Peter Fonda, Tom Jones, and Rabbi Fishman
or Rudy, Larry, and Steve?*

ℐHE BATTLE OF COLUMBIA
AND THE OKIES OF CALIFORNIA

William Shakespeare once wrote, "There is a tide in the affairs of men, which, taken at the flood, leads on to fortune." I soon found out that there is also an undertow.

On July 6, 1978, Steve and Rudy and I got caught in the undertow, resulting in controversy that would haunt us for the next ten years. That fateful day, we sang to thousands of screaming, adoring fans at "The Greatest Country Music Show on Earth," in Columbia, Tennessee.

It was hot and so were we. "Night Time Magic," from our *Love Is Just a Game* album, was a number-one hit, and our latest album,

Oh! Brother, was climbing the charts. We were cute and young and full of ourselves. We could really sing and our band was hot—real hot. We sang for an hour and the crowd went crazy. So we did a couple of encores, and they stood up and stomped and clapped and screamed and hollered. It was a great performance for a great crowd. Everything was looking good. We had a great record company behind us, and the fans loved us. Then "Shakespeare's tide" swept over us, and the undertow took us by surprise.

I was soaking wet from head to toe. I was so hot I could barely breathe. I was so thirsty I could not talk. I thought I was going to pass out. I had drunk all the water I had on stage, and I was still totally dehydrated. We ran off the stage, and our agent D. J. McLachlan tried to get us to our bus, but a crowd of about fifty or sixty people blocked our way. They didn't have backstage passes—they were not supposed to be there. Period. Backstage is for performers and crew and invited guests only.

I was already hot, and I got hotter. They were fans who had somehow gotten past the security guards, and they were standing between me and a cold Bud, Coors, or Miller Light or glass of cold water. They started grabbing at my sweaty shirt, begging for hugs and autographs, and I lost it. I pushed and cussed my way through them, climbed hurriedly into our bus, ripped off my sweat-soaked shirt, and sat down. I had at least three or four of the above-mentioned adult beverages. Little did I know that a reporter from the *Nashville Banner*, Bill Hance, saw the whole thing.

A little while later, after a clothes change, Janis and I spread a blanket on the ground, toward the back of the backstage area, and laid out a picnic lunch for us and our kids, Kristin and Josh. (Someone had gotten rid of the herd of backstage interlopers.) About halfway through the picnic, some jerk who was standing outside the backstage barrier screamed, "Hey, Gatlin. Get over here and sign your f—— autograph on this f—— program."

Well, you guessed it. I lost it again. I said, "I'll sign your f— program when I get through with our f—g picnic."

Bill Hance was watching and listening the whole time. After the picnic, I walked over toward an area that had been roped off for autograph seekers. As God is my witness, I signed autographs for twenty minutes. Finally, a sweet little old lady said, "Thank you, Mr. Gatlin."

I looked at her and said, "No, it is I who should thank you, ma'am. You are the first person who has said thank you in twenty minutes."

I smiled at her, signed her program, handed it back her, and walked off. Bill Hance was again in the background, watching and listening.

I don't remember exactly the order of the events that took place over the next few days. Either Hance interviewed me on the phone and then wrote his article, or he wrote the article and I called him—I don't remember. But he wrote an article nonetheless, and it was not flattering. The headline read: "Gatlin Mars His Image with Fans."

I confronted Hance the next day, after his story appeared. He and I cussed each other on the phone, and then I decided to take some action. I went directly to the publisher of the *Nashville Banner* and demanded an apology.

The publisher brought Bill Hance into his office, and we squared off against one another. I called him a liar, he called me one, and I said, "You can't prove that I said all those things." He said, "Oh, yes I can"—I think he had taped our phone conversation, which I think is illegal unless the tapee is told he's being taped.

One thing led to another and I finally left the room, defeated. I knew then I was a goner, the great paradigm shift had begun. The upward momentum of our career was about to come to a screeching halt—like a roller coaster ride that cannot get to the top of the loop so it slowly begins to fall back. That would be us—the ride was not over, but the upward trajectory was. We weren't finished, but this one event in Columbia, Tennessee, and the subsequent newspaper article was a blow from which we would never fully recover.

If I had a chance to do it all over again, I would have been sweeter, more compassionate, and more user-friendly to the fans, and I would definitely not have picked a fight with a reporter. Hindsight is 20/20. But in the heat of the battle, I made a real tactical error, resulting in irreparable damage to our careers. The tide had turned. The slide had begun.

At every stop the story followed me: "Gatlin Lives Up to Reputation" and "Larry Gatlin: Who Is This Man Who Scolds His Audience and Refuses to Sign Autographs?" the headlines said.

For years after this incident, anytime I was interviewed by a magazine or newspaper, the autograph thing reared its ugly head. Very little time was devoted to talking about our music or our careers or anything positive. It was just, "Larry, what is this deal about you not signing autographs and being rude to fans?"

Before I knew it, I was labeled the "Peck's Bad Boy" of the country music industry. Every time the question came up, I tried to explain what happened. I thought that if I kept talking about it, it would all go away. It didn't. The harder I tried to explain the deal, the bigger hole I dug for me and Steve and Rudy and our careers. It got worse by the day and I got madder by the minute. By now, another factor had come into play—alcohol and drugs.

I had been drinking a little bit too much and druggin' a little bit too much for a couple of years now. But until this critical time in my life, it had not been much of a problem. Well, now it was a problem—a big one. Trying to douse a fire with gasoline ain't too smart. Trying to douse anger with alcohol, or other drugs, ain't too smart either. Thus the vicious cycle had begun—anger, booze, hangover, remorse, guilt, more anger, more booze, another hangover, more remorse, more guilt.

Before all of this started happening, I was a most-of-the-time good ole boy from Odessa, Texas, who occasionally got a little hot under the collar and let off some steam. As this weird, awful chain of events began to unfold, I became a most-of-the-time pain-in-the-rear, spoiled, brat who was pretty much mad at the whole world. I became an argument waiting to happen. I became a loser, a loner, and a liar. I became an alcoholic addict. There it is—I've said it.

I fought like a tiger. I made up stuff. I was passionate in our defense. I took every opportunity to try to say something profound. I quoted the part of the Bible where our Jesus took a boat across the Sea of Galilee to get away from the press of the crowd. I quoted Rousseau (I think) on the importance of songwriters to the world: "Take me not to the men who write your laws—for they will lie. Take me to the men who write your songs—for they will not."

Oh, I was really something. I was eloquent. I was passionate. I was persistent. And I was wrong 90 percent of the time. Booze and drugs and their effect on my mind, my body, and my soul had rendered me incapable of real feelings—of real integrity and of real truth. I was hooked, and the forces of darkness were reeling me in.

There is something noble and good about a person taking the moral high ground and drawing a line in the sand and saying, "This is what I believe—this is what I stand for, and I will fight for my convictions at all costs." There is nothing noble and good about a person taking the low road of lying and deception and half-truths and arguing that he has a right to his feelings at the cost of integrity, honor, and trust.

Meanwhile, country music was really taking off, and more and more artists were trying to cross over to the pop charts while retaining their base of support from country music fans. Mac Davis, Roger Miller, Glen Campbell, Dolly Parton, and a bunch of others had been successful in crossing over, and I wanted to cross over too.

About this time, I made a very painful decision. Monument Records, Fred Foster's company, was gradually slipping away from him after CBS's deal to handle distribution ended. Sales had declined significantly when Fred switched to an independent distributor, and I realized that we could not compete with the other Nashville artists if we didn't have a viable, strong record company behind us. So I worked up my courage and went to see Fred.

It was one of the longest meetings of my life. This man was and is my friend. He had given me a chance. He had spent money on me. He had given me my head and allowed me to make music the way I wanted to. He had believed in and supported me, and he had done everything for me that he could. That was the problem: he couldn't take us all the way. He had done it with Roy Orbison and Ray Stevens and Boots Randolph and Kris. But the record business was changing, and Fred was too nice a guy to do some of the things that had to be done to succeed. That's not to say that all record people are heartless, crooked, unethical people, but the business was changing from the good ole boy mentality Fred had worked under to a hard-edge, dog-eat-dog big business.

This is all very clear to me from a nineteen-years-later vantage point. But back in 1978, I knew in my heart of hearts that Fred and Monument were doomed. Well, I walked into Fred's office and started my speech.

"Fred, I love you and I appreciate all you've done for me, and this really hard for me but . . ."

"But," he interrupted, "you want to leave Monument."

"Yes, Fred, I do. I want to get in the game. I want to really have a chance at the big time."

It was a good speech. I'm not lacking in passion or oratory skills, and my pleas were falling on compassionate ears. Fred is a good man with a good heart, and he knew I was right. His company was in serious trouble. That day, in that office, he agreed to shop the Gatlins to a major label.

Soon the word was out on the street, "The Gatlins are for sale. Fred's going under, and Larry wants out."

Fred had had some preliminary discussions with some of the big bosses at the major labels, but nothing significant. I got tired of waiting, so I took matters into my own hands. I flew to New York and Los Angeles and talked to all the "big boys" at the major record companies about a future with the Gatlins. I talked to all of them—CBS, RCA, United Artists, and Warner Brothers—trying to make the right deal. Here I was with only six months of law school, talking to the presidents of major record labels who negotiated contracts every day; I was in way over my head.

On a trip to Los Angeles, I met with Jim Massa at United Artists and with Mo Austin at Warner Brothers later that same day. As I recall, my meeting with Jim went well, and he was very interested in us coming to United Artists. Kenny Rogers had sold zillions of records for them, and I figured it would be a good place for us to be. Jim and I talked, and I proposed some kind of deal. He looked at me funny and made a counteroffer. I remember it didn't sound too bad, but it was about $250,000 less than I thought we ought to get.

Again, I had no business handling the negotiations. There's an old saying, "The lawyer who represents himself has a fool for a client." Well, I was not a lawyer (six months in law school does not qualify), and I was foolish to try to deal with those guys by myself.

I left the meeting with Jim Massa saying I would give his counteroffer serious consideration, and then I got stuck in a big-time traffic jam on my way to meet with Mo Austin at Warner Brothers in Burbank. I was held up in traffic near the Hollywood Bowl, when I noticed a car in front of me. It was a '59 Mercury station wagon with Oklahoma license plates. There were kids hanging out all four windows, a rocking chair tied to the roof, and there were pots and pans, boxes, and suitcases. The only thing missing was Granny Clampett, sitting on the rocking chair, and Flatt and Scruggs on guitar and banjo playing *The Beverly Hillbillies* theme.

I laughed out loud at these Okies in their '59 Mercury with all their worldly possessions loaded in cardboard boxes and their skinny kids hanging out the windows. I stopped laughing as I realized this was not a TV show, and these people were not the Clampetts. I realized that all of my people, before they moved to Texas, had been poor Okies with skinny kids and cardboard boxes and pots and pans, with no dreams and no future. My laughter turned to hollow noise.

There I was, only one generation out of "poor Oklahoma white trash" myself. (My grandparents were not trash, but I'm sure that most people a few rungs higher on the economic ladder called them that.) And here I was laughing at these poor people—this father and this mother and their skinny kids and their cardboard boxes and their '59 Mercury station wagon with Oklahoma plates. I had no business laughing. In desperation, they had left Oklahoma just like the Joads of the thirties and headed for the "promised land"— California. In a flash, I saw their future and I said to myself, "Dear God, have mercy on these poor folks."

While I was still stuck in traffic, the image and words came to me: they have come to California to find the golden dream, and what they're going to find is that "all the gold in California is in a bank in Beverly Hills in somebody else's name," and "California is a new ballgame." California is going to chew these people up and spit them out, break their spirits and send them packin' back to Lawton or

Chickasaw or Oklahoma City or Tulsa or wherever they came from "'cause it don't matter at all where you've played before—California is a brand new game."

When I pulled in the Warner Brothers parking lot, I scratched down a few lines and the basic idea on a piece of paper, threw it on the front seat, and walked into the building for my meeting with one of the smartest record men in the history of the music business: Mo Austin.

I laid out my plan for Mo, which involved buying Fred's last two albums, adding three more for $1 million or so, and I seriously thought I'd made a good case. Mo just chuckled and said, "That isn't going to work," and made me a counteroffer. It was probably a fair deal, and maybe I should have taken it, but I told him I would get back to him soon, and I left.

My brain was on fire. I almost ran out of the building to my car. When I got in, I grabbed the pencil and paper and the song wrote itself—or, as I like to say, God writes the songs, I just copy 'em down. It came all at once—the words, the correct rhyme, rhythm, feel, and melody. It took maybe ten minutes—probably more like five. The opening lyrics went like this:

> *All the gold in California*
> *Is in a bank in the middle of Beverly Hills*
> *In somebody else's name—*
> *So if you're dreamin' about California—*
> *It don't matter at all where you've played before*
> *California's a brand new game—*

I have seen that '59 Mercury station wagon in my mind's eye many times over the last nineteen years. I've wondered what became of that father and that mother and those skinny kids. I hope they made it in California, and if they didn't I hope they got back to Lawton or Chickasaw or Oklahoma City or Tulsa or wherever safe and sound. Those poor folks were the inspiration for a song that has made me God-only-knows how much money. I doubt seriously if that father had a hundred dollars in his pocket when I was stuck in that traffic jam with him and his little family at the Hollywood Bowl in 1978.

●　　●　　●

In a moment of lucidity, I decided to sign with CBS Records. They had most of our old masters from the time Monument was affiliated with CBS, and I knew all the people. In going with CBS, I was reunited with my old friend, Rick Blackburn, whom I had known from my Monument days. Rick was now head of CBS Records in Nashville, and a longtime Gatlin fan.

Rick and I discussed some ideas for our first album, and I flew to Houston the next day for a concert at the Summit. I taught Steve Smith "All the Gold in California" in the dressing room before the show. He and I played it together, and at the end of the song, he looked at me and I looked at him, and he said, "That's the one. Let's get home and record it. Quick!"

We did. We hired producer Chip Young to help us cut the song. I called him and said, "Chip, I've got one that's a smash song. Come help us make it a smash record."

Chip, Steve, Rudy, Mike Smith, Phil Fajardo, Ralph Geddes, Steve Smith, and I got together and recorded the song at Chip's Young 'Un Sound studio. I think we got it on the second or third take. Steve and Rudy and I overdubbed some vocals and then we went back and listened. It was in the pocket. Almost twenty years later, it's still in the pocket. I'm really proud of the song and the record.

In September 1979, "All the Gold in California" was released as a single from the *Straight Ahead* album. It was a smart move to sign with CBS since they had incredible distribution, which extended from coast-to-coast around the world. "All the Gold in California" debuted on the Billboard Hot Country Singles Chart at number 55 with a bullet its first week, and by the following week it was the hottest song in America. It went to number one in just a few weeks. *Straight Ahead* became our first album to be certified gold.

Marty Klein was one of the hottest agents in the world, and his specialty was television. Steve and Rudy and I did every show there was to do, thanks to him—*Sha Na Na, Hee Haw, Dinah!, Merv Griffin*—you name it, we did it.

Of all the TV shows we ever did, I really believe the most important one for our careers was the night we sang "All the Gold in California" on *The Tonight Show* for the first time. We tore up the place, and The Tonight Show Band played it along with our guys—Steve Smith, Mike Smith, Ralph Geddes, and Phil Fajardo.

On the last chorus, I got Doc Severinsen and the show's band to sing along. The place was rockin'. I walked over to sit down, and Johnny was very complimentary. We had gotten along very well since the night he threw me some question or comment that was not on his "list," and I had handled it and had given him something back to play with. We had gone back and forth from there and laughed and had a good time.

Johnny said something like, "You guys almost didn't get in today because of the fog." (We'd flown in that morning, and the fog had been so thick the pilot almost couldn't land the plane.)

I said something like, "Yes, Johnny, we almost didn't make it." Then I started winging it about the L.A. Airport.

"Yeah, Johnny, the plane was late. Our limo was not there, and we heard that deal about the 'white zone' is for loading and unloading passengers only." Then I did it in pseudo-Spanish. "La zona blanca is para el loading and el unloading of passengers—solamento."

Well, I don't know why that struck him as funny—but thank God it did. So he went off on some airport comedy thing, and then I said, "Why in the world do people bring pineapples back to L.A. from Hawaii? You know, they've got 'em in the overhead bins and all over the floor, and they can buy 'em at Farmers Market in L.A. cheaper and they don't have bring 'em all the way from Honolulu."

Johnny laughed and giggled, and I did the "la zona blanca is para el loading" thing again, and he laughed again, and we went to commercial.

Later that night, *The Tonight Show* coordinator, Debbie Vickers, told me that Johnny instructed her to put us on "the A list." We had been on "the D list." That means that everybody from Gene-Gene the Dancing Machine up through Fred DeCordova (then the show's producer), Peter L. Salle, Bobby Quinn, and Johnny had to okay an appearance on the show. After that *Tonight Show* about la zona blanca, all we had to do was have Marty Klein call Debbie when we were going to be on the West Coast, and if there was an open slot, we did Carson. I loved it. We always did well. Thanks, Johnny.

Meanwhile, the autograph controversy persisted. As much as I tried to distance myself from it, I couldn't. Steve and Rudy and I were working in Dallas at the Fairmont Hotel. One morning in the middle of this insanity with the press and the autograph thing, I went to the lobby bar of the Fairmont to have a Bloody Mary.

I walked up the step to the couch under the huge chandelier and sat down. One of the great characters of Texas jurisprudence, Percy Foreman, was sitting on the opposite couch. I walked over and introduced myself. We had a couple of Bloody Marys and finally I asked for his legal advice.

"Mr. Foreman," I asked, "is there anything I can do about the terrible things that people are saying about me in the paper?"

"Mr. Gatlin," he said in a slow Texas drawl, "I'm gonna give you the best legal advice anyone will ever give you. Number one, don't ever get in a stink fight with a skunk, and number two, don't get into an argument with a man who buys ink by the barrel."

We laughed and had a couple more Bloody Marys and then he had to leave. Looking back, I know he was right. It was the best legal advice I was ever given. Too bad I didn't take it. I went right back to fighting the battle, and it was a battle that I could not win.

CHAPTER 11

*Barbara Mandrell, Charlie Daniels, Bob McDill, Frances Preston, Eddie Rabbit,
Michael Martin Murphy, me, and Ed Cramer*

☞HE BEST OF TIMES, THE WORST OF TIMES

One afternoon in Toronto, Phil Fajardo, my old college buddy and our drummer at the time, rolled an old wino over onto his stomach on a park bench. He was struggling to breathe and was heaving, and we thought he was going to choke to death. Some other guys in the park saw what happened and came over to thank us. I hung out with them and played poker and drank wine for a couple of days. It was great in a weird sort of way.

A few days later, we had some great Chinese food in Saginaw, Michigan, and, after the meal, I said to the boys in the band, "If there's no Chinese food in heaven, who the h— wants to go?" Later that night, I wrote what I still believe is one of the most insightful, and compassionate songs I will ever write, "The Midnight Choir," about a wino down at the Union Mission in Nashville.

I still remember sitting up in my bed at the hotel and grabbing a piece of paper and writing down the lyrics—

> *The door to the Mission opens at seven*
> *and the soup will be ready about nine.*
> *Right now it's 6:30 and they're ragged and dirty,*
> *But they're standin' and sittin' and layin' in line.*
> *First they'll do a little singing, then hear a little preachin'*
> *Then get saved for the third time this week.*
> *A bowl of soup later and a pat on the shoulder*
> *And by midnight they're back on the street.*

The next day, we were all together for a sound check at the Regency Hotel in Detroit, Michigan, and I started playing the song for the band.

> *They walk to the corner of 4th Street and Broadway.*
> *Then take the first alley on the right.*
> *One of them asks a stranger "How 'bout a hand."*
> *But he just gives 'em one finger at a time.*
> *Then they spot an old buddy—*
> *With a bottle of heaven—*
> *Then pass around what means everything*
> *One bottle for four,*
> *Thank God, someone scored.*
> *Now the Midnight Choir starts to sing.*

The band joined in, and we arranged it on the spot. (We had worked on it a bit on the bus on the way to the gig, and Steve Smith gave me the line, "He just gives 'em one finger at a time." Great line, Steve. I'm only about—what?—fifteen years late giving you credit.)

Will they have Mogen David in heaven?
Dear Lord, we'd all like to know.
Will they have Mogen David in heaven?
Sweet Jesus
If they don't
Who the h— wants to go.

Well, we sang the song that night, and the crowd went nuts—they loved it. We had to sing the last verse and chorus a second time, and they went nuts again. I will state right now that I thought we had a smash hit on our hands. A few months later, when we recorded the song for the *Straight Ahead* album, we decided to make it as authentic as possible. We all drank a bunch of Mad Dog 20/20 Mogen David wine, and then turned the recording machine on and let it roll. Looking back now, I know it was overkill and in bad taste. At the time, it seemed like the thing to do.

After "All the Gold in California" really put us on the map, it was time to release another single from the album. In January 1980 CBS released "The Midnight Choir," and it would put us at ground zero for an attack from all sides—newspaper and magazine reviews ripped us. I got cards and letters from "good Christians" calling me every name imaginable. One radio station vowed to never again play a Gatlin Brothers record because one of their advertisers was a Jewish merchant who refused to buy time on the station since he thought we were making fun of Mogen David, a Jewish ceremonial wine. (I can't believe this happened, but that's what people at CBS Records told me.) Many listeners in other areas of the country called their local radio stations, demanding the record be taken off the air.

To top the whole thing off, a radio station in Little Rock, Arkansas, threw a record-burning party. That's right. Some really spiritual, intelligent God-fearin' folks got together and burned the Gatlin Brothers recording of "The Midnight Choir"—a simple song about a bunch of drunks trying to *pray.*

I went ballistic. We had been singing the song on every show, and the live audiences loved it. Add that to the fact that I believed then (and still do) that the song was divinely inspired. Add that to the fact that I was already on the defensive because of the newspaper/autograph situation. Add all that to the fact that I had started drinking and drugging more and more frequently and you can easily see, the situation was very volatile.

I quoted Rousseau—"Take me to the men who write your songs. . . ." I explained that it was not the Gatlin Brothers who were saying, "If there's no Mogen David in heaven—who the h— wants to go," but that it was these poor old winos who were confused, sick, and hurting and in need of help—and whose only idea of heaven was a bottle of Mogen David and temporary relief from the pain—a little piece of heaven, if you will. I went so far as to question the public's musical discretion when "rape and murder is acceptable [from "Coward of the County"] but winos talking to God is not." It was all to no avail. Again, I had picked the wrong battle, at the wrong time, with the wrong enemy.

Meanwhile, a Portland, Oregon, radio station sent a telegram to Joe Casey, the national promotion man for CBS Records. I'll do it from memory, so it's not exact, but it read:

> Dear Mr. Casey. We will not play the Gatlin Brothers'
> recording of "The Midnight Choir." Stop. It is not the
> purpose of this radio station to air views of a bum. Stop.

When I read the telegram I couldn't figure out whether I was the bum or the winos were the bums, but either way things were on the downhill slide. I was incensed. I went on a rampage, a holy war, a Texas jihad. I was gonna tell 'em all where to go, and I was gonna stand up for the winos.

Steve, Rudy, and I drafted our own response to radio stations that were not playing our song, and sent it to every station in the country:

> Dear Friends:
>   We are sorry if our record "The Midnight Choir" has
> caused you or your radio station any problems. However,
> we are not sorry that we released the record. We searched

our hearts and did what we thought we had to do. (If nobody thinks the song has done anything positive, they should check with Rev. Harry Smith at the Atlanta Union Mission, Atlanta, Georgia.)

If you are playing the record, we thank you! If you have played it and have taken it off the playlist because of adverse public reaction or because you do not like it, we understand your predicament. Thanks for trying!

God help the winos . . . doesn't look like anyone else is going to!

Sincerely,

Larry, Steve & Rudy Gatlin

A week after our letter went out, we appeared on *The Tonight Show* to sing and plug "The Midnight Choir," trying once more to state our case. It didn't help. If anything, it made things worse.

The chaplain at the Nashville Union Mission called me and suggested that I bring my lawyer to a meeting at the mission. He chastised me for making fun of his flock, and threatened to sue me. He ranted and raved and I just listened. When it was my turn, I tried to explain that he and I were on the same side—I was only trying to paint a compassionate picture of the hopeless men who lived in the alleys and under the bridges close to the mission. I got mad. He got mad. My lawyer and business manager and brother-in-law, Don Malone, tried to resolve the situation with a little calm, good advice to both of us, but it did not work. The meeting turned ugly. Nothing was resolved.

I want to stop right here and come clean. In light of my own sobriety, with a new sanity and new spirit in my heart, I know that I went about all of this the wrong way. Make no mistake about it—I am not apologizing for "The Midnight Choir." I am proud of the song and thankful to God for it. What I am apologizing for is my attitude and the fact that our treatment of the song in the studio and the recording itself were heavy-handed. If I had been in my right mind, I would have been more sensitive and recorded a more compassionate version. But I was a mad crusader in a holy war—a war that could not be won.

As I got into my car after the meeting with the chaplin, I saw a policeman across the street rousting an old wino who was asleep under a bench. I told the chaplin that while he was calling me names and threatening to sue me, one of his flock was being hassled by the local gendarme. Perhaps, I suggested, his time would be better spent minding his flock and his business and leaving me to take care of myself. End of conversation. End of meeting. End of the beginning of a great career.

In May of 1980, controversy erupted again, this time at the annual Academy of Country Music Awards, held at Knott's Berry Farm's Good Times Theater in Buena Park, California. We were winners in three major categories: album of the year, for *Straight Ahead*; single of the year, for "All the Gold in California"; and Larry Wayne Gatlin for male vocalist of the year. We won over some real heavyweights, and I was surprised by the triple win.

"Is this really mine?" I remember murmuring backstage, clutching one of three cowboy hat-shaped trophies.

The celebration was short-lived. As it turned out, *all* of the academy's ten awards that night went to singers signed with CBS. (Our boss Rick Blackburn was embarrassed by the situation, especially when someone pushed him on stage during our last acceptance speech, on live national television, and I said, "Blackburn, what are you doing up here?" I was joking.)

The brothers and I were getting ready to go on tour with Anne Murray when the story broke. Several record executives charged that the CBS victories resulted from bloc voting by CBS employees. As I understand it, the complaint was that three hundred employees at CBS got to cast their votes, increasing their voting strength. It was not a valid argument as the academy then had more than two thousand registered members.

Finally, I wrote a letter to the academy saying: "We're thankful we won, but we don't want anything that doesn't belong to us. If someone can show me, if it can be proven, that something was done illegally or unethically or not in keeping with the Academy of Country Music charter, I'll send the awards back in the same box they came in."

Well, the entire matter was dropped, nothing illegal or unethical was proven, and that was the end of it.

My friends Bill and Fran Boyd had started the ACM awards a few years earlier; it was a California version of the Country Music Association Awards. Over time it has grown to a big organization that puts on a great show, which Dick Clark always produces.

Well, after winning three ACM awards in 1980, a funny thing happened at the Country Music Association Awards the following October. "All the Gold in California" was nominated for single of the year. I was up for entertainer of the year. And here's the strange part—Larry Gatlin and The Gatlin Brothers Band were nominated for vocal group of the year and instrumental group of the year. So what's so strange? Read on.

At the meeting of the CMA board two months before the final voting, one of the board members made a successful motion to the effect that no one could be a finalist in the male vocalist category and also be in a group nominated for vocal group of the year. In other words, Larry Gatlin could not be a finalist in both categories. (It's not too much of a stretch to figure this out, since I was the only one in the preliminary balloting in the top five of each category.)

Well, Rick Blackburn, who was a CMA board member, was given the unenviable task of asking me which category I wanted to be in. I opted for the group category. (I would not have felt right about accepting the vocalist nomination at the expense of Steve and Rudy.) To those of you who are not terribly familiar with the politics of Nashville and the dealings of the movers and shakers of that little town, this whole deal may seem like small potatoes. But believe me, it wasn't. For years, everyone in Nashville had told me that I was going to win CMA male vocalist and I hadn't (previously I had been nominated three times), so it was always, "Next year is your year, Larry."

Well, 1980 was to be my year. I had had a solo career for seven years in Nashville before this CMA nomination, and the fact that my peers had made me a top-five finalist as a soloist and in the group category told me that the industry itself had no problem with the dual nomination. But someone on the board did, and that someone had a lot power.

The Statler Brothers won the group award, and George Jones won in the male vocalist category. (Two very good choices, I might add.) As for my brothers and me—we were shut out that year. And we were only nominated for two awards the following year, then one award the year after that, then none the next year, and none to this moment in time. (There's always tomorrow, Scarlett.)

I *was* very bitter about this deal, but I'm not mad anymore. It took me a long time to realize there will always be political shenanigans, not just in politics, but in business. Many years down the road, I realized that on occasion, I had pulled political shenanigans myself. I was just getting back what I had given.

I was sitting on the bank of a little stream in Florida one night during the firestorm over the autographs and "The Midnight Choir." I was trying to write a song. I heard a car behind me, and I turned to see what was going on. Well, lo and behold, it was one of my heroes—Mr. Arnold Palmer—and Mrs. Winnie Palmer. There they were—unloading groceries. That's right, the general of "Arnie's Army." The Man. The King of Golf. Unloading groceries, like a good husband is supposed to.

I walked over and began to reintroduce myself to Mr. Palmer. (We had met a year or so earlier at, I believe, the Houston Open golf tournament.) He promptly interrupted me with, "Hello, Larry. How you doing? How are Steve and Rudy?"

I was flabbergasted. This man remembered me and my brothers. We had only met briefly one time, but he remembered it and was thoughtful enough to ask about my brothers. I was stunned.

We talked for a while and then I said something like, "Sir, even if you never hit another green or sink another three-footer, I will always admire you and respect you for the way you have handled your success. The way you treat your fans is just admirable. I'll admit it. I'm not very good at it sometimes."

This great man put the sack of groceries back into the trunk of the car and looked right at me. Then he said something I will never

The Gatlin boys and the General—Arnold Palmer

forget: "Larry, you have to remember something—you may be the most important thing that ever happens in their lives."

I couldn't say anything. I just nodded and finally mumbled something about good advice or something. We shook hands. Then Arnold Palmer picked up the grocery sack, closed the trunk of the car, walked up the stairs to his condo to join his wife, and I just stood there, transfixed as if I had been in the presence of God.

Guess what? I was.

I'm not trying to be cute, and I certainly mean no sacrilege. Arnold Palmer was not and is not God. But what Arnold Palmer, child of God, told me that night in Florida was divinely inspired. It was *from* God Almighty, and I was deeply moved. I have never forgotten what he told me, and now—years down the road, after a spiritual awakening that changed my life—the truth behind what Arnold Palmer told me that evening is a cornerstone of my new life.

Understand this, I do not practice this truth perfectly. I still "short out" on occasion and am not as gracious as I should be. But I can say I am better. (Kris once said to me, "Gatlin, you are better, but you ain't well.")

A couple of years later, I had the great pleasure and privilege of being paired with Arnold Palmer at the Gatlin Brothers Senior Golf Tournament in Reno, Nevada. He was as gracious and down-to-earth as before.

We had a great time playing golf together and even went to the casino and saw a show together and played a little blackjack. On the occasions we have been together since that time, Mr. and Mrs. Palmer—Arnold and Winnie—have treated me like an old friend. In other words, as if meeting them might have been the most important thing that ever happened in my life. (Sound familiar?)

After I played the pro–am round with the General on Thursday of the Reno tournament, I did not return to the golf course until the awards ceremony on Friday. (I don't even remember who won.) My brother Steve had to make an emergency call to get through the "hold" I had ordered placed on my hotel phone. I was sitting alone in my room, drinking vodka and snorting cocaine. The White Demon now had me totally in its power. My life was no longer about family or friends, or music or golf, or God or anything else. My life was about *Where can I get more cocaine?*

I really lost it one night in Reno. I had returned to Interlaken, the fabulous house Bill Harrah bought years ago for his stars. The place was complete with maids and servants and cooks, tennis courts, swimming pools, and hot and cold running everything. When I stayed at Interlaken, there were also cocaine and Valium and Quaaludes and vodka and insanity, all rolled into one.

One night after the second show at Harrah's, I drove (God knows how) the four or five miles from the hotel to the house. I stumbled into the kitchen, poured myself a tall vodka, ladled up some home-made vegetable soup into a huge wooden salad bowl, and sloshed my way up the stairs toward the master bedroom. The next thing I remember was my brother-in-law Don Malone shaking me and telling me to wake up. I was not asleep. I was in a drug and alcohol-induced coma—a blackout. I was closer to death than I had ever been. Steve was there, too, and he and Don went to work.

Don pulled me to my feet, and they both talked to me and walked me around until I could stand on my own. I really believe that Don and Steve saved my life that night. I don't know how many Quaaludes I had taken. I don't know how much vodka I had drunk. I do know that for rock 'n' rollers, jazz cats, and "ordinary" country boys, Stoli (vodka) and 'ludes equal blackout/coma. Adios. Curtains. Don't he look natural. A little organ music, please.

This became a portent of things to come.

In Lake Tahoe, the same thing happened. We were booked there after our Reno engagement, and I hadn't slept in four days. I had only eaten some mixed nuts from the bowl in the dressing room and a few olives and lemon wedges from the setup by the bar. Well, between shows I decided to take a Valium to stop the cocaine shakes and maybe get a little hour-and-a-half nap. Valium plus no food plus vodka and beer equals blackout/coma.

At 11:50 P.M., ten minutes before the midnight show, I was nowhere to be seen. Ron Carpenter, our road manager, found me—passed out on the bed, still in my stage clothes from the first show. He got me up and walked me to the backstage area. My hair was a mess, my clothes were a mess, my whole life was a mess. I remember little else about this episode. But I do know I did the show, even in my fragile condition. Maybe to the audience, nothing looked strange. But I knew I was not right. In fact, I remember falling asleep while singing "The Heart." My brother Steve later told me that it was the longest five minutes in show business history. The song is only about two-and-a-half minutes under normal conditions. At this point in my life there was no such thing as normal conditions. Everything revolved around booze and drugs.

From Lake Tahoe, it was on to Las Vegas—same deal. I was up all night doin' coke and almost missed the show. It was a merry-go-round that had spun out of control—and the problem was, I couldn't get off. No, let me take that back. I didn't know how to get off.

Steve and I began to argue about my drug use, and we even came to a serious pushing contest one night in our tour bus in Massachusetts. Later in Reno we got into a horrible argument. He told me that I had to stop doing coke, and I told him, "I work hard and I'm gonna play hard and nobody is gonna tell me I can't." We almost came to blows. Steve tried hard to help me. Looking back, I know that I made his life miserable.

Don't get me wrong, folks. There were some good times. Some great times. We did great concerts, television shows, award shows. We had some fantastic evenings at the Grammys and the CMA and ACM awards shows. We were there the night The Doobie Brothers rocked the Grammys with "What a Fool Believes." We were there the night Barbra Streisand and Neil Diamond walked onto the stage unannounced and sang "You Don't Send Me Flowers Anymore." And when Ella Fitzgerald, Sarah Vaughn, Michael Jackson, Bob Dylan, Donna Summer, Dionne Warwick, and Diana Ross electrified their peers and the live television audience. We saw some wonderful performances by some of the greatest artists of all time.

One night I will always remember was the Grammy awards in 1981 in New York when Patti LuPone sang "Don't Cry for Me Argentina" and raised the roof. (Lionel Ritchie and I bet on every award. I won $100.)

Barbra Streisand and Barry Gibb did a great duet from the *Guilty* album, which Barry had produced (and which won in the category of best pop performance by a duo or group). After the show, at a CBS party at the Four Seasons, I walked up to Barry and tried to introduce myself. Before I could get my name out of my mouth he said, "Dear God, mate. My brothers and I love you guys. You sing the best harmony in the world."

Holy Saturday Night Fever, I thought. *Barry Gibb knows who I am, and he and his brothers love The Gatlin Brothers—what a deal!*

We talked for a while and he introduced me to Maurice (Robin was not there), then invited me to the Waldorf Astoria after the CBS party for a drink and a visit. Janis was very tired and I think she knew what was coming, so she went back to The Plaza Hotel.

It turned out to be one of the most memorable evenings of my life. Picture this: my brothers were not there to sing harmony on "All the Gold in California" and "Broken Lady" and "I've Done Enough Dyin' Today," so Barry and Maurice Gibb sang their part with me. It was marvelous. Robin Gibb was not there to sing his part on "I Started a Joke," "Words," and about twenty other Bee Gees songs, so I sang it. It was a totally cosmic musical experience.

Don't get me wrong, I wouldn't trade my two brothers for any two other humans on earth. I'd rather sing with them than any other two cats alive. But if they can't make the gig, Barry and Maurice Gibb would be pretty good pinch-hitters. Can you believe it? The Bee Gees know our songs.

When I got back to the Plaza around dawn and fairly drunk, Mrs. Gatlin was not thrilled. She just looked at me with a "Good Lord, Larry, are you ever going to quit acting like this" look on her face. Then she rolled over, and went back to sleep. She is a real trooper, a women of incredible strength and faith.

As I've said before, it was the best of times and the worst of times. We were still a hot act. We landed a fabulous deal with Ed Wachtel and Herb Goldstein, the owners of Members Only jackets. We became spokesmen for the company and made some good TV commercials (got a lot of free Members Only jackets too). How they ever put up with me, I do not know. The ad campaign was a great success. There was a huge sign on the Queensborough bridge with us in our Members Only jackets. It was a kick. I'd walk down Fifth Avenue and a cab driver would holler, "Hey, Larry, where's your Members Only jacket?"

Can you believe it? A kid from Odessa, Texas, being recognized by a New York cabbie. Is this a great country or what?

The first time I really started thinking about asking for help was in October of 1982. I found myself at a pay phone in the Phoenix Airport, following another awful night of drinkin' and druggin'. We were in the middle of the Kenny Rogers tour and had just played the Phoenix State Fair. C. K. Spurlock, Kenny's promoter, had asked if we'd be interested in touring with Kenny that year. Well, Kenny was red-hot and we were not as hot as we'd been. We decided the P.R. would be great, even though the money was not as good as it would have been doing our own tour, and we would be singing for more people with Kenny than by ourselves. So it all came together.

I was hungover and sick and lonely and depressed and guilt-ridden. In other words, the prodigal had spent himself and his fortune in riotous living. I was not literally in a pigpen, but I was in dire straits.

There was no thunderclap, no bolt of lightning, no audible voice, but there was something inside that kept saying, "Call Papa Joe. Call Papa Joe."

I had not seen Papa Joe Neely, my preacher when I was in college at the University of Houston, for thirteen years, but that morning in the Phoenix Airport, I spent the better part of two hours tracking him down. Something told me I had to get to him. I found him in Belton, Texas. I don't really remember how I did it. I had three days off from the Kenny Rogers tour so I changed my reservations and flew to Temple, Texas, and on a hot July night in 1982, I walked into the back door of the tiny Assembly of God church outside Temple and sat down toward the back.

Papa Joe was telling the small congregation about his trip to Greece. Then all at once he looked at me and I saw tears of joy fill his eyes. He stopped his presentation and said, "Folks, I have just seen a man walk into this church who has been like a son to me for over twenty years. I haven't seen him in thirteen long years, and I just cannot help it. I must go and hug him right now."

Papa Joe walked toward the back of the church as I walked toward the front. We held each other tightly for I don't know how long. We cried, and he prayed and thanked God for bringing me back to him. Then we went to his little trailer house after the service, and he and Mildred, his angel of a wife, talked with me until the wee small hours of the morning. Papa Joe showed me to the guest bedroom and literally tucked me in and said he'd see me in the morning. I slept more soundly than I had in years and only woke up when I smelled bacon and coffee.

Papa Joe's specialty (aside from great preaching) is pancakes. He piled them high on my plate, and I covered them with maple syrup and butter and tears. Finally I said, "Pop, I've done some really horrible, horrible things in the last few years."

There was a slight pause and he said, "Son, I don't care what you have done. I still love you. And just think of how much more capacity God has to love you than I do."

I cannot express exactly what happened next, but it felt like a warm oil being poured over my head. I wept like a baby, and Joe Neely—wonderful son of God—held me in his arms as a father would hold a small child. I would like to tell you that my troubles all vanished and that everybody lived happily ever after and that the prodigal had returned forever to the fold. But that is not what happened. I was still a slave to alcohol and drugs and anger and lying and self-will run riot.

But the words of love and forgiveness had been spoken, and two of God's great prayer warriors, Joe and Mildred Neely, had recommitted themselves to bombarding heaven on a daily basis for the restoration of Larry Gatlin to the whole, sane, sober man he had once been. There was still a difficult road ahead, but I was on my way.

CHAPTER 12

Larry G. (Burrhead) and Glen H. (Big Foot)

$\mathscr{L}$ARRY G.

A few months after my visit with Papa Joe, Janis and I had our worst argument ever. It seems that I had passed out at the dinner table in front of Jerry and Suzie Pate, Ben Crenshaw, Tom and Christy Kite, and others before the meal was even served. It was February of 1983, and we were on vacation in Hawaii.

It embarrassed Janis terribly, and when I stumbled up to our room at the Kapalua Hotel, she read me the riot act. It was not a pretty sight. I fought hard and valiantly (not physically, but verbally), defending my right to drink whenever and wherever and whatever I chose. Janis Gail Moss Gatlin didn't buy it.

I got another room and spent the night alone, fuming. Well, not really the whole night. I ran down to the bar and had myself a couple of beers and some vodka and blacked out—alone and fully clothed—while the prettiest, sweetest, and most loving woman in Hawaii prayed and cried and slept not very soundly, all alone in a room registered to Mr. and Mrs. Larry Gatlin.

The next day, I slunk back to our room looking for a deal. I apologized for my behavior and promised Janis I would never drink *in front of her again*. I didn't promise not to drink. Oh, no, that would have been selling out my right to do as I pleased. No, I just ran a little scam on my sweetheart and in desperation—having no alternatives but divorce or murder—she took the deal.

"Do you promise, Larry?" she said, crying.

"Honey, I promise."

Nice try, kid. I would learn later that "half measures availed us nothing."

Following our Hawaiian vacation, it was back to business. Steve and Rudy and I resumed our concert schedule. Earlier, we had laid down some new tracks for our upcoming *Houston to Denver* album, which included our number-one hit song, "Houston (Means I'm One Day Closer to You)," and the Top 10 hit, "The Lady Takes the Cowboy Everytime." We made the usual rounds of television talk and variety shows, including performing at Burt Reynolds's dinner theater in Jupiter, Florida, for a taping of Dinah Shore's television program.

Dinah was doing a couple of weeks of taping at Burt's dinner theater during the day, and there was some play going on at night with Martin Sheen. Burt was on Dinah's show, as were Lee Majors, James Brolin, Joe Namath, Paul Williams, and Kathie Lee Johnson (now Kathie Lee Gifford). It was wild and wonderful, and we all had a good time. We were all Burt's guests at the performance of the play that evening. A beautiful meal was served in Burt's private box, but I didn't eat a bite. Cocaine removes any desire to eat.

Well, things got a little rowdy at dinner, but I got through it. We adjourned the party to the bar, where Paul Williams and I tried to drink all the vodka in the house. Siberian coma was what Paul called the drink—vodka and soda, tall with a slice of lemon. We got blasted and soon ran out of cocaine, so I told Paul I would call our pilot, Bill Blair, and have him file a flight plan to Miami.

"Paul, old pal," I said, "let's go to Miami and get ourselves some more of that white powder." (Again, I wouldn't mention names except for the fact that Paul has cleaned up his act and is doing great.)

I told Paul I would meet him in the lobby in fifteen minutes, after I'd had a shower. I was drying off when I heard a knock on the door, so I wrapped the towel around me and opened it. I expected Paul. It was Kathie Lee. She walked in. I went to the bathroom to put on some clothes and told her I had to leave soon to go to Miami on business.

Kathie Lee told me that Brother Steve—and maybe Rudy, I'm not sure—had sent her to talk to me. She told me that she knew that I was going to Miami with Paul to try and get some more drugs and that she was not going to let me go *anywhere*.

I was getting sicker and more paranoid by the minute. I cannot describe what it is like to be crashing from a coke high. But it is hell on earth.

I said, "Kathie Lee, I've got to go."

"Larry, you are not going."

I remember crying and I remember her holding me in her arms and rocking me back and forth on the couch and praying for me and soothing me and calming me. It was not a sexual deal. It was an act of compassion and love and healing that helped saved my life.

After I calmed down a bit, Kathie Lee helped me get into bed. I can see her now kneeling by my bedside, asking God to deliver me from the demons that were tearing me apart. She was Florence Nightingale and Mother Teresa all in one. She was an angel of mercy sent by God who arrived on the scene in the nick of time.

I'm sure that by now you are tired of hearing all the gory details about my insane behavior, so you probably do not want to know about my week at the Helmsley Palace in July 1984—locked and bolted behind the door, with a chair wedged against the knob. No food or sleep for almost a week. I only went outside the room once, to go see number 99, Wayne Gretzky, play in the NHL All-Star Game. Then it was back in the room, bolted and locked and wedged in—because "they" were out there and "they" were going to come and get me. More vodka, more cocaine, more Valium, more insanity. Perhaps a step backward down the mountain. Curtains pulled closed. No maid service. No bath for almost a week.

When I returned to Nashville from New York, Janis confronted me right away. "Larry, are you doing drugs?"

"No, honey, I'm not," I said. "I promised I wouldn't. I'm just tired and upset and the pressure—you know how it is. I need a vacation."

Janis believed me—then again, maybe she didn't and just acted like she did. We took a vacation to the Cayman Islands in mid-April of 1984 and had a good time. I didn't get drunk once. I was still trying not to drink in front of her. It was a scam.

I was a very naughty boy in Dallas at our Gatlin Brothers MDA Golf Tournament in June of 1984. I don't mean to trivialize it. I was, very simply put, totally out of control. Some of my other episodes almost pale to insignificance compared with this little three-day number.

Me and The Great Son and The Great One and Lord Stanley's Cup.

Darrell and Edith Royal were upset with me. Steve and Rudy were upset with me. The universe was upset with me, because, as I said, I was out of control. There I was at a wonderful charity event for a great cause, with friends and relatives and guests and big-dollar donors, and I was going to the men's room every five minutes to do more "blow."

I even wrote Janis a goofy letter, claiming I was hooked on Percodan because of my aching back and that I was going to see a back specialist who promised to get me off the stuff, and, no, I was not doing cocaine. Boys and girls, it was fantasy—pure fantasy. It was pure fiction. Nothing about this deal was real except that I was in real trouble.

A few days later I finally realized I needed help, so I called Darrell Royal and he flew to Atlanta to see me. When he told me I needed treatment I said, "Darrell, I can do this on my own. I ain't goin' to no funny farm to hang out with a bunch of losers. I'll do this on my own."

Well, he very gently, but firmly, told me he didn't think it was possible to kick this thing myself. I made him a deal. "OK," I said, "if I can't kick this thing on my own, I'll go with you. I promise."

"OK. If you really mean it, it's a deal."

He knew I could not do it, so he shook hands on it and went back to Austin to await my call for help. I went seventeen days without any cocaine, but on the eighteenth day, I got hooked up with some coke heads in Dallas and I was off to the races. This time, it was different. I smoked the stuff for the first time. I'd never felt anything like it in my life. It was the greatest euphoria I had ever felt. I cannot explain it, but it was wonderful. We were working at the Star Garden Theatre in Dallas. I was loaded on opening night. My friends, the Haggars—Joe and Ed and all of their families—came to see us, and I was so high I could barely talk to them. I was awful. I went on a three-day binge the likes of which I had never experienced.

In the midst of it all, Rick Blackburn, the boss at CBS and a good friend, showed up at my hotel suite. He quizzed me about my life and what was going on, and I lied like a dog and said I was doing great. While I was talking to him in one room, my new coke head buddies were freebasing cocaine next door. Rick was trying to help me, but I wasn't ready to be helped. Less than twenty-four hours later I would be.

The cocaine was gone. It was Sunday morning, November 29, 1984. I was crawling on my hands and knees, looking for little pieces of cocaine to put into the pipe that my "friends" had given me. I had crashed before on many occasions, and overheated before, but nothing—nothing, had ever felt like this.

It was the flu, a hangover, the guilt of the whole world and knowledge that I was utterly helpless—all at the same time. Add to that the fact that I was sweating like a pig and crawling around the floor like a crazed animal and you begin to get the picture. I crawled into the bathroom and caught a glimpse of the devil in the mirror. Surely it was the devil. Surely this reflection in the glass was not Larry Wayne Gatlin, good Christian boy from good Christian parents—God-fearing—praying—Bible-verse reciting—Rousseau quoting—college-educated—Larry Wayne Gatlin.

Surely this was not the same guy who had written "Help Me" and "Light at the End of the Darkness" and "It Must Have Rained in Heaven on Crucifixion Day." Surely this was not the same guy. But it was. It was not the devil in the mirror. It was me. I just looked like the devil. Neither before that time nor since have I seen anything that scared me as much as my reflection in that Holiday Inn mirror.

While still on my knees, I prayed, "God, if you don't help me, I'm going to die."

God did help me. I somehow got packed and into a cab.

"Sir, do you like country music?" I asked the cabbie.

"It's my favorite," he replied.

"Do you know The Gatlin Brothers?"

"They are my favorite group," he replied.

"Well, I'm Larry Gatlin and I'm broke, and I'll send you the money tomorrow if you'll get me to the airport."

He said, "You don't look like Larry Gatlin."

I sang one line of "All the Gold in California," and he nodded and said, "You're Larry Gatlin, and you've got a deal."

We headed for the Dallas/Fort Worth airport.

I was a wreck. I was sick. I was mad. I was hurting real bad all over. Most of all, I was scared. I didn't know what to do. My brain was so toxic that thinking clearly was impossible. I just breathed in and out and prayed and took a cab ride for which I had no money.

When the cab pulled up to the American Airlines entrance, I got out and started to unload my baggage. I heard a voice behind me.

"Hey, Larry."

I turned around and saw Michael, the bartender from the Admiral's Club inside the airport.

"Hey, Michael," I said, "can I borrow some money?"

Michael gave me some, and I thanked the cabbie for being willing to let it slide until I could get home and send him a check. Michael helped me into the terminal and with checking my bags and took me to the Admiral's Club. He knew that I was in bad shape.

I don't remember everything that happened, but I do remember giving him my phone number and asking him to call Janis. I overheard part of the conversation.

"He's alive, but he's in pretty bad shape," Michael said into the receiver.

I got home around noon and went to bed. I slept until the next morning. Janis was in the bathroom doing her makeup when the phone rang. I answered it. It was Ron Carpenter, my good friend and road manager.

"Larry, let's have lunch." He said it in the strangest tone of voice. It wasn't like him. Something inside me said, "He's gonna quit." He can no longer be part of this insanity. He is not willing to hang around and watch you kill yourself, Larry. It was over. I knew it. I couldn't run anymore. I had a choice—life or death. I chose life. I picked up the phone and called Darrell Royal.

"Jefe," I said, my nickname for him (Spanish for chief or sheriff).

"Why, hello, Larry Wayne," he said.

"I didn't make it, Darrell."

"Well, I knew you wouldn't, but that's OK."

"So, where are we going and when can we?" I asked.

"You name it and I'll come get you."

We agreed to meet in Fort Worth and I thanked him and hung up

PHOTO COURTESY OF RICK HENSON PHOTOGRAPHY

Mrs. Coach and Coach, Edith and Darrell Royal

the phone. I walked into the bathroom and said, "Honey." Janis turned around. "I just talked to Darrell. I'm going to go to treatment. He's gonna take me."

She started crying and laughing at the same time and came over and hugged me real tight and said she was glad and she knew that everything would be all right. I wasn't so sure about that part, but I did feel a sense of relief.

I was scheduled to do the *Family Feud* with some of my fellow Grand Ole Opry members—it was a "Celebrity Family Feud"—on December 9, 1984. Jerry Clower, Ricky Skaggs, Bill Anderson, and Jan Howard, I think. Anyway, we did the show, and then Darrell and I got in the limo and told the driver to take us to Orange County.

On the flight to Los Angeles, he hadn't pushed or told me what I was going to have to do or anything else. He just told me that everything would be fine and that I was going to be glad I had made the decision to get help.

On our way to the CareUnit of Orange, California, we saw a Mexican food place, so we asked the driver to stop. We had a wonderful

Mexican dinner, and I had four Tecates with lime wedges. It was great. I looked up at Darrell and said, "Darrell, I'm going to stop doing that cocaine and those pills, but by God, nobody's gonna tell me that I can't have a couple of beers with Mexican food every now and then."

"Well, cowboy, why don't you just take it easy and let the experts tell you what they think you really need to do, OK?"

Reluctantly I said, "Yeah. OK." After all, he was the head coach, and I decided to follow his game plan. It was too late to back out now.

We pulled into the driveway in front of the CareUnit of Orange, California, at around 8:00 that night, and I checked in at the front desk. Darrell asked the lady behind the desk to call Dr. Pursch in his office and tell him we were there. Darrell and Dr. Pursch had been in touch for a few days, and the "Doc" had agreed to stay late that night to wait for us.

I finished the paperwork just as he came up to the desk. "Hi, Larry, I'm Dr. Pursch," he said in his beautiful Yugoslavian accent. "I'm glad you're here."

He and Darrell shook hands, and after some small talk he showed me my room. We all talked for a few minutes, and then Darrell hugged me and said he would come to see me the next morning.

After Dr. Pursch told me good night, the two men walked down the hall and out the door. I was alone. This was it. The funny farm. The looney bin, all alone with a bunch of drunks and druggies, losers, winos, needle freaks, and "coke whores." Larry Gatlin—smalltown Pentecostal Christian kid from Odessa, Texas, all alone in the Care-Unit of Orange, California. I had never been more alone in my life, but without question it was exactly where I was supposed to be.

A nurse came into my room and said, "Larry, I'll have to take your shaving kit."

"Why is that?"

"Well," she said, "we don't want you to drink your aftershave or eat your deodorant."

I laughed out loud. "What?" I asked.

"They have alcohol in them, Larry, and we don't want you to have any alcohol."

"I'm not an alcoholic. I have a cocaine problem, but booze is not the problem. I'm *not* going to drink my aftershave or eat my deodorant."

"I'm taking it anyway," she said. And she did.

My education had begun. I was soon to find out I had a lot to learn.

The next morning I stormed down to the main nurses desk.

"Lady, there has been some kind of mistake," I said to the woman behind the desk.

"What's the problem?" she asked.

"The problem is that I have no shower in my room. I didn't notice it until this morning, but this is not going to work. I want a private room with a shower. I do not want a roomie. Where are the good rooms?" (I was talking rather loudly by now.)

"The shower is right down the hall," she said calmly, pointing to her right.

"No, you don't understand," I said, a little louder. "I want a room with a shower."

"The shower is right down the hall," she said calmly again.

"Lady, you still don't understand. I can afford a private room. Last week I stayed in the $1,000 per night Presidential Suite at the Hyatt in Fort Worth. I'm a star. I want one of the good rooms," I screamed.

"Mr. Gatlin," she said, even more calmly. "You are not a star in here. You are just an alcoholic and a drug addict like everybody else. The shower is right down the hall."

I turned on my heels and very slowly and calmly walked in the direction she had pointed. I walked into the men's communal shower and washed the previous day's residue from my body and the very fresh three-egg omelette off my face.

Let me stop here for a moment for an observation. My life has been one "God moment" after the other. One moment after another of God placing exactly the right person in my path. The incidents are recorded throughout this book. But never was there a more badly needed God moment than my meeting with the "lady drill sergeant" who was working at the nurses station that morning. She took no guff. She was not intimidated. She did not get mad. She simply and calmly pointed out the obvious: Mr. Gatlin, you are not a star in here. Thank you, God, for placing that nurse in my path. Thank you for that God moment. The cleansing, physically and symbolically, had begun.

I will not try to tell you everything that happened during the next twenty-eight days, but I think it is important to hit some of the high points.

After my shower, I dressed and walked around a little while. I noticed an old man using an aluminum walker, barely shuffling along. I asked the nurse, "What's his deal?"

"He's a speedballer," she replied. "He's probably not gonna make it two or three more days. His body can't take anymore."

"What's a speedballer?"

"He shoots heroine and cocaine at the same time."

"So he goes up and down at the same time?" I asked.

"Yep," she replied. "And the human body was not meant to do that."

The old man shuffled toward the courtyard door, and I hurriedly walked over and opened it for him. It was a bright, sunny, beautiful day.

"Let me help you," I said.

"Thanks," he replied.

"No problem," I said. I helped him get through the door, out into the courtyard, and over to a wooden chair.

I sat down in a chair across from him, and he opened up to me. "My back is killing me," he said. "Back always hurts every time I try to kick."

"I'll be glad to rub it for you, uh . . ."

"Vick," he said.

"I'd be glad to rub it for you, Vick, if that would help."

"OK, kid, that would be great. Thanks."

So I massaged his back for a while, and we talked. The guys back in New York had "shot him up" for his sixteenth birthday present, and he had been a heroine addict ever since. A few years before, he said, he'd found a new toy. "Speedballin'. I've tried to quit a hundred times. But this time I've got to make it. I'm getting too old for this. My body cannot take any more of this."

Then I asked him, "How old are you, old timer?"

"I'm fifty-one," he said.

My hands stopped moving on his back, and I'm sure my mouth flew open. I was stunned. He looked at least seventy, as God is my witness. Something inside of me said, "Larry, this could be you." Take heed. Pay attention. Your body can't stand any more of what you've put it through. Old Vick—the right person, at the right time, at the right place. A God moment!

I heard someone say one time that if a doctor would come into a new town, hang up a shingle, and just *listen* to patients for the first year, half of them would get well. Dr. Joseph Pursch must have heard *and* believed this to be true. At our first meeting, he spoke very little. Perhaps because I pontificated for most of the hour, but also because he is a wonderful listener and a compassionate soul. I ranted and raved and paced the room like a caged tiger, and he smiled and listened and asked an occasional question. He asked me to sit down and I did, but that didn't last very long. I was back up pacing, preaching, performing, and pontificating, trying to impress this guy I had heard so much about.

I expected him to fight back. I wanted him to fight back. I wanted a challenge. I wanted chaos. I wanted a confrontation. I was always at my best in the middle of battle. Well, he just sat there and smiled and listened and smiled some more. The right person, at the right time, at the right place. The caged tiger paced himself into the ground. A God moment!

Another God moment occurred during group therapy on my third day in treatment. At first my reaction was, "What a bunch of losers." A bunch of mealymouthed nut cases all sitting around in a circle, crying and whining and blaming every one but Santa Claus and the Tooth Fairy for their problems. This was my worst nightmare come true.

"Well, my mother did so and so," one girl whined.

Some guy said, "My dad did so and so."

And there in the middle of it all was some guy in a polyester suit, taking notes and encouraging everyone to be open and share their feelings. I wanted to barf. What I really wanted to do was get out of there. But something inside said, "Larry, this is your only shot. Do it whether you like it or not."

Well, the topic for sharing was one of the twelve steps of recovery, and different people talked about different steps and what they meant and how to do them. Finally, it was my turn. "I did all twelve of those son of a b— this morning. Why don't I feel any better?"

The Polyester Cowboy with the clipboard looked at me and said, "Larry, why don't you just try step one for a year and get back with us?" The right person, at the right time, at the right place, saying exactly the right thing. A God moment!

I went to my room. I got on my knees and I took the "Big Book" of Alcoholics Anonymous and opened it on my bed, to the place where it says, "There will come a time when no human power can keep you from taking a drink."

I read it out loud. I prayed. "Father, if it be possible, take this cup from me. Nevertheless, not my will but Thine be done. I cannot do this on my own. Please, dear God, save my life and remove the desire from me to drink and use drugs. In Jesus' name."

Then I shut up. I stayed on my knees for a few minutes. The God moment of all God moments occurred then and there. God removed the desire completely. From that moment to this, I have not wanted a drink or a drug. Praise be to Almighty God. Ain't God good?

From that God moment to this one, I *have* had life management problems like everybody else, but I have not wanted a drink or a drug. The miracle is real!

During my second meeting with Dr. Pursch, he immediately identified my problem. "Your problem is not drugs and alcohol—your problem is Larry," he said in his matter-of-fact, Yugoslavian accent. "You are the problem."

Hallelujah, I thought to myself. *Now we can get on with the fight, and I can show this old boy that he ain't dealing with one of those mealymouthed losers. I got a brain and a personality and a college degree, and I'm standing my ground.*

We jockeyed back and forth, feeling each other out. Then I started complaining about how Nashville didn't understand me or my songs, and how all the producers were playing the publishing game and wouldn't let their artists record my songs, and how people were spreading horrible stuff about me, and how I was the best songwriter in the world for Steve and Rudy and me and that nobody could write for us like I could. It was a rant worthy of Dennis Miller.

"Why do you feel so passionately about doing your own songs?" Dr. Pursch asked softly.

"Well, Doc," I said. "One night in Montreal, a lady came up to me and said, 'Larry, someone sang your song "Help Me" at my two-month-old daughter's funeral last year, and it really helped me get through it. God bless you and your brothers.' Well, Doc, what if we hadn't put 'Help Me' on that album? What if we had sung 'Rocky Top' or 'Tennessee Waltz' or one of those other songs that the Nashville crowd wanted us to record? (No offense intended to Felice and Boudeleaux Bryant who wrote "Rocky Top" or Pee Wee King who wrote "Tennessee Waltz.") Huh, Doc? Answer me that. That lady might have never heard 'Help Me.' Huh, Doc? Explain that one."

He looked at me with a tear in his eye and softly said, "Larry, you were an instrument of God's peace to that woman. Why can't you be an instrument of God's peace to yourself?"

A holy silence fell on the room. The meeting was over. The right person, at the right time, at the right place, saying exactly the right thing. A God moment if ever there was one.

I walked back to my room in silence. God had spoken to my heart. Anything I might have said would have been "clanging brass and a tinkling symbol." But God was not through yet.

After an AA meeting in the cafeteria that night I went over to meet a guy, "Big Foot" he was called, who had *quoted* chapter 5 of *The Big Book of Alcoholics Anonymous* during the meeting: "Rarely have we seen a person fail who thoroughly followed our path," he said and so on. He was doing it from memory—the whole thing. I was impressed.

"I enjoyed your chapter 5," I said.

"Thanks."

"My name is Larry, and I'm an alcoholic."

"My name's Glen and so am I," he said. "Are you the one who's supposed to be a hot-shot singer or something?"

"I'm Larry Gatlin of The Gatlin Brothers."

"Never heard of you," Glen H. said.

"Don't you have a TV?" I asked.

"No."

"Don't you have a radio?" I asked.

"No."

I was stunned and humbled and decided to shut up. The right person, at the right time, at the right place, saying exactly the right thing. Not impressed by who I was; the only person in the room without a TV or radio. Another God moment.

A couple of days later I asked Glen H., a.k.a. "Big Foot," to be my sponsor, and we have been wonderful friends ever since. Big Foot has played a major part in my recovery. I love you, Big Guy. You're a winner (that's what he always tells me).

Unfortunately, not everyone who enters treatment is successful in recovery. An anesthesiologist was undergoing treatment in Orange County around the same time. I can't remember his name so I'll just call him "Doc." Doc and I ran together every morning. A van would take us six or eight blocks to a junior high school track, and Doc and I would run two or three miles while the other folks would just walk around or sit and do nothing.

"Look at all those losers," we would say as we surveyed our fellow "inmates." Then while running, I said one day, "I'm gonna make it."

"Yeah, me too," Doc said. "I feel real good. I'm getting out in four days.

"You keep up the good work and keep running two or three miles and you'll do fine."

"Yeah, you too," I said.

"I just know I'm gonna make it," he said.

Four days later Doc checked out after twenty-eight days of meetings, prayers, twelve-step classes, one-on-one consultations, and intense psychological evaluation. Two days after he checked out, someone brought him back in with 108 needle holes in his arms. He'd been skin-popping heroine for two days. He was almost dead. I looked at him in disbelief. His words rang in my ears: "I just know I'm gonna make it." The right person, at the right time, at the right place, saying exactly the right thing. It was a very frightening God moment, but a God moment nonetheless.

Doc was too sick to stay at the CareUnit. They transferred him to an emergency intensive care hospital. I never saw him again— until about ten minutes ago when I saw him in my mind's eye as surely as if he were running beside me on the track at the junior high school. "Look at those losers," he said. "I'm gonna make it. I just know I am." I hope you did, Doc. I really hope you did.

I don't know whether or not Doc made it, but Tim K. did. Tim and I didn't really meet each other until I had already been in treatment for nearly two weeks, but when we hooked up with each other it was instant friendship. We had a lot in common: vodka, beer, cocaine, pills. We were both successful businessmen, from good homes, with college educations. We had something else in common. We knew we were going to die if we didn't stop snorting cocaine. It was that simple.

We talked for hours and hours at the CareUnit and after "graduation" we stayed in touch. Tim came to New York to see me in *The Will Rogers Follies* back in 1993. I haven't seen him in a while. I tried to call him yesterday, but there wasn't anybody at home. But even though I didn't get an answer, I got a good feeling. I just know that Tim is OK. He always has been a good guy, and I hope he's still sober. Meeting Tim was a God moment. I can't wait to see him again. He's a winner and a brother. (I talked to him today, and he's OK. Thank God.)

Not only were there no showers in the rooms, there were no phones. The one pay phone down by the nurses station was a hot commodity, and someone was always on it. I was not allowed to call out or receive calls for a few days. But finally I called Janis, and we had a great talk. Dr. Pursch told me that he thought it would be OK for Janis and the kids to come out for Christmas. So we planned a big get together at the Disneyland Hotel.

Dr. Pursch gave me a day pass, and I picked up my little family at the Los Angeles Airport, and we drove to Disneyland. It was December 24, 1984. I had been in treatment for fifteen days, and I felt pretty good. I was so glad to see Janis and Kristin and Josh, I just laughed and cried and hugged them and then laughed and cried and hugged them some more.

After we opened our Christmas presents, the kids went downstairs to look around and Janis and I spent some "quality time" together. I won't go into the details, but it was quality time. I knew that I had never loved her more than I did at that moment. My emotions had been so numbed by booze and drugs for the preceding three or four years, I had somehow lost sight of what a wonderful blessing this good woman had been in my life. Our quality time and love making and communion with each other was the most precious it had ever been in our entire married life. We knew we had almost lost each other, and in finding sobriety and a new sense of purpose and a new way of living, we found each other again. It was a God moment, par excellence. I can honestly say that even after almost thirty years of marriage, when the spirit moves us and we engage in a little "quality time" together—it is *still* a God moment. Ain't that wonderful?

The right people, at the right time, at the right place. Janis, Kristin, and Josh; Christmas '84; Disneyland—a God moment I'll never forget.

The CareUnit experience: a.k.a. twenty-eight days of one God moment after another, the right person, at the right time, at the right place, ordered by God to bring the prodigal son back to a glorious, loving, forgiving, and restoring reunion with his Father, his family, and the whole universe.

CHAPTER 13

Josh, me, Kristin, and Prince Ugly

$\mathscr{F}$AMILY WEEK
AND GOING PUBLIC

"Family week"—the week from hell . . . and it was.

Talking calmly and objectively and lovingly—especially about substantive, serious family problems, a.k.a. "dirty laundry"—well, that's never been one of the Gatlin family's strong suits. We're more into screamin' and hollerin' and rantin' and ravin'. Add to that the fact that talking back to grown-ups was something that just wasn't done, and you can understand why this family week had all the makings of World War III. And there would be strangers in the room and some shrink types—well, World War III it was.

That week was one of the most nerve-racking, awful, painful

weeks in any of our lives and, without question, one of the most important. The shrink types were actually two very nice, loving, caring, well-educated, and highly trained individuals who had seen this stuff hundreds of times and knew exactly what to do.

Family week consists of several distinct parts. First, the counselors establish some ground rules—love and honesty and no fistfights— then they show some films about family dynamics. After a day of beating around the bush, family members start beating on each other. Not literally, but verbally.

The deal is this—alcoholics and addicts live in a world of out-and-out lies and half-truths. During these sessions family members sit face-to-face with the patient and tell him or her what he or she has done to hurt the person sitting opposite them. The patient is not allowed to retaliate in any way to this "things I don't like about you" deal. Then the spouse or son or daughter or brother or sister or father or mother tells the patient what he or she likes about him or her. Finally the process is turned around, and the patient gets to do the same thing. Believe me—it is very difficult to confront a father with his faults and failures. And I'm sure it was difficult for my dad to confront me with all of mine.

One thing that happens during this time: you begin to walk around in the other person's shoes. So it was with me and my dad.

My dad had some pretty tough breaks as a kid. His sister disappeared into the East Texas night. His dad was sick with Parkinson's disease. He only got to finish the tenth grade. He worked his fingers to the bone eight hours a day, seven days a week, with every penny going for the necessities and the few amenities we could afford. There were no unions to help regulate oil field workers' hours and working conditions. Life really stinks when you have to drive seventy miles one way to get to a stinking oil rig in 100 degree heat or 10 degree cold for barely enough money to get by. On top of that, a guy had cheated him out of an interest in an oil well that would have made us rich for life.

During family week I began to walk that walk with him, now that I, too, was a dad and knew something about how he felt.

He was tired. Physically. Emotionally. Spiritually exhausted, all the time when I was a kid. He was the kind of tired that twenty-four hours of sleep won't fix. He was tired of drilling rigs and seventy-mile one-way trips and paychecks that weren't big enough. But he kept on keepin' on because a man takes care of his family and puts bread on tables and clothes on backs and shoes on feet and gas in cars. And when just the wrong combination of tired-to-the-bone and sick-of-heart and mad-at-the-world collides with a son whose hair is a little too long or who is a little late getting in from a date or who doesn't exactly toe the line in some matters . . . well, sometimes things got a little hot.

I love what Mark Twain said about fathers and sons: "When I was a boy of fourteen, my father was so ignorant I could hardly stand to have the old man around. But when I got to be twenty-one, I was astonished at how much the old man had learned in seven years."

Dad and Mom had moved to Nashville in 1982, and Dad became my farm foreman. He and Mom lived in a house across the street. We still argued on occasion but since it was my farm and since Dad was now working for me, he did his job in the same workmanlike fashion that he would have if I'd been his boss on a drilling rig. My dad could overhaul the space shuttle with a pair of pliers and a screwdriver, and the farm was always in need of his skills and knowledge.

During and after my time in treatment, we began to feel each other out. As we did, we started liking each other again (we always loved each other). Occasionally, he'd say stuff like, "Well, I probably should have done that a little differently" or maybe, "I was too hard on you and I shouldn't have been," and over a period of three or four years a wonderful miracle occurred. The spirit of love that had lain dormant in each of us was slowly rekindled, and we began to do things together again—like bird hunting and playing golf—and the hurts and fears and angers and resentments of the past were relegated to their rightful place of nonimportance. Or as my Mexican buddy Louie Murillo says, "No le hace" ("It don't matter").

At times in the past, they had mattered to both of us. We were both tired and beat up and vulnerable and scared and confused, and we struck at each other. And we were both right at times and wrong at times. But we made it to the other side of the hurt and anger. We both threw down our crosses and gave up our roles as bleeding messiahs and in the spirit of the true Messiah, forgave each other as He forgives us. And we are now great friends.

Oh, sure, we still disagree about a lot of stuff and sometimes we ruffle each other's feathers. Big deal. *No le hace.* We give each other some room. We count to ten or twenty or a thousand, and we no longer take the Butch Cassidy and Sundance Kid leap off the cliff into the swirling water and bone-crunching boulders below.

It's wonderful; it really is. The past is healed. It was what it was. Today and tomorrow are now far more important to me and my dad than yesterday ever was. The good things of yesterday are stored in our memories. My first 22-caliber rifle at Christmas when I was six years old. Our first rabbit hunt. Going to the rig with Dad and the roughnecks. Baseball and football games. A lot of good stuff is stored in our memories forever.

Family week is a gruesome, awful, bloody, tearful thing—that's the bad news. The good news: a mystical, magical, spiritual healing begins to take place as family members clear out the family closets and face one another in a loving and truthful confrontation. Confession is good for the soul. So is accusation—if it is followed by reconciliation and forgiveness. Our family was surely dysfunctional, with secrets upon secrets, layers of neurotic behavior and fear, doubt, anger, and jealousy. It was, in other words, a pretty typical All-American family (if you don't believe it—just look around).

We cried and prayed and sobbed and hurt each other, and after about $50 worth of Kleenex and a bucket of tears, we all embraced and forgave and promised to start over and try to be more open and more loving. It has not worked perfectly, but I will tell you without a doubt, the Gatlin family is much healthier and more open and more loving and caring today than it was before we went through the "Week from Hell."

Steve and Rudy and I still disagree on occasion. Sometimes things get a little hot—but we know how to cool it and just let things take their course. We are still very passionate, volatile men, but we are now more practical and mature. Thank God. The same goes for my relationship with my folks. They are wonderful people who have always done the very best they knew how for their four kids. Yes, it was a week from hell, but when a family goes through hell together—which is exactly what we did—that family is stronger, smarter, and more able to withstand the trials and tribulations that are a part of every life. As I have often said, "I believe that old Daniel had a lot more faith when he came out of the lions' den than he had when he went in."

Family Week was awful, but it was a God moment of lions' den and fiery furnace proportions. So I thank God for the week from hell.

• • •

In the twenty-eight days I was at the CareUnit of Orange, I learned a lot of things that would serve me well on the outside. One was that Dr. Joe Pursch is, very simply, the best alcohol and drug man in the world. His touch, his voice, his heart, his knowledge, his intelligence, and more than anything else, his genuine love of God and God's children—all are remarkable. We became very close during my stay and to this day remain great friends. I "go to the couch" on occasion even now. All I have to do is call and Dr. Pursch comes to the rescue. He has never given me bad advice.

On the occasion of our last meeting at the CareUnit, he told me I could make this thing work if I put Larry's ego to death and allowed God to rule my life. He was right then. He is right now. When I act out of Larry's ego, things come unraveled. When God is allowed free reign in my life, things work out for the best.

Dr. Pursch's favorite saying must be "Let go and let God." Over the years I have remembered many times his saying it as he stood at the front door of the CareUnit and waved good-bye to me. He said, "Larry, remember, let go and let God." It was a God moment I'll always cherish.

The other things I learned were some steps that are suggested as a program of recovery:

Step 1: *Admitted I was powerless over alcohol—that my life was unmanageable.*

I was in the CareUnit almost a week before I admitted my alcohol addiction to anyone. Finally an old timer told me in no uncertain terms to quit messin' around and get with the program. The next day, at a small AA meeting, I said the hardest words I've ever spoken: "I'm Larry, and I'm an alcoholic."

For some reason it was easy to admit I was a cocaine addict. I guess because for so long doing coke was a status symbol. All the cool people, all the beautiful people, did coke. To sit in a meeting of strangers and admit that I was an alcoholic—a drunk, no better or worse than the winos I had written about in "The Midnight Choir"—well, that was something else. But I did it. Another God moment. I felt free. I felt I had turned a corner, and I saw that the light at the end of the tunnel was not an oncoming train.

Step 2: *Came to believe in a power greater than myself that could restore me to sanity.*

I've always believed in God. The problem was, I believed in Larry and Larry's version of sanity more than I believed in God and His version of sanity. The Bible says, "All our righteousnesses is as filthy rags." Well, my sanity was filthy rags and total insanity. It seemed perfectly sane to snort and smoke cocaine with total strangers and walk through Central Park in New York at 2:00 A.M. looking for drugs. It seemed sane to leave my wife and kids for weeks at a time to hang out with druggies in Los Angeles. All of that was Larry's sanity, which was obviously totally insane.

My higher power's sanity is love, happiness, patience, persistence, smiles, goodness, and the blessings of a loving Father. It is my wife and kids, brothers and sisters, and friends and neighbors drinking Coke instead of doing coke. It is a wonderful gift.

Don't get me wrong—sometimes I'm still crazy, but I'm no longer insane. God has restored me to His sanity, and I'm grateful.

Step 3: *Made a decision to turn my will and my life over to the care of God as I understand Him.*

Or, as I say, don't understand Him. It would be arrogant to say I understand a God who scattered the stars and planets into the void of space, who breathes life into a baby's lungs at the moment of birth, and who transports us into the next world at the moment of our last breath in this one.

I do not understand it all, but to the degree God has let me understand, I turn my will over to Him, gladly, because my way does not work. I tried living life my way, and I woke up on the floor of a Holiday Inn smoking carpet lint.

Believe me, friends, this part of the program is very hard for me. I want to stick a steering wheel in the ground and drive the world around. But if I could do that, I would get us all in a big wreck. Turning my will over to God is a daily deal with me. When I do it early in the morning, my day is usually great. When I wait until noon or midday, my day usually stinks until I get alone somewhere with that God who did all the star-scattering and breath-giving and say, "OK, Father, forgive my arrogance. You can have your world back."

Oh, did I say it was a matter of *daily* surrender to God's will? With Larry Wayne Gatlin, surrendering to God's will is a minute-by-minute thing.

Step 4: *Made a searching and fearless moral inventory of myself.*

I wrote it all down. It was not pretty.

Step 5: *Admitted to God, to myself, and to another human being the exact nature of my wrongs.*

Poor Glen H., a.k.a. Big Foot, he had to sit there and listen to all my garbage. But he was very patient and loving and understanding. I thought I was really shocking him. But after this little process was over, Glen looked at me and said, "No big deal, Burrhead. I've heard it all before and done most of it myself."

Step 6: *Was entirely ready to have God remove all my defects of character.*

I have always had trouble with this step too. I guess it's my West Texas work ethic. I believe that I'm supposed to have to work for everything. The concept of grace and of God doing the work is still hard for me. I feel guilty. I feel like I have to do something to rid myself of all my defects.

On a daily basis, I have to turn this defects deal over to God. Slowly but surely, He is making of me what His vision of me is. Here are three ideas I like: (1) I'm not perfect, just forgiven; (2) God does not make junk; (3) G.R.A.C.E.—God's Riches At Christ's Expense (Mickey Rooney told me that one). As I become ready on a daily basis for God to remove my defects, He does it in His time.

Step 7: *Humbly ask Him to remove my shortcomings.*

Ask is the key word. To become ready is one thing. To ask God, in childlike faith, to remove defects and shortcomings takes courage and faith. I mustered up just a thimbleful of each and the miracle began to happen.

Step 8: *Made a list of all persons I have harmed and became willing to make amends to them.*

There ain't enough paper, ink, or time. I offended thousands, or even millions, at a time on TV or in newspaper articles. When I was doing research for this book, I ran across some newspaper and magazine articles I did back in the "good old days." I was shocked. Dear God, did I really say all of that? In keeping with my promise to myself, my family, Dr. Pursch, Big Foot, and God Almighty, I began making a list. It was long and painful. It was also an eye-opener to see how many people I had hurt because of the volatile combination of booze, drugs, an opinion on everything, and a big mouth.

Step 9: *Made direct amends to all those I had harmed wherever possible except when to do so would injure them or others.*

I really believe that I have done this part fairly well. Do not get me wrong; I'm not a saint. There are those in my life from whom I have not asked forgiveness—face-to-face. Whoever you are, wherever you are, I'm really sorry. Please forgive me.

Step 10: *Continued to take personal inventory and when I was wrong, promptly admitted it.*

I do not always do the right thing. During treatment I was taught that amends must be made when my self-inventory indicates a wrong done to another. I have had to learn to ask for forgiveness and say, "I'm sorry."

Fast-forward to me and my boy, Joshua Cash Gatlin, circa 1994. Let me set the scene for you. I was tired—well past tired, exhausted, by the comings and goings of my life and for better or worse (obviously worse) my bleeding messiah complex had kicked in. I was in a terrible mood because the world did not appreciate me and nothing was going right and yatta, yatta, yatta.

I was physically and mentally and spiritually exhausted—I was sucking my thumb and couldn't get anybody to suck their thumb with me. Then along comes this kid Josh Gatlin. He says something or does something (I don't remember what), and it hit the bleeding messiah in the wrong place and—whammo!—I came unglued. I screamed. I ranted. I raved. I threatened. I shamed my wonderful son into thinking for a little while that he was a low-life worthless piece of dog droppings who had no feelings for me and the sacrifices I'd made for him and who took advantage of my big heart on every occasion.

Silence filled the room, then tears welled up in Josh's young, totally innocent eyes. Then the bleeding messiah—Larry Wayne Gatlin—went off to the other room, taking his cross and dragging it with him, leaving behind a kid whose world had been temporarily shattered by his best friend, his hero, his dad.

Alone in my room, I laid the cross in a corner and stretched out on the bed. Within minutes—no, within seconds—the poison and anger, shame and guilt, and genuine self-loathing so overwhelmed me that I got up and almost ran to the other room to find my boy. I didn't take the cross. I was no longer the bleeding messiah. I was the pleading father.

"Josh, I was wrong," I said. "You haven't done anything wrong."

Those same innocent eyes turned to me, now full of tears of forgiveness, and the best boy I've ever known said, "That's OK, Pop. I knew you didn't mean all that stuff."

I stammered, "Please forgive me, Son. I was wrong."

"It's OK, Dad. There's nothing to forgive. Go take a nap, and we'll go get some Mexican food after a while."

We hugged. I went to the bedroom and took a nap, and later I had the Number 3 enchilada plate with a side order of grease, and Josh had the soft tacos and a double order of tamales at Matt's El Rancho in Austin. No harm done. Forgiveness asked for and freely given.

Step 11: *Sought through prayer and meditation to improve my conscious contact with God as I understand Him, praying only for knowledge of His will for me and the power to carry that out.*

Prayer—what a privilege. Meditation—what a blessing. I try to get alone with God at least twice a day. One of my favorite times to pray is on my daily run. I love to run on the sand in Myrtle Beach or along Town Lake in Austin or across the Golden Gate Bridge in San Francisco, in Central Park in New York or in Central Park in Zagreb, Croatia, on the streets of Moscow or on the Left Bank near the Eiffel Tower in Paris. I could go on and on. I love to run and pray. God can keep up with my eight-and-a-half-minute pace, and some of my greatest times of prayer are during those jogs through His beautiful world.

My other favorite thing to do is this: I get somewhere alone and lean back in a chair and just think stuff like, "I will greet this day with love in my heart" from Og Mandino's book, *The Greatest Salesman in the World.* These times of silence—alone with God—are marvelous. "Be still, and know that I am God." In stillness there is strength and healing. I love the stillness. God lives there.

Step 12: *Having had a spiritual awakening as a result of those steps, tried to carry this message to other alcoholics and to practice those principles in all my affairs.*

Many of us exclaimed, "What an order! I can't go through with it." Don't be discouraged. No one among us has been able to maintain anything like perfect adherence to these principles.

Folks, I have had a wonderful spiritual awakening as a result of following these steps. I do not do them perfectly, but that's why they call it "practicing the steps."

I have done my best to carry the message, from Moscow to Memphis, from Minneapolis to Mogadishu, literally all over the world, and I will continue to do so. The truth in those steps has saved my life. Those truths were first laid down by the master Teacher, Jesus, on the side of a mountain almost two-thousand years ago, and they still work. A reborn, sober, sane, and upwardly moving Larry Gatlin is living proof.

A little historical perspective before I move on to the next period of my life.

One of the traditions of AA is that those in the program will remain anonymous at the level of the press, radio, and TV. I have asked my sponsor and others how to respect this tradition but still write this book to tell my story. Glen H. told me very simply, "Newspapers are 'the press.' Your life story in book form is not a newspaper. TV is TV. Radio is radio. Neither of them is a book. So, Burrhead, don't spout about AA in the paper or radio or TV. Write your book and pass on the good news of recovery, and quit trying to make everything so darn difficult. Keep it simple."

When I talked about my recovery with Johnny Carson on *The Tonight Show*, or with my old buddy Larry King on *Larry King Live* and on Larry's radio show, I never said AA or Alcoholics Anonymous. It is true I talked a little about the program. To talk of my recovery and not at least refer to "a program of recovery" would be less than truthful. And getting to the truth is what recovery and sanity are all about. In my heart, I have honored our AA tradition of anonymity at the level of the press, radio, and TV and will continue to do so.

Dr. Pursch told me I would need the support and understanding of my road group—the band and crew—to be successful in my recovery program, so I flew the boys to Orange County for four days, and he explained the deal to them. They agreed then and there to help and support me. The band and crew vowed they would not drink or drug while we were on the road, for a period of one year. We said a prayer, hugged each other, and we were off.

Dr. Joe waved good-bye, and we headed to the airport. On January 6, 1985, I left the CareUnit of Orange and flew home to Nashville, to Janis and Kristin and Josh and a new start. I felt great. I was not nervous. I really believed I was going to do this thing—with God's help and the support of my family and friends. So when the *Good Morning America* folks called two weeks later to ask if I would come to New York and discuss my treatment at the CareUnit and my plans for the future, I immediately said yes.

Kathy Gangwisch, my weird, wonderful, zany, and very good P.R. lady, called me at my hotel the night before the show.

"Larry, there's been a slight change," she said. "Joan and Charlie are out sick [or something], and there will be a guest host tomor-row. Do you still want to do it, even if it's with someone you don't know?"

Well, I was nervous now. The boys and I had done the show with Joan Lunden and Charles Gibson on other occasions, so we were all acquainted. Naturally, I was looking forward to being with one of them. The prospect of doing my "recovery interview"—my first national TV show posttreatment with a total stranger—was cause for a bit of anxiety.

"Well, Kathy," I said, "that really stinks (or something like that—I'm not sure). Who is the stand-in host?"

"They aren't sure, Larry Wayne," Kathy replied, "but I think you should do it and get it out in the open and get on with your life. Don't you?"

"Yes, I do," I answered. "Let's do it."

The next morning I woke up at about 4:30 and did my run in Central Park and prayed and asked God to take charge of the situ-ation and keep me clean and sober, one day at a time. I did all the "steps," lovingly drilled into me at the CareUnit, as best I could. I went back to the St. Moritz, showered, and went downstairs to the car provided by *Good Morning America*.

When I got to the studio, the production assistant met me with a smile and a clipboard (contracts to sign) and cheerfully said, "Larry, Kathie Lee Johnson will be doing your interview today. Do you know her?"

I can almost hear Rod Serling now—"Next stop, the Twilight Zone!"

What a coincidence, I thought then. (I have since learned there really are no coincidences, or as we say in "the program," coinci-dences are God's way of remaining anonymous.)

"Why, yes, I do know her," I said. "She's an old friend."

An old friend indeed. Perhaps even a lifesaver, as I discussed ear-lier in this book. The faith and confidence of Kathie Lee Johnson—not yet Kathie Lee Gifford—was very settling to a thirty-nine-day clean-and-sober addict–alcoholic. She very gently led me into a dis-cussion of what had gone wrong in my life, what had helped me to see the light, and what was going right with my new life. A God moment. The right person, at the right time, at the right place, saying exactly the right thing.

I got to ask America's forgiveness. I got to do a big universal ninth step. I got to apologize to people I didn't even know for my hurtful actions. It was one of the most healing and cleansing moments of my life. It was a God moment.

When the interview was over, Kathie Lee and I hugged, and I thanked her for being my friend and for hanging in there when I was less than lovable.

I walked out of the *Good Morning America* studio, up toward the makeup room to take off my "face." When I sat down in the chair, Kathie Lee was on the TV monitor. She said, "We'll be back in the next hour with Ann (so and so)," and she named the wonderful lady who was to be her next guest.

I said to the makeup lady who was wiping the "goo" off my face, "I didn't know Ann was doing the show today too. I would like to say hi to her. I've known her a long time."

Well, the production assistant overheard this conversation and said, "Larry, I'll go tell Ann you're here and want to say hello. She doesn't go on for another twenty or twenty-five minutes."

After the makeup removal ordeal, I walked down the hall to Ann's dressing room. She burst out of the door and held my face and said, "Oh, Larry, you were wonderful just now. I'm so proud of you. I didn't know you were a friend of Bill W." (code for "I'm a recovering alcoholic in the AA program too.")

Well, again I would hear Rod Serling in the background—"Next stop, the Twilight Zone!"

That sweet lady—who shall, in keeping with our tradition, remain anonymous—is one of Hollywood's all-time biggest stars, most beautiful women, and greatest talents. But all of that pales when compared to her great heart and compassion. She hugged and encouraged me and told me to stick with it and that she and her husband would pray for me.

Well, I cried, she cried, and another wonderful moment of healing and peace and forgiveness swept over me. In the retelling of the events of that *Good Morning America* morning, I am again over-come with emotion and gratitude. There is, however, a difference today. I no longer hear the voice of Rod Serling. I now recognize that voice for what it really is—the still, small voice of God, our Father, whispering to us that all is well. Whispering to us that "though I walk through the valley of the shadow of death, I will fear no evil; for You are with me. . . ."

What a comfort that voice is in times of trouble. Over the years I have even learned to listen to that voice when I'm not in trouble. I go off by myself somewhere and listen. And He speaks. Not in audible tones, but in that still, small voice. And while I have not per-fected the art of listening, I am better at it than I was. My journey from being a full-blast, dominate-the-conversation kind of guy started that morning in January of 1985 with Kathie Lee Johnson, soon-to-be Gifford, and with Ann. Listening to the voice of God.

What a concept!!

No. . . . What a reality and what a blessing!

CHAPTER 14

Me, Ava Gabor, Merv, and the Chairman of the Board

$\mathcal{T}$HE CLIMATE
WAS A CHANGIN'

After I "graduated" from CareUnit High, I resumed my singing activities with the brothers and the band, and Janis and I started putting all our stuff back together. The kids were growing, and life was really good.

After the *Good Morning America* show I flew to Washington for "The Second Reagan Inaugural Gala Performance" at the Kennedy Center in Washington, D.C. It was a star-studded evening. Frank Sinatra was the host, and there were big names galore—Don Rickles, Robert Wagner and Jill St. John, Ray Charles, Crystal Gayle, Jimmy Stewart, Mikhail Baryshnikov, Twyla Tharp.

It was on this occasion that my old pal Merv Griffin told Mr. Sinatra about my song, "I've Done Enough Dyin' Today." I was thirteen days out of treatment for drugs and booze, sitting in a chair a few feet from the stage with Steve and Rudy, waiting for our rehearsal. Merv walked up and said hello and we visited for a couple of minutes. Then he got a huge smile on his face and said, "Frank, this kid has written one of the greatest songs I've ever heard. He did it on my show a few years ago and absolutely stopped the whole show. Larry, what is the name of that song?"

"'I've Done Enough Dyin' Today', Merv," I said.

Merv was still bubbling all over. "Frank, it's a great song."

Mr. Sinatra looked at me and said, "Larry, what's the name of it?"

"Well, Mr. Sinatra—"

"Frank. Call me Frank."

"Yes, sir. Frank. It's called 'I've Done Enough Dyin' Today.'"

The Chairman of the Board looked at me for another couple of seconds and said, "I know that song. Why do I know that song?"

"Frank," I said very respectfully, "do you remember when Don Costa played you some songs in Vegas a few years ago by a Nashville songwriter?"

Frank nodded. "Yeah. I remember that. There were a bunch of great songs."

"Well, sir, that songwriter was me, and the songs were my songs."

About that time, Gary Smith, the producer of the show, hollered some instructions to Frank (actually, they were more like suggestions. Nobody, but nobody, hollers instructions to Frank Sinatra).

As Frank walked off toward Gary, he looked over his shoulder and said, "Kid, get me a tape of that 'Dyin'' song."

"Yes, sir, I will."

I sent a copy of the song to Frank, and a couple of weeks later I received a letter, in which he said:

> About the tape . . . played it several times. . . . I think it's as good a saloon song as I've heard in a long time. I will probably, in the near future, put it in the book for the one-nighters,

concerts, etc., etc . . . as I will not be recording for some
time. And there I needn't tell you why; material today does-
n't fit me. . . so I have to wait 'til I find some more things.

So, if you come upon an idea for something similar that
will work for me, shoot it to me and then perhaps I can find
enough material to knock off an album.

Frank never recorded the song, but just to know he liked it is
something I will never forget. The Man, the Chairman, the Voice.

Another time I remember with Frank was at the reopening of the
Statue of Liberty in July of 1986. It was another Smith-Hemion spectacular, "Liberty Weekend," televised on ABC. At one point, backstage, I looked up and realized I was actually having a conversation
with Frank Sinatra, Shirley MacLaine, and Elizabeth Taylor. How I
was included in that circle I still do not know. But they were talking to me and I was answering back and we were nodding and laughing and I felt like one of the gang. I had visited with Ms. Taylor the
evening before at some fancy reception (we met at the presidential
inaugural gala for the first time). She was very sweet and are those
eyes violet! We have some things in common regarding prescription
medication, and we talked about healing and love and forgiveness.

I was like a kid at Disneyland, all these legendary performers and
me and my brothers on the same stage. I just knew in my heart that
this was a special night and that our career was going to take off
again. (Well, part of the feeling was accurate.) It was a special night.
Frank Sinatra sang "Quarter to Three" ("No one in the place, but
just you and me"), while Mikhail "Misha" Baryshnikov did this
beautiful, Twyla Tharp-choreographed number to the song. I don't
know much about dancing, but that Misha fellow is one heck of an
athlete. If you don't believe me, you try jumping up in the air and
turning two complete circles and landing squarely on your feet. This
was followed by Jimmy Stewart, Don Rickles, and R. J. Wagner and
Jill St. John, Crystal Gayle, The Gatlin Brothers, and the Reverend
Ray Charles. It was a terrific evening and, I hoped, the start of the
rejuvenation of our career.

After the inaugural gala, a whole gang of us went back to the

Blue eyes galore—me and Elizabeth Taylor, a very sweet lady

Mayflower Hotel and had dinner. It was fun. Life was good. I was sober and really excited about my life. Janis and I were staying with our good friends, Jim and Ann Free, and we were all planning to go to the inaugural parade and then to President Reagan's swearing-in. Well, that never did happen. It got so cold that night that the whole deal was canceled. So Jim Free and I went to Maryland with another friend of ours, Jim Bugg, and went goose hunting. Real smart. It's too cold to watch a parade but just right to sit in a duck blind on the little Choptank River and wait for a goose to fly over. (Kinda makes you wonder which one is the goose.)

The Reagans were always nice to all of us. We went to several different functions at the White House, and Nancy and I did a bunch of "Just Say No" programs together. Jane Erkenbeck, Mrs. Reagan's assistant, would call me and say, "Larry, this is the Golden Girl. [She always has a great tan.] Mrs. Reagan will be in Atlanta (or San Francisco or wherever), and she would love for you to come and sing some songs and tell the kids about drugs and alcohol."

I'm not sure how many of those programs I did, but I always loved being with Mrs. Reagan. She is a sweet lady and really does care about people. She got a bad rap about being cold and hard to know. Nancy and Ronald Reagan are, in my opinion, among the best things to happen to America in a long time. They helped restore pride and dignity to our country and they stopped the commies. That's good enough for me.

After the inaugural week, it was on to Radio City Music Hall in New York for "Night of a Thousand Stars" (and one million stage hands). I'm not even gonna try to tell you about this night. I'm just going to give you a list of the performers: Lucille Ball, Gregory Peck, Sir Lawrence Olivier, Christopher Reeve, Alexander Gudinov, Ann-Margret, The Gatlin Brothers, and many others.

Radio City Music Hall, New York City, national TV—and Larry Gatlin and The Gatlin Brothers were part of this fabulous show. One thing I will always remember about it is seeing big, big stars with autograph books backstage, working the room, asking each other for autographs. It was a hoot!

Next, Steve and Rudy and I performed at the CMA awards show in Nashville, my first time since coming out of treatment. My throat was bothering me a little, but I just knew, now that I was taking better care of myself, it would get well and everything would be all right. (When my throat had bothered me in the past, a little rest usually did the trick.) I never gave it a second thought.

Before I knew it, everyone wanted to hear my story of recovery. I got a call from the principal of a Nashville high school, who asked if I would talk to his students about drugs. I said, "Sure."

Well, the local paper did a little blurb, which was picked up by the AP and UPI wires. The next thing I knew I was inundated with requests to talk to schools and civic groups. This began one of the most meaningful times of my life—sharing the good news of recovery with young people. I spoke all over the country and even went to Moscow to a big AA convention, where I sang and told my story. It was a fabulous experience. To see a big ole, red-faced, gray-headed, stubbly bearded Russian crying like a baby and thanking the God of his understanding for delivering him from the grip of vodka was truly inspirational. It brought home to me again that the disease of alcoholism knows no geographical borders or economic boundaries. More importantly, it reminded me that God is a loving God of all people, rich or poor, Christian or Jew, black or white, Russian or American. When God is brought into the situation, the situation changes for the better. He knows no borders and is no respecter of persons.

Fast-forward two years to March of 1987. I got a call from someone in Houston (for the life of me I cannot remember who) while we were there to sing at the Houston Livestock Show & Rodeo at the Astrodome. "Your ole buddy 'Wondrous William' [not his real name] is in city jail and about to go to Huntsville. I'm sure he'd like to see you," said the someone whose name I can't remember.

When I was playing football at the U of H, Wondrous William was our star running back. On his good days, he was simply the most electrifying football player on earth. You know all those things Michael Jordan does with a basketball? Well, William did the same kind of things with a football. When he really wanted to play (which unfortunately was not very often), he made it look like a game of men versus boys. William was the fastest human being for 30 or 40 yards anyone had ever seen. Lord knows, he was hard to catch.

Well, someone did finally catch him—the Houston Police Department. I walked into the city jail and signed in and they searched me. Then I was taken to see William.

"Sweet, what took you so d— long to get here? Man, I need you. Get your a— over here," William said with a big laugh. He always called me "Sweet" because I used to have to jump and dive to catch passes. What would be an easy catch for most guys was a remarkable catch for me. I was short and slow, not a good combination for a wide receiver. William always hollered "Sweet" every time I made one of my diving catches. "It is so sweet the way you catch the ball." Well, it stuck and he called me Sweet from then on.

William had been busted for possession of cocaine and not for the first time. There was also a little matter of burning down his girlfriend's house because she had turned him in. It was a mess. We talked, laughed, and reminisced about old times and all our old U of H football buddies, and then he said, "You gotta get me outta here, Sweet. They are trying to send William to the Big House in Huntsville. I can't do that deal, Sweet. You gotta help me. The judge said something about one of the treatment places, but I don't know if I can do that either. You gotta help me, Sweet. You're my only hope. Do something, man. You're a big star, and the judge, man, he'll listen to you."

I told him I'd do what I could, and I left. It was great to see him again, but it was terrible to see him behind bars.

I talked to his parole officer, and I even made a videotaped plea for leniency to the judge.

Well, it worked. The next thing I knew Wondrous William was in the Faulkner Center in Austin, and I was on my way to see him. I walked in with my son, Josh, who was then ten years old. We were on our way to Vegas, and we were looking forward to some time together.

William was out of control. The counselor told me he was the most uncooperative person she had ever seen. All he did was prance around and say stuff like, "You don't even know who I am."

He even had someone send a bunch of old newspaper clippings to his counselor so she would show him some respect. It would have been laughable had it not been so tragic. I tried to talk to him.

"William, this is your last chance. If you don't use the tools these people are trying to give you, you are gonna wind up back on the street. And then you're gonna rob somebody or hurt somebody or burn somebody's house down or sell some dope to another under-cover cop, and you are going to go to prison."

"But, Sweet," he said, "they don't know who I am." (Folks, does this sound familiar? "I'm a star. I can afford the room with the shower. I'm rich." Remember?)

"William," I said, "you are not a star anymore. You don't score touchdowns anymore. You are a drug addict, and you are a felon. If you don't do this deal right, you are going to prison."

"But, Sweet," he said again, "they don't know who I am."

After about an hour I just threw up my hands and said, "OK, they don't know who you are."

We went to a Cocaine Anonymous meeting after lunch at the

Faulkner Center, and William immediately broke my anonymity, telling everybody who I was. "That's my man, Sweet. That's Larry Gatlin, big country star. He's my buddy from school, and he's come to help me."

I couldn't believe it (so much for it being an anonymous program). He spouted off some more and then the meeting got down to business. It was a great meeting. I shared a little bit of my experience, and we all said the Lord's Prayer. Then before we broke up, the group leader said, "Does anyone have anything they want to say?"

Josh raised his hand.

"Yes, young man. You want to say something?"

"Yes, sir, I do. I'm Josh Gatlin, and I'm ten years old. I don't do drugs or alcohol but my daddy did. If God can heal him from drinking and doing drugs, He can do it for you."

The room got very quiet as the Holy Spirit filled it with love and healing and wisdom, spoken by a ten-year-old boy who understood. Josh got it. He understood. William did not get it.

Two weeks later, after William was released from the treatment center, he broke his parole agreement and off to Huntsville he went. I've heard various stories about him since then. I think he got out for a while and then went back in. It's a shame.

(William, I know who you are and more importantly God knows who you are. I just hope you have figured it out.)

After I got clean and sober, another guy on my prayer list was Mickey Mantle. (I would not use his name if he had not been very public about his problem and his program of recovery.) I kept hearing stories about his drinking escapades and deteriorating health and wish now I had contacted him and tried to help.

I first met Mickey at the Tony Lema Memorial Golf Tournament at Marco Island sometime in the '70s. He and I hit it off real well. It was all I could do to keep from slobbering like a baby. (I mean, come on! This ain't Joe Schmo we're talkin' about here. This is The Mick. Number 7.)

The next time we met was at the Amana Tournament in Iowa, maybe a year or two later. One night after the pairings dinner and the show, I had the distinct pleasure and honor of sitting with some of my heroes outside by the pool until 3:00 in the morning, talking baseball. Are you ready for this? Mickey Mantle, Billy Martin, Yogi Berra, Whitey Ford, Stan "The Man" Musial, Joe Garagiola, "Mr. Cub" Ernie Banks—I think Roger Maris was there too.

Well, I will remember it as long as I live. Story after story after story about baseball—home runs, famous catches, double plays, bad hops—everything, you name it. I was a kid in a candy store with an American Express card. Wow, what a night!

Some of us got pretty drunk. We laughed and slapped each other on the back, and they allowed me into their circle. It was heaven on earth for someone who had grown up idolizing every one of them.

Mickey went back home to Dallas on Monday after the tournament and almost died of some kind of stomach rupture deal—I don't know exactly what. But I do know the heavy drinking at the tournament in Iowa could not have done Mick's insides any good, especially considering that Mickey had been drinking heavily for years. I'm not trashing my hero. I'm really not. Keep reading; it gets better.

The brothers and I were working at the Venetian Room in the Fairmont Hotel in Dallas in 1981, and Mickey invited me to play golf at Preston Trail.

I was hungover from the night before, but somehow I got my rental car to Preston Trail and went to the pro shop. The guys at the shop told me Mickey was waiting for me upstairs and wanted to have lunch. So I went up and found him and we had a sandwich, then went to the men's locker room where Mickey changed out of his sports coat and tie and put on a pair of old ratty-looking golf shorts and a wrinkled white golf shirt. He put on his shoes (no socks) and said, "Let's go play golf, kid."

Well, off we went—just me and The Mick. It got very hot so we drank some cold beer. Mickey got really hot so he took off his shirt and so did I. (There are not many rules at Preston Trail.) And we played on. (My Lord, what a pair of shoulders and forearms the man had. No wonder he could hit a baseball so far.)

Mickey always teed off with a 3-wood. I have seen the greatest golfers in the world hit a golf ball, but to this day I have never seen a golf ball leave the face of a club the way it did when Mickey Mantle hit it. He had very little idea where it was going, but wherever it was going, it got there in a hurry. We laughed and messed with each other and drank more beer and then drank more beer.

Then it started to rain. I mean really rain. So right after Mickey birdied the ninth hole, he turned to me and said, "That's it, kid. You lose. We got in nine holes. We're rained out. It's a match. Let's get outta here."

We dried off in the locker room, and he put on his slacks and shirt. He and our friend Mack Rankin played backgammon for a while and then Mick said, "I'm hungry. Let's go get some Mexican food."

We were really "in the bag" by now. But Mickey was a little farther gone than I was, so I drove. When we got to the Mexican restaurant, I thought it would be cute to drive on the sidewalk. So I pulled the car up over the little concrete divider. (You know, the little barrier placed about a yard in front of the sidewalk to keep drunk, obnoxious country singers from driving on it.)

Well, the front wheels got wedged between the concrete divider and the sidewalk, and I could not back up. The car would not go back over the barrier, so I just slapped that little unit into *P* for park, shut down the engine, got out of the car, and Number 7 and I went inside for some Mexican food and about three pitchers of margaritas. When we walked out an hour later, we could not spell *cat* or count to four between us. Now we were really in a tough spot. I had to get Mickey back to Preston Trail, and I had to get back downtown to the Fairmont Hotel to get ready for the show in less than an hour and a half.

The front tires of my car were firmly wedged between the divider and the sidewalk. It would not budge. At this moment—when panic was about to render me null and void—my hero, Mickey Mantle, Number 7, pulled off one of the greatest athletic feats I've ever seen. (Stay with me, folks, this is the gospel truth.) He got out of the car and said, "OK, kid, throw her in reverse and when I count to three, gun it."

So he counted to three, I gunned it, and he lifted the front end of the car enough to unwedge the front tire. I went flying back about 30 feet before I could get that little unit stopped. He laughed at me, and I laughed at him. He hopped into the car and I drove him back to Preston Trail. Then I went to the Fairmont and I sang like a mockingbird. (Tequila, mockingbird—get it? To Kill a Mockingbird? Never mind.)

In 1985, after I got out of treatment, I heard stories from our mutual friends about Mickey's drinking problem. I kept telling myself I should write or call him, but I just never did. I was afraid he wouldn't like me anymore. (Way to go, Larry—way to lay it all on the line for the home team.)

In 1989 I was really overcome with joy when I heard that Mickey had checked into the Betty Ford Center and was working on a program of recovery. One of the most moving things I've ever seen was the TV interview he gave where he talked about his fears—about his doubts and his faults and his failures—about his wife, Merlyn, and his boys and how he had not been a very good dad at times. Then he shyly and humbly asked for forgiveness and to be given another chance.

He told young people to stay away from booze. It was wonderful. I was moved—literally—to tears. I was so happy for him and his family. Of all the great and courageous things Mickey Mantle ever did—playing on tissue-paper knees, diving for line drives, sliding into second base to break up a double play, knowing a spike catching the wrong way in the dirt meant another blown-out knee, running out routine ground balls—I really believe his finest hour was that hour on television when he looked into the camera and won our hearts all over again.

What a guy. What a player. What courage. What an inspiration.

• • •

For a while, everything looked so promising for our career. We had done the CMA show and "Night of a Thousand Stars." We had been featured guests on the inaugural gala show with Frank and Ray Charles and Liz and Robert Wagner and all those other legends. We had been to the White House and sung for President and Mrs. Reagan. I was positive we were on our way. Boy, was I in for a surprise.

Rick Blackburn was still our boss (and senior vice president and general manager) at CBS Records in Nashville when I got out of treatment in 1985. He had tried to help me with my drug problem, and I'll always be grateful.

I met with Rick one day in Nashville to discuss plans for a new album, and he suggested I try to write some different kinds of songs and maybe get some new "ears" to produce our records. It really made me mad, but I decided I would do it anyway. After all, Rick was the record man. Since our career was not doing very well, I decided to try to do it his way.

A few weeks later I went to Rick Blackburn with an idea. I said, "I'm going to Florida to write some songs with Barry Gibb, and maybe he'll want to produce some stuff. How does that sound?"

Rick said that he thought that would be a good deal, so I went to Florida.

Writing songs with Barry Gibb was a fascinating project. The man is a songwriting machine. His melodies, his chords, his timing and phrasing—it was wonderful. He just grabs a guitar and starts going.

I stayed with Barry and his wife, Linda, for four or five days in Florida, and we wrote songs . . . and wrote songs . . . and wrote songs. It was a gas! The man is a genius.

One morning when I walked into the writing room of Barry's home, he said, "Larry, let's write something about an Indian summer. Isn't that a lovely idea, Indian summer?"

"It's a beautiful image and it sounds good. Let's do it," I said.

So the Gibb Genius and the Gatlin Whatever took over. Barry grabbed a guitar and started strumming, and I followed along.

"Indian Summer" turned out to be a really good song. When we finished, Barry looked up and said, "Mate, that sounds like a Roy Orbison song."

"It sure does. Let's call him."

To make a long story somewhat shorter, I called Roy's home and talked to his wife, Barbara, and we arranged for them to stop in Miami on their way home from England to record "Indian Summer" with the Brothers Gibb and the Brothers Gatlin. Barry had idolized Roy for twenty years but had never met him.

When Roy got out of the limo and walked over to Barry and I

introduced him, he smiled from ear to ear and said, "Roy, you are one of my heroes."

Roy shook Barry's hand and said, "Well, thank you, Barry. You're one of mine."

It was a great moment, and we hadn't even sung a note yet.

We recorded "Indian Summer" and made a video all in the same day. Larry, Steve, and Rudy Gatlin; Barry and Maurice Gibb (Robin was not there—again. Remember, he was absent the night at the Waldorf also. Robin, you need to hang around with your brothers a little more. You're missing some good stuff.); and the one and only Roy Orbison. The song came off great. We passed the solos around and sang harmony and laughed and just enjoyed ourselves. When I received the mixed copy of the song and the edited copy of the video, I thought we had a smash hit and a great video. Boy, was I in for a shock.

"Indian Summer" was put on the *Smile* album with some songs we'd done with Larry Carlton. Larry is, in my opinion, from another planet. One night back in 1982 or 1983, my dear friend and very favorite guitar player, Steve Smith, got in The Gatlin Brothers Touring Bus and said, "Larry Wayne, you gotta hear this." He put a tape into the machine and sat down on the couch.

Steve Smith has played guitar for The Gatlin Brothers for almost twenty years, and I believe he is the best when it comes to doing the right thing at the right time behind a vocal group. Well, when he told me I ought to listen to some guitar player, I sat up and listened. Larry Carlton is so fast, so clean, and his choice of notes is amazing. I have never, before then or since, heard a man play guitar the way I heard it played that night on that tape.

Anyway, I'll cut to the chase.

I was doing a project with Johnny Mathis and needed a couple of guitar solos, so I got in touch with this Carlton fellow's manager. At that time, Larry had left the Jazz Crusaders and was doing a lot of solo gigs and studio work in Los Angeles. His manager said, "L. C. will be glad to play some guitar." That was my first experience with Larry.

Years later, I flew to Los Angeles with four or five songs I'd written and a couple more ideas. Larry was sitting in the studio downstairs. We hugged and talked a while, and I told him I just wanted us to play around and see what happened. He said that was cool, and then he said, "Listen to the melody I've been working on," and he went into the studio, picked up his Gibson 335, and played one of the prettiest melodies I've ever heard.

I said, "Man, put that down on a tape and I'll put some lyrics to it."

Hal, the engineer, said, "I just did. I recorded it while he was doing it. I always turn the machine on when L. C. walks into the studio and picks up that guitar." He smiled, and over the next few days I learned why.

Mr. Carlton does not fiddle around when he picks up his ax. He plays, and it always sounds wonderful.

"Larry," I said, "that's a gorgeous melody. I'd love to work with it if you don't mind."

Larry said he had to meet a guy for an interview, but he'd be back in a couple of hours.

With that he left me and Hal and that beautiful melody.

I said, "Turn it on, Hal. Let's get to work."

"You're Always Welcome Here" was the result, one of my favorite songs. It was written, recorded, and had harmony voices on it by the time L. C. got back from his meeting. We later added some bass. And guitar, which L. C. played, and some keyboard, which L. C. also played, and we added Steve and Rudy. Then Hal and L. C. mixed it, and it went on the *Smile* album.

Over the next few days we recorded "Say" and "Can't Stay Away From Her Fire," which I had written only a couple of days before I flew to Los Angeles for a visit with Larry. (He played a solo on that track, which is one of the greatest guitar solos in the history of the world.) Working with L. C. was a tremendous experience and one I'll always cherish.

When we had the *Smile* album together, we had a big "listening party" in Nashville at CBS. Larry Carlton flew in from Los Angeles, and he and the Gatlins were really excited about playing our new album for the brass. The company executives flew in from New

York. We all sat down around a table and turned it on. Steve and Rudy and L. C. loved it. I loved it. The brass at CBS from New York hated it. They didn't dislike it. *They hated it.* They didn't think the music was commercial.

"Barry Gibb and Roy Orbison are not on our label. We don't want to release that 'Indian Summer' song. Larry Carlton is not on our label." It was a very sad day.

The brass got back on the company plane and flew to New York. Larry Carlton got on American Airlines and flew back to Los Angeles, and I flew into an absolute rage. On the way home to Brentwood, just south of Nashville, riding with Steve and Rudy, I called the CBS boys everything in the book—idiots, bean counters. That's the nice stuff I called them. We had worked very hard and thought we had some really good music for them, and the pin-striped suit guys hated it.

The handwriting was on the wall. I did not see it yet, but it was there. Our days at CBS were numbered. Our days in Nashville were numbered. Our record career was history. Our career, in general, was in serious trouble.

CBS did release two songs from *Smile*—"Nothing but Your Love Matters," which fell short of becoming a Top 10 hit, and "Runaway Go Home."

I had written "Runaway Go Home" in June of 1985. We were on our way to play golf at the Joliet Country Club and had already missed our tee time; the cab had been late picking us up, and we had gotten lost. Somewhere in Joliet, while en route to the golf club, I had seen a billboard on the side of the road for Trailways Bus company. It said: "Runaway, go home free on Trailways."

We played golf that morning, but I couldn't really keep my mind on the game. Those three words kept going through my head—*runaway go home.*

I asked my sound man, Tom Hensley, to get me a guitar from the bus. Back in the hotel room, I scratched out a song on some Shorewood Inn stationery in fifteen minutes.

I got the boys together that night—Steve and Rudy, and band members Steve Smith, Mike Smith, Ralph Geddes, Shannon Ford, and Ron Carpenter—and said, "Boys, I want you all to hear something," then sang "Runaway Go Home."

Everybody teared up and to a man said, "That is a great song. We have to learn that right away."

By the next day at the sound check at the Rialto Theatre, we had learned the song. We sang it that night, and the people loved it. We all thought we had a winner. Wrong again.

Well, half wrong.

It was not a hit record, but then, my life and our career—Steve and Rudy's and mine—has never been just about hit records or making money. It's been about feeling and emotion and the human experience. And that song and that record felt like the right thing to do, and we knew it.

CBS *did* try to promote the song for a while—by distributing a one-minute audio version to radio stations and 275 runaway centers across the country, to be used as public service spots. It was also used as the theme for "Project Safe Place," a national campaign launched by the U.S. Department of Health and Human Services to heighten public awareness of the problem of teenage runaways, and a two-minute video of the song aired on MTV.

The song peaked at Number 43 on the *Billboard*'s Country Singles Chart.

A friend of mine, Don Langford, the program director for KRAK-Radio in Sacramento, told me the CBS record people didn't like the song—didn't want us to record it—and they were not going to promote it. Well, my buddy Don played it anyway. He called me one day and said, "Gatlin, my boy. Your song sent a runaway kid home to Idaho today. She has been hanging out in a city park in Sacramento. She's an eighteen-year-old hooker. She was on a lunch break, sitting in the park eating a sandwich and listening to her transistor radio when she heard the song. She called me crying and said, 'Thanks for playing that song. I'm going back to Idaho. I just called my mom.'"

And there were others.

One night a lady pushed past the security backstage in Hamilton, Ontario. I had the flu and really felt terrible. I didn't much want to see the lady but—there she was. She walked up to me and said, "Mr. Gatlin, this is my sixteen-year-old daughter."

With that she handed me a small picture. "Two weeks ago, she was working as a prostitute in Montreal when she saw your video of 'Runaway Go Home' on TV. She's come home to me, Mr. Gatlin. God bless you and your brothers."

I was speechless. We hugged and she disappeared.

After the *Smile* album, we did a couple more for CBS and managed to scratch out only two more Top 10 hits—"She Used to Be Somebody's Baby" and "Talkin' to the Moon."

But the climate in Nashville was changing. As the new guys and gals came in at CBS (Rick Blackburn left in 1987, and CBS was sold to Sony Music), they didn't seem to have the same feeling about the music. I think we all just lost touch with each other. Business is business, and they didn't think our stuff was the stuff of hits. As I said, the handwriting was on the wall and now I was seeing it all too clearly.

CHAPTER 15

PHOTO COURTESY OF KATHY GANGWISCH

"Brothers": Patrick and me

$\mathcal{B}$ROTHERS

It was either Thoreau or Whitman, or one of those philosophical biggies, who said, "What you are speaks to me so loudly that I cannot hear what you say." In other words, actions speaks louder than words.

I've been privileged to know some great people who walked the walk and talked the talk. Jack Boland was truly one of those people.

Dr. Joe Pursch called me one day and said, "Larry, I want you to call a friend of mine, Jack Boland. I think you would enjoy talking to him and getting to know him."

So I called Jack Boland at the number Dr. Joe gave me. The voice on the other end of the phone answered, "Church of Today." *Oh, no*, I thought to myself. *One of those newfangled, "Fern Bar" churches with sandals and Kumbaya.*

"Yes, hello, could I speak to Jack Boland, please? This is Larry Gatlin. Dr. Joe Pursch asked me to call."

"One moment please."

Then I heard Jack's voice for the first time. "Larry Gatlin. I love you," the voice said. "This is Jack Boland."

"Well," I said, "I love you too."

And I did love him. From that moment until right now. Jack Boland exemplified the Christ truth as well as anyone I have ever known.

One day in Detroit at the Church of Today, I told Jack I was having to fight the music business and the people in Nashville to get anything done. Jack said, "Larry Gatlin. If you will get in tune with the spirit of the universe, that friendly universe will stand by and applaud for you. And you will find a parking place in front of every building you need to enter."

"Jack, I've been working on trying to get my motives right."

"Larry Gatlin, your motives are going to be wrong most of the time because you are a self-centered, egotistical, alcoholic–addict. Quit worrying about your motives and just *do* the right thing. Love everybody—starting with yourself."

"Jack, I can't even afford two new buses."

"What's wrong with the buses you have now? Did they get up here to Detroit OK? New buses aren't the problem. A new heart for Larry Gatlin, that's the problem and the solution. How about asking God to give Larry a new heart? He may give you two new buses along with it."

"Jack, why do I keep having all these problems? I'm sober. I'm trusting God. What am I doing wrong?"

"Larry Gatlin, these problems you're having are very simply God banging on your hood. He wants to get your undivided attention, and rest assured, sooner or later He will."

"Jack, some people just bug me. There are some people I just do not like."

"Larry Gatlin, every person who comes across your path comes across your path for one of two reasons: to heal you or to be healed by you." (Read that again, folks. It's pretty wonderful stuff.)

One Sunday I saw Jack Boland stand in a crowd of a hundred people, all wanting to talk to him after a Sunday morning church service. He was tired from two services. He'd been awake since 3:00 A.M. (He always got up at that time to prepare his Sunday morning lesson.) He was hungry, but he was also filled, filled with the Spirit of God. He talked to every person. More importantly, he listened to every person. I stood over to the side waiting, and waiting, and getting more and more annoyed by the minute. I said to myself, *Why don't they leave him alone and let him go sit down and get some lunch?* What I really meant was, "Why don't they leave him alone so he can take me to lunch and I'll have him all to myself." He never once shorted anyone. He was their earthly shepherd, and he loved his flock and cared for them as the Good Shepherd commanded him to.

In January of 1990, Jack's cancer showed up again. A year later he decided he wanted to say good-bye to some of his friends, so the local family of the Church of Today in Detroit and some of the greater family—Og Mandino, Wayne Dyer, and Larry Gatlin— gathered in February of 1991 to have a farewell party. Jack was the color of split pea soup. The doctors had tried everything to kill the cancer, to no avail. We all knew this was the end. All of us except Jack. He called it "a beginning." He stood in front of us and gave one of the most inspiring and enlightened and anointed messages I've ever heard.

He told this story: A friend of Oliver Wendell Holmes wrote him a letter in which he asked, "How is my friend Oliver Wendell Holmes?"

The old, sick, and dying judge replied, "The earthly house in which Oliver Wendell Holmes resides is old and is falling down and in ill repair. But as for Oliver Wendell Holmes, he is well. He is well."

Then Jack said, "The earthly house in which Jack Boland resides is indeed old and falling down. But Jack Boland is well. He is well."

He went on to tell us all not to be afraid, and he told us how much he loved us and how much God loved us. Then we took turns telling him how much we loved him. When it was my turn, I stood and said, "I am a crier, and I'm going to cry now."

Jack said, "Go ahead, Larry Gatlin. It's OK to cry."

Then I said, "Jack Boland, I love you very much, and I'm going to miss you very much."

He smiled. Then I continued, "But Jack Boland, I do not worship you. I worship the Lord Jesus Christ who is in you and when you leave this earthly plane, I claim the blessing Elijah gave to Elisha. I want a double portion of the power, the love and the wisdom, and the grace that God has given you."

He smiled, and I sat down.

One week later, I spoke to Jack on the phone. He asked me to sing "Amazing Grace" and with tears in my eyes I did—"Amazing grace! How sweet the sound. . . . "

Jack died two days later. I miss him terribly, but he speaks to me almost every day. And guess what? Most of the time—90 percent of the time—I find a parking place in front of the building I need to go into. Ninety percent—pretty good average, I'd say. And a few times I have felt that double portion of power, love and wisdom, and grace. I'm not all the way there, but I'm gaining.

Many times I remember his words: "Larry Gatlin, every person who comes across your path comes across your path for one of two reasons: to heal you or to be healed by you."

Father, grant me that Spirit of Love that You gave your servant Jack Boland and Elijah, Elisha, Joe Neely, and . . . oh, yes, that Jesus Man.

•   •   •

1985 was the year *North and South*, the great TV miniseries about the Civil War, thrust Patrick Swayze into the national spotlight as Confederate General Ory Mane. It was in 1986, at the Texas Sesquicentennial, that he burst into my life, or I guess we burst into each other's lives. That spring, a huge television special was taped in Austin celebrating the 150th anniversary of Texas joining the Union. It featured a who's who of Texas talent, including Tommy Tune, Sandy Duncan, Van Cliburne, The Gatlin Brothers, and General Ory Mane, a.k.a. Patrick Swayze.

I was getting into the elevator to go to the lobby, and there he was, looking like a model out of one of those fashion magazines.

"Hi, Patrick," I said, "I really loved *North and South* and thought you did a great job."

"Thanks, Larry," he said. "You're my favorite singer. I love to listen to your records."

"Thanks, man, I appreciate it." I got into the elevator, and he got out. That was it—for the time being. Short and sweet.

One morning in 1989, I was in the locker room at Maryland Farms Racquet Club in Brentwood, putting on my workout gear for my twenty minutes on the Stairmaster or Lifecycle. Larry Hamby, a record executive with CBS, walked up and said, "Larry, you and Patrick Swayze are friends, aren't you?"

"Well, we met in an elevator for a few minutes, and we like each other's work. That's about the extent of it."

"Well," Larry Hamby said, "he's doing a movie called *Next of Kin* and we [CBS] are doing the soundtrack. Would you be interested in writing a song for it?"

"Sure, what's it about?"

He went on to tell me it was about some brothers. One of them gets murdered, and the whole clan decides to go get the killer. After Larry filled me in on the story line, I told him I would love to give it a shot. I went to the exercise room and got on the Lifecycle.

As I was riding away, Larry stuck his head in the door and said, "Maybe a duet. You know, something you and Patrick could do together."

I said OK and kept riding. In the twenty minutes it took to finish the Lifecycle workout I had written—

Patrick's part: *You've always known if anyone tries to get to you, they'll first have to get through me.*

Larry's part: *And you've always known I'd be by your side, no matter what the situation might be.*

Both: *When we were just boys we vowed our allegiance. Shoulder to shoulder against all others. Brothers. Brothers.*

I called Mike Smith at Gatlin Brothers Music and said, "Fire up the machine. I'm on my way."

I walked into the little studio in Mike's "basement" and said, "Turn it on, Mikey."

He did, and I recorded "Brothers." We did some overdubbing to show Patrick what the duet and the harmony would sound like, Mike mixed the twenty-four track down to a cassette, and I headed for Larry Hamby's office.

Larry told me about the project at 9:15 that morning. At 11:15, I was standing at his desk with the tape.

"See if this will work," I said as I handed it to him. We listened together.

"It will absolutely work," he said. "I'll get in touch with them."

Rosi Hygate, Patrick's assistant, called me late that afternoon from the set of *Next of Kin* in Chicago and we started making plans. I don't remember the exact time frame, but in a few weeks, I was in Los Angeles in a studio eating Thai food with Patrick and figuring out how to do the song. Some other folks had already done the track. (Sorry, I don't remember the guy's name. But it was a good track.) And all we had to do was sing our solos and then do the duet part.

Patrick and I became pals at once. We're both from Texas, we're both extremely talented, and we're both really handsome—and modest and humble. He is really a sweet spirit. He's a little rambunctious at times (at least he was back then). I mean he rides horses as fast as they'll go. Motorcycles as fast as they'll go. Cars as fast as they'll go. Airplanes as fast as they'll go—and then he jumps out of them. (One of life's great mysteries: why would anyone jump out of a perfectly good airplane?)

One night I said, "Patrick, why don't you slow down a little bit."

He laughed. "I'm not sure how long I'll be here. I've gotta do everything now."

It was a funny moment that turned serious in a second. I saw a look of, not desperation, but at least anxiety on his face. I do not believe it was a fatalistic death wish thing, but he certainly was serious about doing everything as quickly as possible. I thought I was pretty much a full-speed kind of guy. Well, Patrick makes me look like I'm standing still sometimes. (Remember this was before *Ghost,* and I think Patrick was probably pressing a bit. He's a little more relaxed now, down to warp speed.)

Next of Kin came out and didn't do very well. I thought it was really good. There were some wonderful performances—Patrick's and Liam Neeson's. It was a terrific story, and I was disappointed it wasn't a big hit for Patrick. The song was only played for a few seconds in the movie. I was disappointed about that too. But what can you do?

CBS decided to release "Brothers" from the soundtrack, so they asked Patrick and me to do a video of the song. Later that year I did a charity horse show with Patrick and his beautiful, charming wife, Lisa. I invited Patrick to come do the Houston Livestock Show & Rodeo with us in January. It was a fabulous night. Some of the greatest thrills the Gatlin Brothers Band ever had were our performances (ten, I think) at the Houston Livestock Show & Rodeo.

The night Patrick joined us on stage we did "She's Like the Wind" (Patrick's big pop hit from the movie *Dirty Dancing*) and "Brothers" for almost fifty thousand screaming cowboys and cowgirls. (I think the cowgirls were doing most of the screaming.) He's my buddy, and I love him—Lisa too!

After a concert at the Vail Arts Center one night in 1989, Steve and Rudy and I went to dinner with R. J. Wagner and Jill St. John. They are a hoot, collectively and individually. R. J. is nuts—wonderful—and handsome as can be. Jill is not nuts. She is very level-headed—also wonderful—and pretty as a picture. Nice kids.

At dinner that evening, R. J. and Jill's other guests were Bob and Connie Lurie from San Francisco. I had heard of Bob because I am a great sports fan, and Bob at that time owned the San Francisco Giants baseball team. We had a wonderful dinner and just as it was about to break up, I said, "Bob, your team is only one game out of first place. The brothers and I are going to root real hard and pray real hard, and if you make it to the World Series, we want to sing the national anthem at one of the games."

"Deal," he said, and we shook hands.

Steve and Rudy and I immediately started rooting, praying, and checking the box scores in the paper and *Baseball Tonight* on ESPN to monitor the progress of our now-beloved Giants.

Well, folks, I'm not sure God answers prayers about baseball (I am sure He does not answer prayers about golf). But the Giants won the National League pennant and were to meet the Oakland A's in the 1989 World Series at Candlestick Park, a.k.a. "the Stick."

I flew to San Francisco from New Orleans. The plane was late, and I was upset. There was to be a dinner party at the Lurie's home that night. I called Connie from the plane and told her I was going to be very late and maybe I should just wait until the next day, game day, to get together with them.

"Nonsense," she said. "Jump in a cab and come on over. We'll save you some food."

"But, Connie, I'm in my airplane clothes, a pair of jeans and a denim shirt. I do not look like I'm going to a dinner party. I look like a . . . well, I look like a country singer on an airplane in a pair of jeans and a denim shirt."

"Larry," she said calmly, "it's OK. We all want to see you. Come on over as soon as you get to San Francisco."

With that she gave me the address and some directions. I hung up the phone, the plane landed at San Francisco International Airport, and I took a cab to the Lurie's home. There I had dinner with the mayors of San Francisco and Oakland, the presidents of the American and National Leagues, Dr. Bobby Brown and Bill White, and their wives, and other distinguished guests. Oh, yes, also the commissioner of baseball at the time, Fay Vincent.

The boys, Steve and Rudy, came in the next day and my son, Josh, came with them. We fooled around most of the day and then we all assembled for the fifteen-minute ride to the Stick for the game. An old friend of mine, Penn Parrish, was living in San Francisco then, and I had invited him to go with us. We had another guest, Chris Jimenez, a wonderful young man from the Bay Area. I'll get back to the baseball part of this story in a little while. First, let me tell you about the Jimenez family.

One night a year or so before this World Series deal, I received a note backstage at Harrah's in Tahoe. I'll paraphrase—"Our son Chris is a big fan of the Gatlin Brothers. He loves your music. He is very ill with lupus, and the doctor says he won't reach sixteen years old. [I think he was about twelve or thirteen at the time.] He would really love to meet you guys and take a picture if possible. Thank you. Love, Mrs. Jimenez."

I instructed the maitre d' to please bring the family backstage. They were really nice people, and I enjoyed visiting with Chris and his mom and dad. I invited him to our Harrah's Reno engagement in a couple of months and asked him to come out to the big Interlaken house and go swimming in the indoor pool with me. He promised he would.

When we were at Harrah's Reno for our two-week engagement, the Jimenez family came for a visit. It was on that occasion that Chris's mom and I sat outside under a shade tree and she told me the doctors didn't give them much hope for Chris's survival.

"But he looks so healthy," I said.

"Yes, he does, but his bad days are awful and they come more often and last longer."

She explained what lupus was and how it affects the body and immune system and how it silently kills.

I said simply, "Let's pray and believe for Chris's complete healing."

She responded, "Thank you. That means a lot to us."

I gave her a copy of *The Sermon on the Mount*, by Dr. Emmett Fox, and I talked to Chris and told him to never give up hope, that we would defeat the lupus together with God's help. I noticed he was wearing a Giants baseball cap. "You stay healthy and be a good kid, and if the Giants get to the World Series you can go with us," I told him.

His face lit up like a Christmas tree. "Wow, that's great," he said. "I'll stay well and be a good kid and we'll go to the game."

"Deal," I said.

I began that night to pray for Chris Jimenez, and we remembered him during our circle prayer time with the band.

A few days before the Giants claimed the National League pennant, Chris's mom called me. "Larry, we took Chris to the doctor.

There is no sign of lupus in his body. God has performed the miracle we all prayed for."

Well, I had cried and she cried and I said, "Put Chris on the phone."

When Chris said hi, I told him, "Hey, pal, get ready for the game because we're going." I could feel him smiling over the phone.

I called Bob Lurie and told him the story, and he got us a ticket for our buddy Chris Jimenez.

And now back to the game. We all loaded into the limo for the ride to "The Stick." Steve was sicker than a dog and could barely hold his head up. We pulled into the VIP entrance at the back of the Stick and were escorted by our hosts to the huge tent in the parking lot, just on the other side of the centerfield fence. The Luries were hosting a big party in the tent for the press and dignitaries. It may be the most food I have ever seen in one place in my life. A fabulous spread. Josh and Chris and Rudy and I had a ball. (Steve was lying in the back seat of the limo, thinking he was about to die.)

I asked Connie if she knew any doctors in the crowd, and she introduced me to the team doctor. I told him the problem and he graciously agreed to leave all that food and drink and go out to the limo to take a look at brother Steve.

We walked out to the big white car and I opened the door. The doc stuck his head into the car, took a three-second look at Steve, and said, "You've got the flu, Mr. Gatlin. Not much I can do."

He backed out of the car, and he and I went inside and loaded up some more chips with that cheese ball stuff (great dip—I mean world class). Looking back on the events of the day now it is funny. It was not very funny at the time.

The party started to break up a little bit, and we decided to go on into the stadium to do a sound check and make sure we knew where to stand and when to start "Oh, say, can you see."

Josh and Chris were good friends by now so they walked in the centerfield gate together and Rudy and I walked in together, and we all walked around toward the third base dugout on the red warning track. Steve was leaning against the inside of a golf cart—barely alive—as someone from the commissioner's office drove him around toward our spot on the first base side of home plate.

The players were playing catch and stretching and warming up and talking and laughing, trying not to allow the tension of the moment to show in their faces. I knew some of them—Will Clark and a few others—so we chatted for a while. I waved to Johnny Bench, who was in the radio announcer's booth for CBS getting ready to do the play-by-play. He waved back. Actually, it was an obscene gesture. No, not the one you're probably thinking about (private joke between the Gatlins and J. B.—not really bad at all), and we laughed at each other from two hundred feet away.

Josh and Chris were in kid heaven—around all the players, the pageantry, and the beauty of Candlestick Park. It was an absolutely perfect night for baseball, as they say, and then things began to rock 'n' roll.

I was standing about twenty feet from the Giants' dugout toward the first base line, talking to an old friend, Mike Lupica, the great sportswriter for the *New York Post*, *New York Daily News* and ESPN. We had met several years earlier at the U.S. Open Tennis Tournament in Frank Chirkinnion's production office. We instantly became

J. C. and J. B.

"podnuhs." He's a cocky little rooster and so am I, and we both like a good prank, even if it's on us.

Well, anyway, "Lupe" and I were shootin' the breeze and all of a sudden the ground started shaking and we heard a rumble. At that exact moment a 747 from San Francisco International was flying low over the stadium and I looked up. The shaking got worse.

"Hey, Lupe," I said. "A 747 ain't supposed to make the ground shake, is it?"

"Gatlin," Lupe said, "ain't no airplane causing the ground to shake, my friend. We are in the middle of an earthquake."

We both looked up toward the stands and the whole place was doin' the wave. Not the fans, *the stadium*. The huge concrete sections were weaving in and out like the limbs of willow trees in a windstorm. The ground was rolling under us.

Steve thought someone was jumping on the back of the golf cart, so he looked around to tell whoever it was that he was very sick and would that someone please stop shaking the cart. Trouble was, there was no one shaking the golf cart. Steve then realized what was happening.

It was 5:04 P.M. We were supposed to sing at 5:08 P.M. The quake lasted only ten or twenty seconds, I guess, and after it was over, a strange quiet fell over the stadium for about three or four seconds, then everybody started to laugh. It was almost a festive, party atmosphere. Al Rosen, the general manager of the Giants, and Roger Craig, the manager, were gathered around a small TV behind the Giants dugout. (A fan had brought it to the game.) We all watched the local news flash about the quake. Bridges were down. Parts of San Francisco were on fire. Broken glass was all over downtown, and people were dead. In a matter of seconds baseball became pretty unimportant.

Josh ran up to me and said, "Dad, they had just introduced Kevin Mitchell onto the field when the ground started shaking. I thought it was some sort of special effect deal to announce their star player. I didn't know it was an earthquake."

We all laughed and waited for instructions. After what seemed like two years the stadium announcer said, "Ladies and gentlemen, would you please all exit the stadium. The game has been postponed until further notice. Please exit in an orderly fashion and be careful going home."

That was it. We all started walking toward the centerfield gate and the waiting limo. The traffic was horrendous. The stoplights were out. In fact, all the lights in the "City of Light," San Francisco, were out. And while there was not panic, life as we knew it would not be the same for a long time.

Our hostess finally got through on a cellular phone to a friend in Los Angeles. The friend took all our phone numbers in Nashville and began calling Janis and Cynthia and Kim to assure the wives we were all safe and sound.

Three and a half hours later, we pulled up to the St. Francis Hotel. There were still no lights. A few flashlights and a few candles, but for the most part the old hotel was completely dark. People stood around in groups of three or four or eight or ten and talked nervously about what to do next. We were getting no news. We didn't know if there was structural damage or possible gas leaks or what. We all just went on faith and instinct. The elevators were not working and we had a very sick boy with us, young Steven Daryl Gatlin. He was on fire (his temperature was over 103 for sure), and his room was on the 17th floor.

Rudy and I walked him up to his room and made him as comfortable as we could, then we went back downstairs to figure out what to do. The phones were out. The lights were still out. The toilets were history after the first flush. We had some water and drinks in the little in-room bars and some candy and snacks, so we knew we wouldn't starve. The airport was closed, so leaving was not an option. We had Chris Jimenez with us and his folks had gone back to their house across the bridge, part of which was now lying at the bottom of San Francisco Bay.

I said, "OK, boys, let's just stay calm and have a little faith and go get some sleep. Tomorrow's going to be a long day."

So we paired up. I think the boys took one room and Rudy and I took the other one.

At about 1:30 or 2:00 A.M., I tried to get back to Steve's room to check on him. I looked for a flashlight or a candle, but couldn't find either. The hotel people told us not to use candles. They were afraid someone would accidentally burn the old place down (comforting thought). I took the stairs up to Steve's room, where I found him tossing and turning but OK, and then I tried to go back to our room.

I literally felt my way down nine flights of stairs in pitch dark. Somehow I got lost and ran into a dead end—a stairwell. Things were real confusing, I still couldn't figure out where I was. Thankfully I met a hotel person with a flashlight who asked if she could help. I said I was trying to get back to room 608.

"Not on the staircase, you won't," she said. "Room 608 is in the other wing. You've got to go all the way down and then over to the other staircase. I can't help you. There's some kind of emergency in another part of the building, and they need me. Good luck and be careful."

Well, I wanted to say, "Hey, lady, there is an emergency going on right here. It's pitch dark and I am climbing down these stairs and the whole place may go up in flames or down into rubble any second and you're telling me you're taking the flashlight and your knowledge of this old hotel and leaving me to my own devices?"

That's what I wanted to say. But I didn't. I just said, "Thank you," turned and grabbed the handrail and started unclimbing the wrong staircase. I made it back to room 608 somehow.

At about 4:00 A.M. there were some aftershocks, but I just rolled over and went back to sleep. When there's nothing you can do about a situation, sometimes the best thing to do is just take a little snooze. And that's what I did.

What a night! I wouldn't have missed it. Don't get me wrong, I hope I'm never in another quake, but I wouldn't have missed the one I was in. I know it sounds crazy, but it was the experience of a lifetime.

The next morning I went to a grocery store and got some fruit and water and orange juice for Steve. He was afraid he was going to die of dehydration, so I loaded him up with liquids. There was no run on the store. The owner charged people the same price he had the day before. He helped people as best he could, and everybody acted normally and in a very orderly fashion. Everyone was courteous. I saw cab drivers motion people across the street at intersections where there was no traffic light. I saw people walk across the street and then those standing in line to cross would stop and wave the traffic through the intersection. It was amazing.

San Francisco is a very civilized place. At least it was during quake week. If the quake had happened in New York, there would still be cab drivers screaming at people and there would be fights on every corner. There were a lot of heroes that week. Firemen, policemen, grocers, cab drivers, and a lot of ordinary citizens who pitched in and helped their neighbors—some of whom had lost loved ones and friends—get on with their lives.

There was a lot of uncertainty over the next twenty-four hours. No one knew when the game was going to be played. The airport was still closed. Bridges were out in different parts of town, and engineering crews were checking on the structural safety of the ones left standing. And, of course, there was loss of life.

We decided to wait it out. We didn't have any gigs to play for a few days, and we probably couldn't have gotten to them if we had, so we stayed in San Francisco waiting for a decision on the game. Steve was still very sick. Rudy and I decided to move from the St. Francis to the Sir Francis Drake Hotel because their gas generators were supplying electricity and they had running water. Hot, running water and TV.

It was a very interesting two or three days. Baseball Commissioner Fay Vincent announced the game would be played a week later, so we loaded up and resumed our touring schedule. It worked out that the game was finally played on the only day within a two-week period that we could attend.

Ain't God good? We got to come back and sing after all. It was a glorious, festive evening at Candlestick. We were, first of all, glad to be alive, and second, we were grateful to the people who had done such a great job in keeping the peace, putting out the fires, and rescuing people trapped in buildings, under collapsed highways, and inside crumbling buildings. Many of those heroes were honored that night in a very moving ceremony before the game. About ten or fifteen of the special people were allowed to throw out the ceremonial first pitch. Then finally . . . "And now, here to sing our national anthem, are Larry, Steve, and Rudy—The Gatlin Brothers." Applause, applause, applause. And sing we did. "Oh, say, can you see . . ."

We watched from Bob and Connie Lurie's skybox as our Giants got pounded, 13-7, by the A's (the A's hit a record-tying five home runs in the game). But the game was almost an afterthought. Surviving the Big Quake of '89. That was the big deal.

Steve Gatlin got over the flu, we got out alive (we did a real good job on "Oh, say, can you see"), and best of all, Chris Jimenez is still alive and well. I got a picture of him a few months ago, holding onto a real pretty girl. It was a wedding announcement. Ain't God good?

•   •   •

As I said earlier, our career and things at CBS were not going very well. We had some great gigs like the Houston Livestock Show & Rodeo, where we always had almost fifty thousand people, we were on some TV shows, and we had some good fair dates. But the record career was not in good shape.

It was evident by the time we released our *Alive and Well . . . Livin' in the Land of Dreams* album in 1988 that CBS had lost interest in us. The company had also taken the low road on a royalty deal, so I figured it was time to talk to someone there. I took Roy Wunch to lunch (sounds like a song). Roy was a vice president at CBS. I laid out our grievances and told him I thought it might be time for a friendly parting. I thought he would beg us to stay. After all, we were The Gatlin Brothers. We'd been with CBS for years. Well, not only did he not beg us to stay, he said, "Larry, I think you're right. It would be best for everyone if we all remained friends and went our separate ways."

When I went back to the office and told Steve and Rudy, they couldn't believe it. Here we were with a summer tour booked and no record or record company to support us. I shopped around for a day or two and came up with a deal I thought would work. My old buddy Jimmy Bowen was making some moves in Nashville, considering several different offers to run record companies, so I went to talk to him.

Jimmy said, "Gatlin, I like you boys, and I like the way you make music. You are unique, and you haven't sold out to all the Nashville horse manure [that's sorta what Bowen said]. I don't know where I'm gonna wind up. But wherever I go I'd like to have you boys go with me."

I stood up and shook Bowen's hand. He went to Hawaii to think about his options, and I went back to the office and told the boys.

Over the next two years, we recorded some really good records with Bowen, first at Universal for one album, *Pure 'n' Simple*, then at Capitol for two more—*Cookin' Up a Storm* and *Christmas with the Gatlins*, and finally at Liberty for our last album, *Adios*. They were not commercial successes, but I enjoyed working with Bowen, and I will always appreciate the fact that he gave us a chance. A lot of people in Nashville think Jimmy Bowen was the devil. Not me. (Bowen is a visionary. Funny how a lot of visionaries are called the devil.) He treated me fairly, and if he started a record company tomorrow and wanted me to do a record, I'd do it.

In 1990 we got the management bug. Over the years we had tried different managers for short periods of time. My old friend Sid Bernstein in New York, the man who brought the Beatles to the States and to "The Ed Sullivan Show"—a wonderful man—had been my manager for a few months early in my solo career. Dan Moss, a good friend, had been our manager for about thirty minutes in the late '70s.

We couldn't figure out why we were paying these people 15 percent of our money when we didn't know what they did. Well, for some reason we decided to try it again, so we went on a manager hunt. We looked around Nashville and Los Angeles and New York, and we talked to a lot of people. We settled on Maria Brunner and Greg Janese, partners in The Entertainment Group, a management company based in Nashville. They were young and energetic and seemed to have our best interests at heart. They also had some good ideas about how to try to put some life back into a career that seemed to be stalled. So we took the plunge.

Maria and Greg worked very hard to jump-start our career. One of their suggestions was that we listen to the people at the William Morris Agency. So we took a meeting with Paul Moore and Marty Klein No. 2. (You remember Marty Klein No. 1 of APA, who was my first agent.)

The William Morris Agency is the biggest agency in the business. They have booked everyone from Bob Hope to Neil Diamond. Their main office has always been in New York, and it was not until the mid-1980s, I guess, that they really opened an office in Nashville. Paul and Marty Klein No. 2 are really great guys and we liked their approach. They made a good case for why we should leave APA, where we had been with Marty Klein No. 1 and D. J. McLachlan for eighteen years, and go with William Morris.

Over the years APA had never had a Nashville office and as time went by, their roster contained fewer and fewer country artists. William Morris, on the other hand, had a roster full of country talent, young and old. Paul and Marty Klein No. 2 explained that the packaging opportunities with those other artists would be wonderful for us, so we decided to make the big move.

The flight to Los Angeles to talk to Marty Klein No. 1 was not a pleasant one. I've never had a better friend than Marty. He signed us to APA. He guided our career. He got us on every TV show in America. We grew together. We laughed together, we cried together, and I loved him very much. The thought of asking for a release from our contract was not a pleasant one.

We met for breakfast somewhere in Los Angeles, and I dropped the bomb. Marty knew it was coming and tried to talk me out of it, but Steve and Rudy and I had made up our minds. So, being the gentleman he was, he said, "Well, Larry, I think you're making a big mistake but if that's what you want, OK."

Over the years, our association with all the people at APA had been a great one. D. J. McLachlan, Burt Taylor, Freddie Lawrence, Danny Robinson, Bonnie Sugarman—all of them were like family, and taking our leave was not easy. These people had helped us pay our rent, and they had been part of our dreams and our successes. It was tough, but we had decided to do it.

Paul Moore and Marty Klein No. 2 took over and for a while things got better. Please know I'm not blaming APA in any way for the downturn in our career. During the old days—B. T. (before treatment)—we had acquired a pretty bad reputation for being difficult, and with the autograph deal and that bad publicity and then the record career going into the toilet, we became a tough act to book. I'm surprised the folks at APA got us as much work as they did. Their hard work and the fact that when we hit the stage we sang and played our guts out and over the years built a following of loyal fans, is all that saved us. It was the fan's loyalty. Thanks folks.

Back to Paul Moore, Marty Klein No. 2, and William Morris.

For a while the routing of the shows and the packaging got better. Steve Gatlin was always the one who worked with APA on the bookings, and after years of dealing with one company, I think he needed a change. It was not enough to pull us all the way out of the nosedive, but it was a good thing. Paul Moore, Marty Klein No. 2, and the others at William Morris did right by us.

CHAPTER 16

The Masters Five, The Gatlin Three
Rosie Rozelle, James Blackwood, Jake Hess, Hovie Lister,
J. D. Sumner, me, Steve, and Rudy

AMAZING GRACE

One night in April of 1991, we did two shows at the State Theater in Wheeling, West Virginia. I was not very good. I did the best I could and the people were nice to us. They gave us two standing ovations and hollered and whistled and rang those old cowbells 'til they were blue in the face.

I was exhausted. I was confused. I was hurting like never before. Except for God and my family and friends, the ability to sing is the most precious thing on earth to me, and now I couldn't do it. My voice was shot. Every song was an ordeal. It felt like I had big ball bearings in my throat. I dreaded every show.

211

I owed the IRS $690,000 in taxes and Steve and Rudy owed about $100,000 each, due to major changes in the tax code that disallowed the sheltering of money in certain investments. It resulted in a huge tax bill none of us expected. Janis and I borrowed the money to pay the IRS, and it took us five years to retire the loan, but we paid every penny. Nearly everything I made went toward getting us out of debt.

I got on our bus after the performance in Wheeling and prayed and went to sleep. I woke up in the bus at about 8:30 the next morning, in the parking lot of another in the seemingly endless line of Holiday Inns. I got dressed and grabbed my little shoulder bag with my running shoes and shorts and headed for the front desk to get my room key.

The nice lady gave me the key, and I turned to go to my room. "Where am I, please?" I asked.

"You're in Campbelltown, sir."

"Campbelltown what?" I asked.

"Campbelltown, Pennsylvania."

"What's it close to?" I asked.

"About thirty miles from Philly."

"Oh, about thirty miles from Philly," I replied, as I walked off toward another in the seemingly endless line of Holiday Inn rooms.

I put on my running shoes and shorts and took off. As I said earlier, I like to pray when I run. (God and I are in great physical shape.) Today was no different—at first. But about halfway through my run I had a moment of enlightenment. I simply said, "God, I've told You everything I know. I'm going to shut up and let You talk for a while. One more thing, God, then I'll shut up. I cannot sing anymore." Then I shut up and kept running.

After a few more strides, maybe a half mile or so, God said, "If you cannot sing anymore, don't sing. Trust My voice instead of your own voice."

Now, friends, the heavens did not part. There was no thunder and lightning, no audible voice booming out of the clear blue sky. There was simply the still, small voice of the Spirit of God, giving an answer to a praying, hurting, running, begging child: "Trust My voice and not your own. If you cannot sing, do not sing."

I ran back to the Holiday Inn and called Steve and Rudy to tell them we needed to talk. We met in my room a few minutes later.

"Boys," I said, "it's been a great run. We've done a lot of great things, met a lot of wonderful people, sung a lot of great music, and, I know in my own heart, blessed and uplifted and entertained a lot of people over the last thirty years or so. But it's over. I can't do this anymore. I want to quit. My throat is shot. I hate the road. We are going nowhere. Our bills are killing us, and we aren't getting any younger. Let's leave gracefully with a little dignity before we go crazy and someone has to do a Gatlin Brothers benefit to pay off the last payment on the bus."

It was a great speech. The boys were stunned. This was the first time the subject of quitting or retiring had ever been mentioned. I guess we all just assumed we would stay on the road forever and that someday we'd all ride off into the sunset in our touring bus.

Singing together is really all we'd ever known, so it's understandable that my brothers were shocked that I was standing in front of them— in my sweats, T-shirt, running shorts, and Nikes—proposing we quit. Steve said something like, "Well, yeah, we can do that if you want to," and Rudy said, "How can we quit? We don't have any money." We all laughed a nervous laugh.

I said, "Well, boys, I was just running and I told God I couldn't sing anymore and He told me to trust His voice, not mine. So that's it. I'm outta here."

Steve, always the businessman, said, "Are you gonna do the show tonight?"

"Yes, we'll do what we've got on the books and then we're outta here." (Please do not misunderstand me. Steve was not being cold-hearted or uncaring about the situation. He's just always the practical one.)

We did the show at the Keswick Theatre, in a suburb of Philadelphia, that night. I wasn't very good, but once again the loyal, wonderful Gatlin Brothers fans stood and hollered and whistled and screamed for more. God love 'em. It would be another year and a half before we really threw in the towel, but the wheels were put in motion that day, thirty miles outside of Philly in another, now not so seemingly endless line of Holiday Inns.

We kept the tour going through June but my throat wasn't getting better. I had contacted Dr. Robert Ossoff at the Vanderbilt Medical Center in Nashville, and he was prescribing some medication, including cortisone shots. We were dying in Davenport, Iowa, and so was I. It was awful. We were singing to about forty or fifty people every day at a matinee at the Capitol Celebrity Theater and then to about three hundred to three hundred fifty at the evening performance. After my second shot of cortisone in as many weeks, I called Jack Boland.

"Jack, my throat is bad," I began. "I've prayed. I've had faith. I've asked God through the power of the Holy Spirit, in the name of Christ, to perform the miracle and heal me so I can sing again."

"Larry, it is insane to be sick when you can be well. Do you think if Christ were here in person on earth today he would stand and block the doors of the emergency room and not let people in to get medical treatment? No, Larry Gatlin. He would not do that and you know it. Christ did not have an emergency room at His disposal back when He walked on the earth in physical form. So He healed people the only way He could. Larry, did God give your doctor his skillful hands and the knowledge to make you well again?"

I said, "Yes."

"Well, it is crazy to be sick when you can be well. Stop blocking the door of the emergency room—or the operating room, Larry Gatlin. Get out of your own way. You are the only one keeping you from wholeness. Let the God within Dr. Ossoff, the God within you, heal you. Do it now."

I said, "OK," then hung up the receiver and called Dr. Ossoff. We scheduled the surgery for June 28, 1991. I called Steve and Rudy and told them I had something I needed to talk about.

"Boys, do you remember that little talk we had back in Pennsylvania about hanging it up? Well, this time I'm really gonna do it. I've decided to get my throat operated on, and after that I'm gonna get off the road and pursue something else. This life was great, but it ain't for me anymore."

I think they both thought it was more of the same thing, but when I called Kathy Gangwisch and told her to write a press release, the brothers knew I was serious.

Later that day Kathy called back to say *Good Morning America* wanted to do a live story on my surgery and about our retirement. We agreed to be at the ABC affiliate in Davenport about 6:30 A.M. the next day to do it. Dr. Nancy Snyderman, who was cohosting with Charles Gibson that morning, did the interview. It was really ironic because she is a throat surgeon. We agreed *GMA* would cover the operation from start to finish and that I would report back on my progress.

That morning we also announced we were going to do some kind of final tour and then check it in. I walked out of that studio in Davenport with the weight of the world off my shoulders.

The next day I flew to New York to be with Janis and Kristin. The girls were going to shop for clothes for Kristin's freshman year at the University of Alabama, and I was going to play golf with Frank Gifford at Deepdale Country Club.

About halfway through our round of golf, Frank said, "Larry, why don't you and Janis have dinner with Kathie Lee and me tomorrow night?"

"Frank, I appreciate it, but I'm taking Janis to see *The Will Rogers Follies*."

"Larry, you would be great in that show, and Keith Carradine is leaving. Let's call Pierre and get you an audition."

At that he took his cell phone out of his golf bag and called our mutual friend, Pierre Cossette, the producer of *The Will Rogers Follies*, and put the wheels in motion for me to audition for the lead role. It happened just like that. Here I am at Deepdale, one of the great golf courses in the world, with a terrible throat, with a former great NFL player and a currently great human being, Frank Gifford, and he's stopping his golf game to try to get me an audition for the lead in a Broadway hit musical—on a cellular phone. (Is this a great country or what?)

Pierre was out of the office, but Frank looked at me as he put the phone back in his bag and said, "I'm on the case, Larry. It's your shot."

I was pumped. I took out my 1-iron and ripped the ball about 265 yards over a creek onto a par-5 green. I promptly three-putted for par, but I didn't care. As they said in the movie, "Somebody up there likes me." It was the first of many God moments that occurred over the next twenty-four hours. The right person, at the right place, at the right time, saying the right thing.

That night, when Janis and I turned out the light to go sleep at the Plaza, I said, "Honey, I'm going to get this surgery done and I'm going to recuperate, and then I'm going to come to New York and find the best vocal coach in the world and learn how to sing correctly so this doesn't happen anymore."

The next morning I took Janis and Kristin to one of my favorite places—The Stage Deli—for an omelette and potato pancakes. Norm, my waiter for fifteen years, still cringes every time I put catsup on the potato pancakes, but they are close enough to hash browns for me and I ain't gonna put applesauce on hash browns. Paul and Norm and all the crew at The Stage Deli are like part of my New York family. I love them, and I love the potato pancakes with catsup. (The Larry Gatlin Sandwich No. 17 is very good too.)

Anyway, Janis and Kristin and I had a wonderful breakfast and then went out into the bright sunshine of Seventh Avenue. The girls turned right to go to Saks Fifth Avenue, and I turned left to go back to the hotel to get my guitar. I had, believe it or not, a meeting with Pierre Cossette, to sing him some songs from a musical I was writing. This is all so strange, because, you see, Frank didn't know I was meeting with Pierre, and Pierre had not yet gotten Frank's message about my doing an audition. As I was crossing the street at Fifty-fourth and Sixth I saw a familiar face. "White Eagle," I hollered.

The face turned toward me. "Larry," the man said.

We walked toward each other and embraced in the middle of Fifty-fourth Street. Nothing strange about that you may say. It was very strange.

White Eagle and I had never met before that moment. We shared a mutual friend, Jack Boland, late of "why be sick when you can be well" fame. Jack had sent me a video of this wonderful Sioux Indian tenor named White Eagle. And Jack had sent White Eagle a video of cripple-throated tenor Larry Gatlin; those videos were how we knew each other. We laughed and walked out of the middle of the street and continued our conversation over the sound of honking horns and screaming truck drivers.

"What in the world is a full-blood Sioux Indian doing in Manhattan? Didn't your people sell this place for twenty-four dollars?" I asked.

White Eagle laughed, and said, "I'm here studying voice with the very best vocal coach in the world." A God moment. The right person, at the right time, at the right place, saying the right thing—the exact words I'd spoken fewer than twelve hours before to Janis. *The very best vocal coach in the world!*

I told White Eagle I was going to have surgery on my throat in Nashville in a couple of weeks and related to him my bedtime conversation with Janis. Then I asked, "Could I come back sometime and get a lesson from him?"

White Eagle looked at me and said, "Come to 120 West Sixtieth at 4:30 and you can have my lesson. I'll call Franco and meet you there."

Wow! We hugged again and I walked—or flew—or floated—back to the Plaza to get my guitar for the meeting with Pierre Cossette.

Pierre is a real piece of work, an old friend from many, many TV shows, one of the leading producers in TV history. I sang my songs and explained the story for *Alive and Well . . . Living in the Land of Dreams,* the title of my musical, and Pierre was very nice. He asked questions. He listened. He loved the songs. The problem was he was up to his neck in alligators. He had a backlog of eight or ten projects he had already decided to do, so nothing ever came of the *Alive and Well* deal with Pierre. I decided not to say anything about the Frank Gifford/*Will Rogers* thing. I just told Pierre I had seen the show once and loved it and was taking Janis and Kristin to see it that night. We shook hands, and I left the apartment.

The next three hours are a real blur. I took my guitar back to the Plaza and put it in the room and then walked and prayed and thought.

I ended up at 120 West 60th Street, New York, New York. I went to the elevator and pushed the button for penthouse A, the fiftieth floor. A very excited little girl answered the door. I could tell at once she was smarter than I was. Melinda is her name.

"Hi, come in," she said in a very grown-up way.

White Eagle was there and introduced me to Maestro Franco Iglesias—the very best vocal coach in the world. (I took it on faith then. I know it from experience now.) He was not at all what I expected, a cold, very businesslike, taskmaster sort of old-fashioned by-the-numbers kind of guy. This little round Mexican was just the opposite. We talked for a while. He told me he had seen me and the brothers on TV many times and loved our voices and our harmony. I told him about the troubles with my voice and that I had decided to have the surgery, and then we vocalized a little together. It was fun, but I couldn't really sing.

"Larry, I want you to see my doctor. Barbara, call Dr. Kessler and see if he will see us."

Franco's wonderful lady, Barbara, called and said the doctor was in and that we should come over immediately. The next thing I knew I was being examined by Dr. Kessler, who confirmed Dr. Ossoff's diagnosis.

Then Franco said, "Larry, I'd love to work with you. We can work on your voice after the operation. Go get it done, have faith, and come back and we will go to work."

I am going to take a chance and make a statement about what has proven to be true in my life. If you need a bigger house, start digging the foundation. Let me explain.

I believe things move toward me when I start moving toward them. I put the whole Frank-Franco-White Eagle-Pierre-Will Rogers scenario into motion by simply letting go of all my old ideas and being willing to accept, at Jack Boland's insistence, the help of God—not through some clap of thunder or miraculous healing, but through Dr. Ossoff. One little step of faith toward God, and all the grand design He had for me sprang into action. It was a marvelous thing to watch—still is. If you need something in your life, God has it for you. Move toward it, and it will move toward you.

Two or three days later, at Vanderbilt Medical Center in Nashville, another God moment occurred when Dr. Ossoff said, "I believe I can restore your vocal chords to 90 percent as good as they ever were," after he, Dr. Ed Stone, and I looked at the video of my larynx. My poor vocal chords were swollen and out of shape from all the abuse over the years.

"Well, Doc," I said, "you take care of your 90 percent and me, and the Good Lord will take care of the other 10 percent."

•   •   •

June 28, 1991. Surgery! I really was not scared; I was relieved. Dr. Ossoff told me, "Larry, I'm very good at this and my team is very good and like I told you, I believe that we will be successful. Sometimes it doesn't work, but those cases are very rare. Do you want to go through with it?"

"Yep, Doc. Start whittlin'. Me and God are ready."

They came in and inserted the IV. Dr. Smith, I think—big guy, real nice—did the inserting. And we were off.

"I'm going to put you out now, Larry," Dr. Smith said. "Count backward from 100."

I think I got to ninety-nine and I was gone. . . .

The recovery room was the pits. I couldn't breathe. There was some kind of tube in my mouth. I finally came to, and they took me to my room. I couldn't talk. Dr. Ossoff came by and said everything had gone very well. On a piece of paper he showed me what he had done and assured me I should recover and be able to sing again. I mouthed a "thank you" and he left.

Friends came by all day long. I was glad to see them, and I appreciated their support. I couldn't talk, but we communicated anyway. I wrote notes and gestured and nodded. They all loved it. Larry Gatlin couldn't say a word for three weeks!

The worst part of the deal was that my tongue and mouth were terribly sore and swollen from the tubes they had put down my throat. I was miserable. I rang for the nurse and wrote her a note. Dr. Ossoff had made arrangements for some kind of sleeping/pain pill, so I asked for it. The nurse put the concoction into my IV thing and about fifteen seconds later, I stopped hurting and just sailed off to Happyville.

When I woke up the next day, I rang for the nurse. She came in and I wrote her a note, "Get this thing out of my arm. I'm going home."

She checked with someone, then came back and unhooked the IV. I took a shower, got dressed, and wrote the nurse a note asking her to call my wife. When Janis walked into the room, I was packed up and ready to go. I wrote her a note on the little blackboard the nurse had given me. It said, "Honey, I took some 'pain dope' last night, my mouth hurt so bad. That medicine felt *too* good. I've gotta get out of here. Now. There's too much 'good stuff' in this place for an old drug addict like me to stay here. Let's go get some pancakes."

My sponsor, Glen H., a.k.a "Big Foot," had flown in from Orange County, California, to be with me. We all piled into the car and went straight to the Pancake Pantry. My tongue and mouth were so sore and swollen I could only eat four huge pecan and chocolate chip pancakes. Pretty good for a guy who was having to turn sideways to use the good side of his mouth. (The right side was totally non-functional.)

For the next three weeks, I walked, prayed silently, and thought. I told people later I really believed God was saying to me, "You've told me all you know, Larry Wayne. Shut up and listen to the Creator of the universe. I know what's best for you. So shut up."

Actually, it was gentle, more like, "Be still and know that I am God. . . . I will never leave you or forsake you. . . . Please, be quiet My child and let Me tell you things that you need to know. I love you, Larry. Let Me show you how much."

It was a wonderful time of healing. After three weeks of complete voice rest, I went to see Dr. Ed Stone—the speech pathologist at Vanderbilt Voice Center. Dr. Ed told me some stuff, we did some stretching exercises, and I blew out some air and hummed. Finally he said, "Larry, you can speak gently—a few words."

I said simply, "Thank you, God. It's over."

Dr. Ed put me on a regimen of talking only a few minutes each day for two weeks, and I left the office. I did what he told me, and

Say, Aaaaahhhhh, Liza!

after three more weeks of slow progress, I was talking normally again. With Dr. Stone and Dr. Ossoff's blessings, I was then off to see Franco for voice rebuilding.

But before that I had the opportunity to enjoy a wonderful evening with Liza Minnelli and her troupe.

Liza and I had first met years before at The Ford Theatre in Washington, D.C., while we were both still in our drinking years. Even though we were both a little tipsy (well, I was drunk—Liza was tipsy), we hit it off marvelously. We laughed, joked, and talked about life and music and show business. It was a wonderful, albeit short, conversation (probably ten or fifteen minutes), but I liked her at once.

Years later in July of 1991, a few weeks after my first throat surgery, Liza brought her wonderful show to the Starwood Amphitheater in Nashville. I called her hotel to invite her to dinner with Janis and me after the show. "Larry, I'd love to but I have asked the whole troupe to go and see some of the sights of Nashville."

I said, "Well, bring 'em all. We'll go to the Stockyard for a steak, and then you all can go gallivantin' all over Nashville." I told her

221

all of this very quietly because I was not yet back to full speaking voice.

Her show at Starwood Amphitheater was fabulous. She sang, she danced, she joked, she laughed, she cried. She was Liza with a Z, and I loved every minute of it.

After the show we did the Stockyard thing, and it was like the show had never stopped. Billy Stritch, Liza's significant other at the time (I don't know whether they are still together), played the britches off the old piano in the upstairs dining room. Liza sang and Billy sang and some of the kids from the show sang. The waiters stuck their heads through the push-out windows at the top of the walls and sang. Jim Fogelsong, one of the nicest men on earth, sang, and George Adams, the Stockyard's star singer, sang two or three Larry Gatlin songs, "The Heart," "I've Done Enough Dyin' Today," and "All the Gold in California." I was the only one who didn't get to sing. It was wonderful misery. All of that talent in one room. All of that music and Larry Wayne had to just sit there and listen and applaud. It was great. So was the steak. And just think—it only cost $1,700. Free concert tickets to Starwood wound up costing me $1,700 at a time when money was really scarce. But it was worth every penny.

Actually, I was pretty much broke. Not really down to bread and milk money, but not really in the chips. I had finally paid off the $690,000 tax bill. (I still think you cheated me, you finks at the IRS.) When all of this throat thing happened, while I was out of commission for about three months, Steve and Rudy and our sister, La Donna, did some shows around the country to try to keep us afloat. God love 'em.

I blocked out a two and a half week period to go to New York and work with Franco in August and September of 1991. I was scurrying around looking for a place to stay that I could afford when out of the clear blue, Frank and Kathie Lee Gifford offered me their fabulous apartment in the city. It was a lifesaver, and I will forever be in their debt. I stayed there and walked to Franco's penthouse on the West Side every day for voice lessons.

My time with the Iglesias family in New York was really something. Barbara, Melinda, and Franco treated me like part of the family. Let me tell you about our first day working together.

I was a little nervous when I walked in. I had not really done any singing for about six weeks.

"Larry," the maestro said, in his broken English–Spanish, "thees morning after I walk Melinda to school I stop at the church on the corner to pray. I say, dear God, look down on me. I do not know everything about the voice. I do not know everything about music and singing. But God, I know You know all about everything. Please God, help me to know what to do so we can restore my new friend's beautiful voice that You gave him."

As I looked into the maestro's face, I could see a glow of the Spirit of God all over it and tears welling up in his eyes. Then he smiled and said, "Now, Larry, let us sing." And we did. We sang for about thirty minutes the first day. He worked slowly and patiently and lovingly with me and before I left that morning, I had hit a high B as clear as a bell. What a miracle. Thank you, Franco. Thank you, Dr. Bob Ossoff and Dr. Ed Stone. And thank You, God. And thanks to all of you who prayed for me. You are a big part of my healing.

For two and a half weeks we worked, and it paid off. After almost ten years of throat trouble, I could sing again. There are some notes I can't hit the way I did when I was twenty. That's life. As I tell people in our shows, my throat is 100 percent well. Dr. Ossoff had to take out some of my flesh, and that is a fact of life. My "head voice," or falsetto, from about the middle C to A may never be the way it was. But the part that remains, the physical part of the larynx, is 100 percent well and that's a miracle. I can sing again, and I'm grateful.

During the period after my first surgery, Janis and I were very blessed to become good friends with Dr. Ossoff, his beautiful wife, Lynn, and my little sweetie pie, their daughter Leslyn. Dr. Ossoff, Lynn, Janis, and I decided to go to Paris for a little vacation in April of 1992.

What a wonderful week it was. Paris is, without a doubt, one of the most beautiful and romantic (and expensive) cities in the world. Janis and I really honeymooned for a week. I will not go into the details, but trust me, being in Paris in April with someone you really love (and really like) is about as good as it gets.

I got up one morning to run the streets of Paris. Along the Champs-Elysées—around the Eiffel Tower—up the Left Bank—past the Tomb of Napoleon—back up the Champs-Elysées—past the Grand Palais and the Petit Palais—through the park and toward the Hotel de Crillon. Well, all at once I stopped dead in my tracks. There were S.W.A.T. teams all over the place. It looked like World War III was about to break out—or that it already had. I ran to the other side of the street and went down a block and circled back to get to the hotel. And then I realized the security forces were guarding the American Embassy. I figured a dignitary of some sort was coming or going and that the extra security was for him or her. I was wrong.

I went upstairs and found out what the deal was. The Rodney King verdict had been handed down in Los Angeles. Riots had started in California, and police all over the world were on alert for attacks and demonstrations. I told Janis I could not believe the jury had turned those guys loose when they had that video of them beating Rodney King while he was on the ground helpless. It was amazing to me and still is. I mean, I am a law-and-order guy, and I believe in supporting your local sheriff, but not when your local sheriff is beating people up after they have been subdued.

Janis and I decided to go outside to wait for Dr. Ossoff and Lynn. Unfortunately we walked right into the middle of a demonstration that the morning news had warned us about. Demonstrating for Rodney King in Paris? I couldn't believe it.

The spike heads—the purple-haired, do nothing but sit around on their butts, smoke dope, and spout anti-American crapolla group—had in fact gotten off their butts, long enough to come over from their Left Bank (appropriately enough) lofts and apartments. They came to shout obscenities at and make obscene gestures toward my flag—the same flag brave young American soldiers had carried with them through a hail of mortar fire and machine-gun bullets, just forty-eight years before, to save the butts of these ingrates' fathers, mothers, grandfathers, and grandmothers and liberate their beloved Paris.

I looked around for help, but there didn't seem to be any in sight. I obviously couldn't whoop all fifty of the weird-looking so-and-sos, and since I couldn't speak any French, I couldn't engage them in political discussion. So I decided to do what I do best. You guessed it—I sang. Looking back on it now, I know it was terribly arrogant and very chauvinistic, but I told Janis to turn on the camera and capture this moment for posterity.

I walked a few feet away from the "madding crowd," and I sang at the top of my lungs with my newly healed voice—

O beautiful for spacious skies,
For amber waves of grain.

They all stopped and looked at this nut, singing something in English.

For purple mountain majesties
Above the fruited plain!
America! America! God shed His grace on thee,
And crown thy good with brotherhood
From sea to shining sea!

There was a smattering of applause from, I assume, a few Americans who had witnessed the whole deal. I acknowledged their applause, turned, and smiled at the Purple Heads, and Janis and Dr. Ossoff and Lynn and I walked away.

• • •

About the same time as all this hubbub with throat surgery, retirement, and tax bills, another crisis occurred, involving my old and dear friend, Dottie West. Very simply stated—she is the reason I am Larry Gatlin, country songwriter and country singer. I've already told the beginning of the story and now, unfortunately, I have to tell you the end. Maybe I shouldn't say it that way. After all, who am I to tell God His business and, really, as gruesome and awful as the story is, there's a ray of sunlight in the whole deal.

In 1990 I started getting calls from a lady named Sandy who worked for Dottie. Sandy told me of Dottie's use of cocaine and vodka and pills and I was really stunned. I had done some drugs with her back in Vegas in the early eighties, but after I got clean and sober I didn't see Dottie very much. I was always on the road and she was always on the road, and I didn't realize there was a problem. (How stupid of you, Larry. You used to chop the stuff up for her and hold the mirror to her nose so she could snort the poison!)

Dottie had a multitude of problems. Her career was on a serious downslide. No record sales, not much money for one-nighters, and the Big Kahuna—the good old IRS—was hounding her day and night. I will not go into all the details, mainly because I do not know all of them, but I do know Dottie made some bad investments and some people who were supposed to be taking care of her money got a little bit cozy with it. Plus, Dottie could spend money faster than anybody I've seen. She was generous. She liked to buy things for the people she loved. She was great that way. But when you put it all together, it spelled financial ruin.

I heard she was trying to sell her part of our publishing company, which owned the publishing rights to all of my early songs— "Broken Lady," "Penny Annie," "Help Me," "Bitter They Are, Harder They Fall," "Light At the End of the Darkness," and hundreds more. So I called someone—a lawyer or business manager, I don't remember—and we had a big powwow at my house. I had not seen Dottie in months, but I had been in touch with Shelly and Kerry, Dottie's daughter and son, and they had confirmed to me that Dottie was using and drinking. I told them I would go see her and confront her with this deal, but I would need their support and backing. We talked about it for some time, but I didn't go over there until after the meeting with the three-piece-suit guys about the publishing situation.

The "suits" came to my house and sat down at the kitchen table with Janis and me, and we started discussing the possibilities. The music industry uses a pretty standard formula to determine the worth of a music catalog: you average the last four or five years' earnings and then put a multiple of six or seven or eight to it and there you have—voila!—the price. Well, as I recall, the selling or buying price for the catalog would have been about $180,000, according to a four- or five-year average and multiple of seven. Well, Dottie's asking price was $300,000. I nearly fell over.

The rumor around Nashville was that Dottie owed more than $1.3 million, and I was really sorry about her bad times, but I was in the middle of some rough times myself.

As much as I would have loved to help her, I couldn't pay almost twice what the catalog was worth. The suits sitting around my kitchen table were embarrassed about even bringing me the offer. They knew it was sky high.

I asked, "Fellows, is this your number or Dottie's?"

To a man, they said, "Larry, the number is Dottie's, and it changes on a minute-by-minute basis. We're just trying to help her, but she doesn't even make sense half the time."

Not long after that I got a call from Shelly, Dottie's daughter, asking me to help Dottie. "Just go talk to her, Larry. Maybe she'll listen to you."

So I went to the house. The next two hours would be two of the longest and most painful of my life. I knocked on the door of Dottie's (soon to be the IRS's) beautiful home, and she came to the door.

"Hi, stranger," she said, a little sarcastically. "Come on in."

I walked in and she said, "Let's go into the living room."

We walked in and I sat down on the couch and spoke first. "Dottie, I've come to help you if I can."

Then it started. "Larry, they're going to take my house. I worked hard all my life, and they're going to take all this away from me. Will you help me keep it? Chet [Atkins] and Kenny [Rogers] are going to help. Can you help me? Can you do something?"

I didn't know what to say. I knew Chet and Kenny and all the rest of Dottie's friends were truly concerned for her and they all wanted to help, but I also knew no one was going to come up with $1.3 million to bail Dottie out of the IRS mess. Please understand, I'm not being judgmental in any way toward Dottie's friends. It's just that $1.3 million is really $2.6 million after taxes to Chet and Kenny and me and whoever else could have possibly come to the rescue, and by that time, none of us was making the kind of money we were making in the late '70s and early '80s. Fifty percent money, a band, road crew, airplanes, expensive houses, wives and kids, divorces, and drug treatment—all that stuff costs money.

Anyway, I knew Dottie's dreams of someone riding in on a white horse and saving the day were just that—Dottie's dreams.

"Dottie, the house is not the problem," I said.

"What do you mean, Larry?"

"Dottie, if somehow you came up with the money tomorrow and paid the back taxes to the IRS, the problem of your alcohol and drug use would still be here, and until you face it and do something about it, your life is going to be a wreck."

Well, the proverbial you-know-what hit the proverbial fan. "Larry Gatlin, you ungrateful —. Are you accusing me of using drugs?" she asked incredulously.

"Dottie, I used to buy the stuff for you and chop it up on the glass coffee table in your suite at The Riviera Hotel in Vegas. It's me, Dottie. It's Larry. Not some flunky who's gonna tell you what you want to hear. It's me, Dottie. Larry Wayne Gatlin, alcoholic and coke addict. Just like you, Darlin'."

Then a look that bordered on hatred came across her face and into her eyes.

"Don't you Darlin' me, you little s—. Get out of my house right now."

"No, Dottie. I won't go. Not until I've said what I came to say."

"Well, say it and get out," she hollered.

"Dottie, I love you. I really do. You helped me make my dreams come true. I'd probably be a bad lawyer in Houston, Texas, if it weren't for you. I am so grateful to you I cannot even begin to put it in words. So I'm going to just spill it. You are very sick. Your kids don't even want to be around you anymore. Shelly is afraid to leave the baby [her daughter, Tess Marie] with you because the last time she did, when she came back, the baby was crying in the baby bed and you were upstairs passed out." Dottie stared at me as I continued. "Dottie, your kids have been calling me for months begging me to come have this talk with you. I came today only because I got them to promise we'd all confront you together at some point in the near future to address your problems. Dottie, you need help and . . ."

"Larry, I need someone to help save my house," she interrupted. "If you really want to help me, help me save my house."

It was gut-wrenching. We moved from the living room to the kitchen to the garage, and finally I found myself perched in the seat of an old tractor in her driveway.

"I'm gonna sell that tractor," she said. "And some of my clothes and the bus and I'm gonna pay those SOBs off," she screamed.

It went on for well over an hour. I did everything I knew to do, short of picking her up bodily and taking her to a treatment hospital. God knows, looking back, I wish I had done exactly that. She finally told me to leave, and exhausted from the battle I had just lost, I got in my car and drove off.

On the way back to our farm, I passed a beautiful house on the right side of the road. The house had a lovely, well-manicured front lawn. My mind raced back to a night only three or four years earlier when I had run my Mercedes off the road into this very same well-manicured front yard. I had been drunk on vodka, high on cocaine, and had taken some kind of pain pills. I had just come from Dottie's house a mile or so down the road, where everyone—I repeat, everyone—had been totally wasted on drugs and booze.

As I drove by the house, I remembered sliding sideways and gunning my engine and shifting and somehow getting back onto the paved road, and I looked up to heaven at that moment and said a heartfelt thanks to God for sparing my life that night, on that rain-slick, winding road. That Mercedes had almost flipped over. I do remember that. And it could have, except for the grace of God.

After I offered my prayer of gratitude for God's protective grace, I prayed He would look down on my friend Dottie West and show me or someone a way to get her to face up to her problems and try to solve them with the help of her friends, family, and Him.

One day a few weeks later I was playing golf with Steve, Rudy, and Vince Gill when my cell phone rang. I rushed to the cart, pushed the button, and said, "Hello." It was Sandy, the lady who worked for Dottie.

"Larry, you have to do something. Dottie has gone crazy. You've got to talk to her. Larry, this time it's worse than ever. She's gonna kill herself if someone doesn't stop her. The guys in the band are frantic. They don't know what to do. They are all worried she's gonna die in the bus."

"Well, where is she, Sandy?"

"Grand Rapids, Michigan," came the reply.

Dear God, Grand Rapids, Michigan, I thought to myself. *Why can't she be about "to kill herself" in Franklin or Murfreesboro or even Atlanta? Why Grand Rapids, Michigan?* (No offense, Grand Rapids. But it was hard to get to from Nashville.)

"OK. I'll go see what I can do."

I went back to the second tee box. We'd only played one hole. I told the boys I had to go. Steve or Vince or Rudy, whoever I was riding with, took me back to the clubhouse and I unhooked my golf bag, put the clubs in the trunk of my car, and drove the five or six miles from Crockett Springs Golf Club to our farm in Brentwood. On the way, I called some airline and got a flight to Grand Rapids.

I packed an overnight bag and headed for the airport. I got to Grand Rapids at about 7:00 that night, then I took a cab for about forty-five minutes to the gig. I walked over to the bus, and Tony Toliver, Dottie's bandleader, looked at me with surprise and said, "Man, where did you come from?"

I told him about the conversation with Sandy, and he confirmed the band members' fears.

"Larry, she's really bad. We don't know what to do. They've taken her home away from her. When she's in Nashville she is literally living in the bus in the Kroger [supermarket] parking lot in Brentwood. She doesn't eat anything. We don't know what to do. She's not really here, man, you know what I mean?"

I told Tony I appreciated him and the guys sticking with Dottie and that I was going to make another attempt to talk to her.

"Good luck, man. She ain't gonna listen, but you can try."

Dottie came out of her dressing room and said something like, "Look who's here." I smiled and she smiled and we hugged and she walked past me, down the steps of her bus and into the auditorium.

(It was a familiar place to me. A young, red-haired girl from Oklahoma had opened a show for us in that very auditorium some eight or ten years earlier. Her name was Reba something.)

Dottie waited backstage as the band did a couple of songs. Tony is a great singer and songwriter, and he did a great job leading Dottie's band. He introduced her, and they "played her on." She did an OK show, but the voice was not really there. The heart was not really there, and the crowd was not really there. I don't think there were six hundred people in the place.

Dottie called me up, and I sang something. She said something to the effect that "Larry's working close by and came over to see me" (where she got that I'll never know).

After the show, we sat inside the bus and the battle was on again.

"Honey, Sandy called me today and got me off the golf course in Nashville to come talk to you. Dottie, everyone is afraid you're gonna kill yourself with pills and coke and vodka. You've got to stop this. Please let me help you."

I was literally on my knees in front of her, on the floor of the bus. "Dottie, Kenny and I want to . . ."

She exploded. "Larry Gatlin. You told Kenny Rogers about this. You've ruined my career. You've spread lies about me."

"Dottie," I screamed, "I did not tell Kenny Rogers about this. He called me last week and told *me*."

"You're lying, Larry."

It was no use. After ten or fifteen minutes of begging and pleading and saying everything I knew to say, she got up and walked toward her room in the back of the bus, without a word of good-bye. I waited for her to come back. I thought maybe she was going to change clothes or get a Kleenex (she had been crying) or something.

Tony looked at me and said, "You might as well go on back to Nashville, Larry. She won't come out of the room until tomorrow at show time."

I couldn't believe it, but Tony was right. She did not come back out of the room.

I said good-bye to a confused bunch of musicians and hugged

Tony Toliver and hailed a cab back to the hotel about twenty-five miles away. That was the last time I laid eyes on Dorothy Marie Marsha West alive.

I saw her bus in the Kroger parking lot a few times. I drove by there going to play golf or doing other things around Brentwood. I started to stop on several occasions, but never did. Then one day I read in the paper that Dottie had gotten a new apartment in Nashville after some of her IRS business was supposedly taken care of, and she was planning to make a new start with her career. I called Shelly and got her phone number.

After brief greetings, I said. "Dottie, I just wanted to tell you I saw in the paper about the new things that are going on in your life. I wanted to say I was happy that things were turning around a little bit, and I wanted to tell you I love you and wish you well."

"I will talk to you, Larry, if you promise not to bring up all that other stuff. You hurt me very badly, Larry. After all I've done for you."

"Dottie," I pleaded, "what would you have done if Janis and Kristin and Josh had called you and asked you to help me with my drinking and druggin'? What was I supposed to do, Dottie? Your kids asked me—begged me—to confront you about the stuff.

"What was I supposed to do, Dottie? What would you have done?"

There was a long pause.

"Well, I wouldn't have accused you and gotten into your personal life, Larry. I can tell you that."

There was another long pause.

"Dottie," I asked, "what would you have me do?"

"Just leave me alone."

I said, "OK, Dottie. That's what I'll do." Those were the last words we ever spoke.

A few weeks later, Janis called me from Nashville (I was in California) and told me Dottie had been in a car wreck and was not expected to live. My heart broke. I prayed and cried and remembered. Dottie died on September 4, 1991.

At the funeral "Mo," Dottie's oldest boy, took me aside and wrapped his arm around me. "I know you tried, Larry. Thanks."

"Thank you, Mo," I said. "We all tried."

Four years later, I would get tears in my eyes again when I walked into Michelle Lee's trailer on the set of *Big Dreams, Broken Hearts: The Dottie West Story*, a TV movie about Dottie's life. I had a small role in the production. Michelle was wearing Dottie's clothes and had her hair done like hers. It was haunting. She looked just like Dottie.

Once again, it seems like I'm trying to be the white knight riding to the rescue. Please know I didn't mean it that way. I could not turn aside and not at least try to help Dottie. I'm a recovering drug addict, and I was doing what my sponsor and other friends in recovery do every day. I was just trying to bring another sick, lost addict into the healing and safety and rebirth of recovery. It didn't work. I wish I had been a white knight. Maybe she would have listened to one. She would not listen to me.

I hesitated to put all of this in the book until Kerry, Dottie's son, and I had a conversation a few months ago. He said, "Brother Larry, Mama got right with God before she died and everything is OK. Tell the story, and don't leave anything out. Mom was on the road to recovery when the wreck happened, and I know she's in a better place. So tell it like it was. Maybe it will help somebody."

Until then I had always believed God had not answered my prayer the day I visited her house—or make that, He had answered it. He had just said "No!"

Now I knew that, in fact, He had said "Yes." I just didn't know all the details.

• • •

Many years ago I was doing an interview with someone from some country music magazine. The interviewer asked, "Larry, how will you know when it's time to quit?" I gave him some smart answer and didn't really address his question. I do remember telling him I would rather quit ten years too early than five minutes too late. It sounded very profound at the time.

Three things happened in pretty rapid succession in 1991 that convinced me it was time to leave Nashville and seek, if not greener pastures, at least different ones. I went to New York to try to mend fences with Charles Koppleman and Martin Bandeer, the fellows who owned part of my publishing at EMI Music. My friend Frances Preston, the president of BMI (Broadcast Music Incorporated), set up the meeting, and Joel Katz, my attorney, went to their offices with me. We had a very cordial and good meeting, and we agreed to throw everything in a big pot: songs for which I owned all the publishing, songs for which they owned all the publishing, and everything in between—we'd split it. We all shook hands, smiled, and pledged our support for each other, and I left New York and flew back to Nashville.

A few days later Joel called me and said, "The deal ain't gonna happen."

It seems that Celia Froehlig, the woman who ran Charles and Marty's Nashville operation at the time, said I was "old business" and she did not want to work my song catalog. Strike one.

I was watching TV one night and there was an interview with the woman who was taking over the programming of CMTV. I watched and listened, not really paying a lot of attention, until she said, "My main priority at CMTV will be to break new acts on television." Strike two. (We ain't a new act.)

A few weeks later we delivered our *Adios* album to Liberty Records, and our friend Jerry Crutchfield, who was then A&R director, said "Boys, there's nothing on this album we can get played on radio." Strike three. You're out.

At that point we had decided to do a final tour, but Janis and I had not made the decision to leave Nashville. I had thought we would live there, and I would write songs and maybe do a solo album or gigs, but when the three strikes came within a few weeks of each other, I knew it was time to "get outta Dodge."

The boys and I had canceled about seventy or eighty concerts because of my throat surgery in 1991. So we decided to do a year-long tour, called "Adios," and say good-bye to the loyal fans who had supported us through the years. (We also were trying to make enough money to pay off everything and everybody and have enough money to get out of town.)

It was a good year. We kicked off the tour in January of 1992 and played roughly one hundred forty dates across the country (the *Adios* album was released three months later). We sang great. My voice was good most of the time, and it was great to be able to sing again. We sang at some of our favorite places—Wolf Trap, The Fox, The Houston Rodeo, some great fairs. It was quite a run. We did *The Tonight Show* with Johnny Carson, one of his last shows before retiring, and I had a great visit in the hallway that night with Bill Cosby—a good and courageous man and a big Gatlin Brothers fan.

I guess my ego wanted someone in the music business to make a big fuss about The Gatlin Brothers retiring. But no one really seemed to care. Don't get me wrong, we got cards and letters galore from fans begging us not to quit—and that was very touching and really meant a lot to Steve and Rudy and me. But not from the business—Nashville. It was like, no big deal. Next. . . .

•   •   •

The "Adios" tour came to a close. We did our last concert on the mainland in Asheville, North Carolina, on December 18, 1992. It was a great evening, and I'll always remember it. What a show. What a band. What a good pair of partners Steve and Rudy have been for over forty years.

The Asheville concert not only marked one of our last concerts as a touring group, but it represented something more. It was the 2,461st concert of our career in seventeen years of doing principally one-nighters, accounting for approximately nine years away from home. Or 3,363 days on the road since 1975 (our first year of touring). Or 36,554 songs performed overall. Or 147,660 minutes spent on stage. It was some run.

We did one more show in Hawaii a few days later and it was over. The touring part of our lives was history—adios—("to God" in Spanish), and that's where we left it.

I couldn't have envisioned all that would transpire in the coming years, but getting in and out of buses two hundred days a year was over. I do not regret that we retired from the road when we did. It was time. We left with some dignity. We paid all our bills. No one had to do a Gatlin Brothers charity concert to get us out of debt. We might have been able to hold on for a few more years, but it would have been drudgery. It was too good for too long to leave with our tails between our legs liked whooped dogs. We left all even with the world. Actually, we left while we were ahead of the game.

We had the cards and the letters and the knowledge that, while we were only a relatively minor blip on the radar screen of country music, we had made a difference in a lot of people's lives. For that the boys and I will always be grateful.

Janis and I decided that, as it says in the Old Testament, "Ye have compassed this mountain long enough" (Deut. 2:3 KJV), and although we had had many good years and made many good friends in Nashville, it was time for a change.

In the fall of 1992, we moved to Austin, Texas, to watch the sun come up over the Colorado River; to eat breakfast at Cisco's, lunch at Rosie's Tamale House, and dinner at Matt's El Rancho; and to play golf with Darrell Royal at Barton Creek Country Club on every occasion I could until one of us shoveled dirt over the other. I love Austin. It is home.

PART THREE

NEW YORK

Larry Gatlin, a.k.a. Will Rogers

CHAPTER 17

On the Palace Theatre Stage with the cast of Will Rogers
and Dolores and Bob Hope

$\mathcal{T}$HE
WILL ROGERS
FOLLIES

Janis and I were walking home from The Palace Theatre one night
when Janis said something like, "There may be other places in the
world that are filthier than New York, but I don't know what they
are."

At that moment we were walking along one of the cross streets,
probably Fifty-second or Fifty-third between Broadway and Fifth,
on our way to Trump Tower at Fifty-sixth and Fifth. On all sides
were week-old trash from dumpsters, the stench of human urine,
rotten food—you name it.

We walked into the lobby of Trump Tower, I said hi to Jairo and
John, the elevator guys, and one of them escorted us into the

elevator for the ride to the sixty-third floor. I unlocked the door, and Janis and I walked into our beautiful apartment overlooking Midtown Manhattan—a sweeping view from the East River to the harbor with the Statue of Liberty and the Empire State Building.

Janis and I sat down on the couch and took it all in. Then, looking out the window at the city, Janis said, "You know, Honey, New York is not quite as filthy from the sixty-third floor of Trump Tower."

I laughed and said, "You're right, Darlin'. This is pretty spectacular."

And it was. So was the rather circuitous route we took to get there in 1993.

In 1992 the "Frank and Kathie Lee Gifford Talent Agency" succeeded in getting me an audition for *The Will Rogers Follies*, with a lot of help from George Lane at William Morris. In fact I was the first one to audition for Keith Carradine's job. A bunch of the producers; Cy Coleman, the composer; Betty Comden and Adolph Green, the lyricists; Peter Stone, the book writer; Barry Moss and Julie Hughes, the casting agents; and other muckety-mucks gathered at The Palace.

Someone said, "OK, Larry," and I walked out there and went to it. I had taken some notes when I had seen the show the night before, and I knew I could sing the part, so I was confident the audition would go well.

It was one of those special moments when I was "in the zone." I did a newspaper bit a la Will Rogers, and then Nancy Ringham— Dee Hoty's understudy for the part of Betty Blake, Mrs. Will Rogers— and I did a scene from the musical. It is still one of my fondest memories. We did the "train station on the moon" scene, and it was terrific. I knew we were doing well because the folks in the audience, who had seen this thing hundreds of times, were laughing in all the right spots.

After that scene I took my guitar and sat down on the front of the big stage and looked them all in the eye—if that's possible—and started to sing: "Never met a man I didn't like. High fallutin' gent or bowery bum. Yes, I've come a long way down the pike. Never met a man I didn't like."

I only sang a few lines and then, as I continued playing, I said, "Folks, I really didn't have the time to learn all of this song. I've spent the better part of the last two weeks becoming a self-taught Broadway actor."

Someone in the crowd of ten or twenty people hollered, "Well, you did a d— good job."

I countered, "Thank you. You all already know I can sing the part, so I concentrated more on the dialogue and the acting stuff. I hope you like it. Will Rogers was one of my heroes growing up, and I'd love to play him up here on this stage. So if you'll give me the chance, I'd be much obliged. But if you don't, I promise I will not hold it against you because"—then I sang again—"I never met a man, or a woman, I didn't like." They erupted into laughter and applause. The casting agents, Judy Hughes and Barry Moss, and all of the rest applauded and smiled. I knew I had it.

Phil Oestermann, the associate director, came running up to the stage as I was putting my guitar into the case and said, "When can you come?"

"December."

"Oh, no, we need you in June."

"Well, I've got a tour to do. My brothers and I have promised our fans we will do a final tour before we retire. I won't be finished until December. I'm sorry, I didn't know you needed someone right away."

He said he understood and that he would be in touch. He also said I had done the best audition anyone had ever seen. I was ecstatic and terribly disappointed at the same time. I wanted to start the next day. I walked out, got into the limo, and went back to the hotel to tell Janis the news.

Mac Davis was selected to take Keith Carradine's place as Will. (Actually he wasn't selected, he was begged out of a five-year retirement. Mac had left the music business a few years earlier to spend more time with his wife, Lise, and their boys. He was actually one of the first people that producer Pierre Cossette had wanted for the role when it was just an idea. So when Keith decided to leave, Mac was a natural choice.)

One variable in my *Will Rogers* decision was a Branson deal. The

Gatlin Brothers had been in negotiations with some guys to do a theater in Branson, Missouri, which was to be part of a big hotel and restaurant complex called The Gatlin Brothers Summit. Yes, we were going to retire from the road, but this "brothers thing" we have would not let us turn loose all the way. Some good ole boys from Dallas and Arkansas were promising us The Gatlin Brothers Theatre would be up and running by January or February of 1993. That would have really fouled up the whole *Will* deal. It was a real dilemma. I knew I was born to do Will Rogers, but my sense of loyalty to my brothers was overshadowing all other considerations. Finally I went to Steve's room in Branson and called Rudy in.

"Boys," I said, "I love you both, and if this deal [the Branson theatre] comes through, I'll sing over here for half a year for the next four or five years so that we can put away some money. But I'm gonna tell you this [this part is hard to say even now], if trying to do the Branson deal keeps me from going to New York and starring as Will Rogers on Broadway, I'll never ever get over it. It's not that I'll blame you guys. That's not the right way to put it. But I know I will have a bad feeling about it until the day I die."

There was dead silence in the room, and then Steve said, "Larry, I am not going to be the reason for you feeling that way. Go do what you want to do and if this thing works out, we'll do it when you get back."

Rudy said, "That's the way to do it. Go do *Will Rogers*, and we'll get back together afterward."

I will always be grateful to Steve and Rudy for understanding the situation. It was a hard thing for all of us. We were pretty much broke, and those guys were offering us a good deal of money to come to Branson.

I looked at them both and said, "Boys, I don't believe the Branson deal is ever gonna work. Those guys couldn't put together a toy train set, much less a multimillion dollar theater. I cannot wait for them. I'm going to New York."

Well, guess what? I was right. The deal was no deal. We never saw a penny or a Gatlin Brothers Summit in Branson.

While I was on our "Adios" tour, I watched Keith Carradine's every move in *Will Rogers* on a video Pierre had sent me. I knew the lines, the moves, the expressions, and the choreography pretty well by the time I got to New York in January of 1993 for my first rehearsal. I didn't know if they would want me to copy his performance, or if I could bring my own personality and talents to it, but whatever they wanted—I was ready.

I was "off book" the first day of rehearsal. Peter Von Meyerhauser, the production manager, really was the one responsible for directing me in the show. He was patient with me, and I will always be grateful for his help.

Phil Oestermann came by on occasion to "tweak" the character a little bit, and a wonderful young lady named Patti DeBeck, the dance captain of the show, spent hour after hour teaching me the choreography. She is a champ.

Tommy Tune came to a rehearsal one day and saw several scenes. Afterward he said, "Larry, you are terrific. You can slow down the whole thing just 10 percent and you'll be perfect."

That was it—no big deal. "Slow down the whole thing 10 percent and you'll be perfect." (Tommy later saw my tenth show and said he couldn't believe I could totally assume the character in such a short period. I was thrilled by his encouragement and his comments.)

By opening night I was ready, and I knew it. It was one of the most exciting evenings of my life. I had friends and family there from all over the country: Mom and Dad; Steve and Rudy; Janis, Kristin, and Josh; Darrell and Edith Royal; Jim Bob and Louise Moffett; Bucky and Jolene Wharton from the Waggoner Ranch; Frank and Kathie Lee Gifford; Franco and Barbara Iglesias; and Mack Rankin.

When I climbed onto that big rope, four stories up in the top of The Palace and started down—my heart was beating 200 miles per hour. Nervous? No. Excited? Yes. Then the music started and the applause for me, Larry Gatlin, a.k.a. Will Rogers. I opened my mouth and, thank God, "Never met a man I didn't like" came out. I finished my walk around the stage and stopped in the center. The opening song was over.

"Howdy," I said. The audience returned a feeble, "Howdy."

Backstage at The Palace. Marla Maples, Bob Fitch,
Hal Linden, me, and Nancy Ringham

"Howdy!"

They repeated more vigorously this time, "Howdy!"

"That's better," I said. "That was some entrance, wasn't it? That's Mr. Ziegfeld's idea of how to open a show. I can't complain though, seein's how I like it a whole lot better'n his first idea, which was having me shot out of a cannon."

I was off. The show went great and the cast and I received a thunderous standing ovation.

Nancy Ringham was no longer the understudy. She was my costar and was absolutely great as Betty Blake. Bob Fitch played "Pa" and did a very good job. (Good actor and a tap dancin' son-of-a-gun.) And there was Marla Maples playing Ziegfeld's favorite. Let me say at the outset, I think Marla Maples deserves a lot of credit for keeping the show "up" right after Keith Carradine and Dee Hoty left it. Please know that I mean no disrespect to Mac. He was great as Will Rogers. But the show never really was the darling of the press. In fact, they pretty much hated it, and even though it enjoyed a two-plus-year run, the show was never a smash hit.

So when Marla came into the show, her front-page romance with Donald Trump and all the notoriety that it brought really helped draw people to *The Will Rogers Follies*.

Let me say something else. Marla and I got along very well and worked well together—after we got some ground rules straightened out.

One night at dinner after a show, she and I were in the China Cafe with two of my talented "wranglers" from the show, and Marla was complaining about all the press and about how Donald wasn't treating her right and all that stuff. Finally, I said, "Marla, you have brought all of this on yourself. You are the one who stole another woman's husband and entered into this deal with a very visible, wealthy man. This is your deal. You've made your bed. Now you have to sleep in it. The rest of us are tired of hearing about it all the time. It's really hard to feel sorry for you, Sweetheart."

Understand that I told her all of this while we were all laughing and having a big time over some really great chop suey, but I think she got the point. The cast was at The Palace for eight performances every week, trying to do a great job and keep the show going. All we heard from Marla was Donald this and Donald that, and all we saw in the paper was Donald this and Marla that.

Not long after that, Marla and Donald reached some sort of agreement and things got better. I realize it was a tough time for her, but as I told her, she made her own situation. She is a good kid, and I like her.

Marla Maples is not a great singer, dancer, or actress. But I'll tell you what quality she has that I admire and respect. She's got guts. She's got "try," as cowboys down in Texas would say. She took her abilities, such as they were, and dug into the part. She worked and learned, and she put herself out there on that stage every night and did a very good job. Heck, folks, it's easy to walk out onto a stage if you know you can sing and dance your way into the hearts of the people in the audience. It's something else again if you know you're not really a great singer or dancer, and you still go out there and pull if off. Marla pulled it off.

By the time she left the show in May of 1993, she had improved by leaps and bounds. She did the choreography from start to finish with some oomph, and her acting was solid. She never blew a line or entrance that I can remember. In short, she took her abilities and made something out of what she had.

Now to Donald. He is a prize. Donald Trump has never been anything but gracious to my family and me. When I found out I was to be paid $2,500 per week for a housing allowance, and I told Donald how much I had to spend, he graciously rented us a $25,000 per month apartment for *only* $10,000 a month. It was a beautiful apartment, with a spectacular view of midtown Manhattan.

One day, Donald invited me to play golf at Winged Foot Golf Club, one of the truly great golf courses in the world. We were walking down a fairway when he said, "Hey, Larry, what do you think I should do?"

"About what?"

"About Marla," he replied. (By now the whole world knew Marla was pregnant with their love child and that he was hedging on the "'til death do us part" stuff.)

I stopped walking, looked him right in the eye, and asked, "Donald, do you love the woman?"

"Well . . yeah. You know . . . yeah, I love her," he stammered.

"OK then, stop acting like New York City is your private harem. Marry the woman. Be a good husband to her and a good father to the child and hit your golf ball. It's your shot."

He laughed at me and made some crude remark about my ancestry, hit his ball onto the green, and we had a great day at Winged Foot.

It took Donald and Marla another six months or so to work out the legal ramifications of their holy union, but in December of 1993 they were married at the Plaza in New York. I was honored that they asked me to sing at their wedding, but I had to say no. I was in a very small, temporary trailer house kind of thing, with no running water, in Mogadishu, Somalia. Somewhere on a USO Christmas tour, singing for the troops.

•   •   •

When Marla left the show in May because of her pregnancy, the producers scurried around trying to find someone to replace her. The show was in trouble. We all knew it, and everyone was trying to find the "silver bullet," the one woman who could do what Marla had done eight or ten months earlier—inject some new life and excitement.

I called Priscilla Presley and talked to her about it. She said she would love to do it, but her movie stuff was taking up most of her time and she just couldn't drop everything for an extended period.

The producers racked their collaborative brains trying to come up with a woman. One day, I had an idea and called my friend Patrick Swayze. I had a very honest and forthright conversation with him regarding his beautiful and talented wife, Lisa Niemi.

I said, "Buddy, would Lisa consider coming to New York to audition for the role of Z's Favorite—the role Marla has been doing?"

Patrick started to say something, but I interrupted. "Now before you answer, Buddy, let me explain this deal. You and I know Lisa is beautiful and can really dance and is a good actress and singer. But I'll tell you right now. These people are looking for a 'silver bullet' to try to save the show, and they are going to use you and your celebrity status in the press, just the way they did with Donald and Marla.

"These people are desperate to keep this show going. And if she gets the job, I'm being honest with you, about one-third of it will be because she is a very talented lady and about two-thirds of it will be because she's your wife. I hate to put it like that, but, Buddy, you and Lisa are my friends, and it was my idea to call you guys. I thought you should know the situation before she flies up here and auditions."

There was a pause—then Patrick said, "Lisa is confident of her work, and she knows she could do the job. It would be a good break for her, and we appreciate you thinking of her and making the call."

I said, "Hey man, I know the lady can do the job; she'll be great. I just wanted to let you know the whole story. Put Lisa on the phone. I want to talk to her."

He gave her the phone.

"Lisa," I said, "I'd love for you to consider the Z's Favorite

The Gatlins and the Swayzes: me, Janis, Lisa, and Patrick

audition. I haven't told them about calling you, but I think you would be perfect."

I then recounted the story I'd told Buddy, and she said she understood all the ramifications and absurdities, but that she would love to have a chance to audition. I wished them well, got some phone numbers for them (they were on their way to Europe), and I hung up and immediately called Phil Oestermann. He thought it was a great idea and said he would call Lisa directly and get the ball rolling. (Phil, Tommy Tune, and Buddy and Lisa are all from the Houston area and had known each other for years.)

Lisa flew almost all night from Cannes or somewhere exotic in Europe—Monte Carlo maybe. Whatever. She walked onto The Palace stage with her blonde hair flowing down beside her face, smiled a big-as-Texas smile, and did a great audition. I was sitting in the back row of the theater, silently rooting for her. I knew they'd offer her the job. She was by far the best singer and dancer to audition. A couple of weeks later, Lisa Niemi was Z's Favorite in *The Will Rogers Follies* on Broadway.

Yes, she's Patrick Swayze's wife. And, no, she's never really established a great acting career—yet. But let me say this, Lisa came into the show under very trying circumstances and did a superb job. I enjoyed working with her, and having her and Buddy in New York was great fun for Janis and me.

•   •   •

In May of 1995, when we heard Mickey Rooney was coming to *The Will Rogers Follies* to take Bob Fitch's place as Clem Rogers, Will's "Pa," there was a bit of anxiety among the members of the cast. We had all heard the rumors that he was absolutely crazy and very hard to work with and that he would foul up everything. Well, that was not the case. Yeah, he's different and he's loud and he's dogmatic and he's very passionate about his life, but he is a real sweet man who has seen it all and done it all and wants to see it all and do it all again.

Sir Lawrence Olivier once said Mickey Rooney is "the greatest actor America has ever produced." I agree. I've only worked with a few, but I can say without a doubt that on a stage or a movie set, when the curtain goes up or someone says "action," he is magic. The range of emotions, his facial expressions, and his timing are unbelievable.

One night he fouled up his lines. He "went up," as we say in the theater, so I just went with him. He was making stuff up on the fly, so I made some stuff up on the fly. We worked it out in front of the cast and about one thousand paying customers. Then we broke one of the cardinal rules of theater: we stepped out of character in the middle of the show.

I said to him, "Mick, this play will work a lot better if you'll say those lines that are written down in that little blue book they gave you during rehearsal."

He looked at me and laughed and said, "I ain't been saying them that way for three months. Why should I start now?"

The crowd went nuts. The cast started laughing. The orchestra pit erupted, and I nearly cried I laughed so hard.

I turned to the audience and said, "He ain't kiddin', folks." Then

Nancy Ringham, Tony Bennett, me, "Mick," Betty and President Ford

we went right back into character and continued the show. It was hilarious.

But that's not why I love and admire him so much. I love and admire Mickey Rooney because he is Everyman.

Let me tell you more about my friend Mickey Rooney. First, a short explanation. One time I asked Jack Boland, "How is it that I can do something really selfless and kind and loving and generous, then turn around fifteen minutes later and do something cruel and heartless and totally unloving?"

Jack replied in his mystic way, "There are two Larry Gatlins. There is the Larry Gatlin that God made who is perfect and loving and kind and generous and totally free of hate and resentment. Then there is the Larry Gatlin that Larry Gatlin made, who is a scared little boy, full of resentment, anger, and doubt, and neurosis upon neurosis, defense mechanism upon defense mechanism. The key is to live your life more and more as the Larry Gatlin that God made. That is why we have prayer and meditation."

Jack paused, then he said, "Larry, it is a spiritual journey that, hopefully, leads us back to the person that God made and not the person society and parents and teachers and Madison Avenue and fears made." Now back to Everyman.

Jack's explanation gave me insight into Mickey Rooney as well as myself, and everyone else for that matter. The Mickey Rooney that Mickey Rooney and society and parents and teachers and Madison Avenue and fears made went bonkers one day on the set of *The Legend of O. B. Taggart*, outside of Santa Fe, New Mexico, in 1994.

The O. B. Taggart "deal" is too long to get into, but it was a Western that Mickey and some fellows wrote, starring Mickey, Ben Johnson, Gloria deHavilland, Randy Travis, Ernest Borgnine, and Larry Gatlin. It wasn't very good. It could have been, but there were too many Indians and not enough chiefs. Actually, there were too many chiefs, but none of them could rein in the project and get it under control. It was actually a very good story about families and greed and murder and stuff, but, trust me, the best thing that could have happened did, in fact, happen. *The Legend of O. B. Taggart* opened as a feature film and closed the same day.

One day during the filming, Mick sat in his trailer all day watching the Breeder's Cup on TV. At about four or five in the afternoon when the horse races were over and after we all had been standing around for six hours, Mickey came out and walked over to the set. The sun was going down and the lighting guys were scurrying around, trying to figure out how to light the scene we were doing. They had to start all over from scratch. It was supposed to be a daytime scene and it was dusk. Well, when Mickey found out it was going to take two hours to redo the lights, he exploded.

"I'm going to miss my dinner again tonight because you people can't even light a set. You've had all day." (Right, Mick, we've been sitting on our butts since 10:30 this morning waiting for you.)

Anyway, he went back to the trailer and fumed for an hour, and then we did the day scene at about 8:00 at night. We *all* missed dinner. It was not fun. That was the Mickey Rooney that Mickey Rooney made.

Now let me tell you about the Mickey Rooney that God made.

One of the camera assistants—I'll call her Mary (how original) was having a rough day. I do not know the details, but she was obviously in anguish about something. When Mickey saw she was upset, he threw up his hands and said, "Cut. Hold it. Everybody take a break."

He went to Mary, put his arms around her, and escorted her off the set and walked her down the street. I was walking toward my trailer, which was in the same direction, and I'll admit it, I was eavesdropping. He was wonderful. He was kind and considerate and loving. He talked to her, and she told him about the problem, and they sat down on a bench and talked for ten or fifteen minutes. It was beautiful. It was the Mickey Rooney that God made. Perfect and loving and kind and totally without malice or greed or jealousy. He was a father to Mary. He was a blessing to her. I saw it with my own eyes.

A few minutes later, we were all back to work and everything was OK.

On many other occasions in my life I have seen men and women do something cruel and heartless and totally unloving, then turn around and do something really selfless and kind and loving and generous. I've chosen Mickey to illustrate this because, although he is short in stature, Mickey Rooney is big of heart.

Mickey is no different than the rest of us, even if he is "the greatest actor America has ever produced." He hurts like we hurt. He cries like we cry. He laughs like we laugh. He is Andy Hardy, but he's also O. B. Taggart.

Mickey Rooney is Everyman. And, Mick, your son, Larry Wayne Gatlin, really loves you.

•   •   •

One night before the show, I got a call backstage from an old friend, Lou Bantle.

"Larry, I'm bringing Bob and Dolores Hope and Leonard Firestone to the show tonight. We're having a little dinner in our suite at the Essex House after the show in your honor. You will be there, right?"

I said, "Right, Lou, I'll be there."

Can you imagine, Bob Hope coming to see me at The Palace? I

introduced him at the first of the show (there's a place in Act I when Will could introduce special guests in the audience). The crowd gave him a standing ovation. At the end of our show, he led the audience in giving me and the cast a standing ovation. I'll never forget it.

After the show he and Dolores very graciously came up on stage for pictures with the cast and to sign autographs. I asked him to tell the kids the joke about the two cowboys going to town on Saturday night. And all at once, as if by magic, this ninety-year-old man, who was having trouble seeing, hearing, and walking, came alive. He had an audience, and he was doing what he loved—telling a joke. He was forty years old again. The kids from the cast all laughed, even though I later had to explain the punch line to half of them.

At the dinner in Lou and Ginny Bantle's suite that evening, I visited with all the guests—with my old buddy Leonard Firestone and Caroline, his wife, with Dolores Hope, who said, "The show was terrible, but you were great."

And finally I sat down with Mr. Hope at the dinner table, where we talked about golf and the people we knew. He got a warm look on his face, and he said, "Kid—you're not just playing Broadway. You're playing The Palace. The first time I played it was in 1934 with Beatrice Lilly. Don't forget, kid. You're playing The Palace."

* * *

In the late '50s or early '60s, Steve and Rudy and La Donna and I sang at some big political rally in Odessa. The rally was for a right-nice young fellow from Midland, Texas, named George Bush. He had a wife named Barbara and a house full of good-looking kids, and we supported him. He lost the first time, as I remember, but later, much later, he won the Big One. And our friend from Midland, George Herbert Walker Bush, became the forty-first president of the United States.

We did more rallies for him, and we supported him because we believed in his idea of a kinder, gentler nation and his idea that government was too big and too intrusive into people's lives.

George Bush was a good president. He did a good job, and I'm proud to have supported him. I would do it again. He got beat in the 1992 election because the world was in a recession that was not of his making and over which he had little control, and the other side—the Democrats—and their young, good-looking Arkansas governor, Bill Clinton, convinced the American public George was the reason for the economic downturn. Balderdash!

Janis and I were invited to the White House in late November or early December of 1992 for what came to be known as "The Last Supper." The president invited about forty or fifty of his closest friends, Democrats and Republicans, to a small dinner at the White House, and he asked Janis and me to come. I sat at the table with the president and Justice Sandra Day O'Connor, my old buddy and golf partner, the then Honorable (and later to be judged not-so-honorable) Congressman Dan ("Rosty") Rostenkowski, Admiral Frank Kelso, and some others I cannot remember. Janis sat at another table with Justice Clarence Thomas, Roger Penske, Prince Bandar Bin Sultan Bin Abdul Aziz, and others.

The president was very upbeat and seemed to be having a good time—under the circumstances. I chastised "Rosty" for blaming the economic downturn on President Bush while he and his guys had absolutely destroyed the real estate and savings and loan industries with their draconian tax bills (cost me $690,000). The congressman just leaned back and laughed at me. Then he turned to Justice Sandra Day O'Connor and called me an unmentionable name. I was shocked.

Rosty is a real piece of work. It was sort of in jest. You'd have to know him. I really like him, always have, even though we disagree on politics. I really think that even though he got caught with his hand—slightly, only slightly—in the cookie jar, Rosty was a good congressman and *fairly* honest.

After the dinner, we all went into the Red Room and President Bush said a few words and then introduced me. I sang four or five songs and the party broke up into small groups and in a few minutes it was just Janis and me, President Bush, and Prince Bandar of

Saudia Arabia. We all chatted a bit. (The prince is a prince of a fellow.) And then it was time for bed.

Janis and I were escorted by a member of the White House staff to . . . yes, *The Lincoln Bedroom!*

We were not $100,000 contributors. In fact, I've not even contributed more than $500 at a time, and I bet my total is less than $10,000. I did donate my time, which is also money, but my hard cash contributions were small.

The Lincoln bedroom experience was wonderful. We gawked for an hour at the pictures, the chairs, the desk where President Lincoln wrote the Emancipation Proclamation. It was wonderful.

There was a knock at the door at a very inopportune moment, because after gawking for a while and discussing whether the room was bugged, we decided to avail ourselves of the hospitality of the surroundings and try out Mr. Lincoln's bed.

I thought to myself, *There must be some sign somewhere in the room, "No love making." I know the "sex police" from the basement have heard us on their secret high-tech listening devices, and Janis and I are going to be thrown out onto Pennsylvania Avenue,*

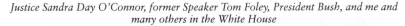

Justice Sandra Day O'Connor, former Speaker Tom Foley, President Bush, and me and many others in the White House

President George Bush, Janis, and me in the Lincoln Bedroom
(I didn't pay $100,000 for this deal.)

at worst—naked—or at best in our jammies." (Actually, I didn't think about all of that at that moment. I was actually thinking about how much I loved the beautiful woman with whom I was enjoying this amorous adventure in President Lincoln's bed.)

We ignored the knock for a while. Then I jumped up, threw on my pajama bottoms, and Janis ran toward the bathroom. I opened the door.

"Sorry to disturb you, Mr. Gatlin."

"Oh, that's no problem. We were just, uh, reading in bed." (A little white lie, not the first one told in the White House, I'm sure.)

The staffer said, "Could you please fill out this card so we can properly prepare breakfast for you and Mrs. Gatlin, and tell us what time you like to have it served?"

"Thank you very much," I said. "I'll fill it out and call you back in a few minutes."

"That won't be necessary," he said, with a smile. "Just place it on the floor in front of the door. I'll pick it up later."

We said goodnight, and I went back into the room. I could hear Janis laughing in the bathroom. I walked in, and we just started howling. My jammies were wrong side out. I'll bet the staff and "sex police" in the basement with the high-tech listening devices (if the room is really bugged—which I do not doubt) had a big laugh too.

In 1993, after President Bush left office, he and Barbara asked Janis and me to bring Kristin and Vaughn, Kristin's husband, and Josh to Kennebunkport, Maine, for a little R&R, while I was doing *The Will Rogers Follies* in New York. We spent a wonderful day and a half with the President and Mrs. Bush.

We went on boat rides. We ate great lobster. We talked and laughed and reminisced. The former president took Josh fishing, and we sat around and just soaked up the sun and enjoyed the fellowship. The "kinder, gentler nation" thing never did take hold of this country, but George and Barbara Bush are kind and gentle, and I'm proud to call them my friends.

A kinder, gentler weekend was just what I needed at a time when I was doing eight shows a week at the corner of Forty-seventh and Sixth. The Bush weekend at Kennebunkport provided that, and I'm grateful.

• • •

Doing Will was a roller coaster of emotion. I loved doing the shows, but we didn't have enough people coming, and we were constantly afraid we were going to close. We had a horrible winter during the big blizzard of 1993. At one matinee we only had about two hundred fifty paying customers. Add to that the bombing of the World Trade Center and the Waco deal; there was not much funny stuff on the front page for ole Will to talk about. Thank God for the Clintons. They were a bright spot in the newspaper. Everything they did for the first six months of their reign was something I could turn into a gag. I had only one real criterion for a joke: Would Will Rogers have made a joke out of it? If it passed that test, I'd put it in.

September 5, 1993, was a very sad day for me. *The Will Rogers Follies* closed in New York at The Palace. I had hoped and dreamed we would have an upsurge in attendance and that the P.R. we did would help, but the show just didn't have the "legs" as they say in the business. I grew from portraying Will Rogers. I became kinder and gentler and more understanding. I know I did. I became more tolerant. I became more like Will. When the curtain dropped for the last time, I felt I had failed everyone, that I wasn't a big enough star to generate more ticket sales. But I also knew I had done my best to revive the show.

To everyone in the cast and crew, I say, it was a gas, one of the highlights of my life. I'd do it again tomorrow night if we could all get together somewhere—just for fun.

After the show closed in New York, I did it on the road for about thirteen months. I met another bunch of great guys and gals with talent galore. Danette Cumming played Betty Blake and was terrific (we are still good friends), and Dana Leigh Jackson was wonderful as Z's Favorite. George Riddle as "Pa" was goofy and forgetful and just perfect—and a Republican like me.

On July 5 (I think), 1994, I closed another *Will Rogers* show, this time in St. Paul, Minnesota. Again, I felt like I'd let everybody down by not being able to sell more tickets. I realize now there are just two things about shows: shows open, shows close.

PART FOUR

$\mathscr{M}$YRTLE BEACH AND BEYOND

L.G. at The Gatlin Brothers Theatre

CHAPTER 18

The Gatlin Brothers Theatre

ℐOU'RE NEVER TOO OLD TO LEARN

When the Branson deal went south, as I knew it would, Steve began looking around for something else for The Gatlin Brothers. Our old friend, Jimmy Kellum, at NationsBank in Nashville, told him about some guys in Myrtle Beach, South Carolina, who wanted to do a Branson-type deal.

Cut to the chase. WCI Management Group Chairman David Bishop and President John Cote, two really wonderful, God-fearing men, built us a theater on their land in Myrtle Beach. It is really nice—great sound, great lights, and great people. The Gatlin Brothers Theatre is a state-of-the-art, two-thousand-seater in Fantasy

261

Harbour, a two-hundred-acre tract along the Intracoastal Waterway on the famed Grand Strand, which is home to many other attractions, shops, and restaurants.

We opened the theater in August of 1994, with a commitment to do two hundred performance dates a year at our new musical home.

That fall I began having some trouble with my voice again. My training with Franco Iglesias had helped me learn to sing correctly, but I was singing too much—eight performances a week is too much.

I went to Nashville to see Dr. Ossoff at the Vanderbilt Medical Center. Thankfully the second throat problem was not as serious as the first one. Still, the nodule on my throat had to be removed.

On January 4, 1995, Dr. O. did a little more "whittlin'." Janis and I stayed with him and his wife, Lynn, for a few days while I recouped. Then Janis and I went back to Austin where I did the three-week, no-talking routine again.

In February of that year, I was privileged to be invited to sing a couple of songs for the Texas Music Educators Association convention San Antonio, Texas. On this occasion, all former members of the Texas All-State Choir, Orchestra, and Symphony Band were invited to perform. Once again Frederick Fennell, our much older, but still vibrant and exciting director, led us in a rousing rendition of "The Battle Hymn of the Republic." It was magnificent.

It also marked the first time I had sung in public since my second throat surgery. I had known I would be OK—and sure enough, I was. And I am. It was just a small nodule, and Dr. Ossoff and Dr. God took care of it.

• • •

One of my favorite sayings is, "You're never too old to learn." I like that one. Now, I didn't used to, mainly because I thought I already knew all there was to know. But, at last a little bit of the light of wisdom has shone on me. *I do not know everything!* But I'm learning. I've learned from people from all walks of life. Rich and poor, famous, not so famous, and even infamous. Let me share a few stories.

1. Lesson on Compassion: Old Harry

Life is not all about George Bush, Ben Crenshaw, Arnold Palmer, and Patrick Swayze. The "Old Harrys" are equally important. I wrote this essay for the Myrtle Beach *Sun-News*.

I'm a lucky man—people are nice to me here in Myrtle Beach. I'm especially lucky that restaurant owners are nice to me: old Bud Ward at Waffle International; Joe Mancuso, Vicky, and the girls at Village Cafe; Jack at Nibils; the folks at New York Prime; and other good folks all along the Grand Strand.

And Old Harry at the Omega Pancake House. He is a cheerful soul, and one day my soul needed cheering. When I woke up at 9:45 A.M. and turned on my television, I was immediately bombarded with bad news. Some crazy man in Scotland had just opened fire on a bunch of schoolkids, killing sixteen of the brand-new angels. He then killed himself.

"My God," I said out loud to no one, "what is this world coming to?"

I got dressed, jumped in my car, and went to Omega Pancake House for breakfast. All the waitresses and cashiers greeted me warmly as I walked to my booth in the back right corner.

That's what I had come to Omega for—their cheerful greetings and Harry's, which came next: "Hello, Larry, my friend. How are you?"

"I'm fine, Harry. How are you?"

"Oh, Larry, God is merciful, I'm fine."

Wow—I felt better already.

I had been to Harry's place on many occasions before, but I had never met Harry's wife, Nicki. She had recently begun a redecorating project, and today she was at Omega to look at her handiwork. (It's very nice, by the way.)

Harry introduced me to his lovely lady, and she sat with me, and we talked for a while about kids and weddings and wallpaper as Harry came and went. (He had on his apron and was helping out in the kitchen.) On one of his visits to my table, a woman approached us with a piece of paper and a pen. I assumed she had recognized me and wanted an autograph. Wrong, ego-head, one-time big star, now medium-sized star!

The lady handed the piece of paper to Harry and quietly asked, "Harry, can you hold this for me until Friday?"

"Why, sure, Honey," he said, as he put her $20 check into his shirt pocket, "I'll be glad to."

The lady said thank you and, with her little boy in tow, went back to her table.

None of this was really for my eyes or ears. This was not a scene from a made-for-TV movie. This was life and love.

In this age of 1-800-credit check, the Internet, "Do you have a picture ID?" and "No, we cannot accept a personal check," Old Harry stepped up to the universal home plate and hit a home run for the home team. "Why sure, Honey," he said, "I'll be glad to."

I thought to myself, *God's in His heaven, all's right with the world.*

"Oh, by the way, Harry, I left my wallet at home, can you hold this check for me till Friday?"

"Why, sure, Larry, old friend; don't worry about it. Pay me next time."

2. Lesson on Having a Sense of Humor: Minnie Pearl

Sarah Ophelia Cannon was one of the funniest people I've ever known. Relatively few people knew her as Sarah Ophelia Cannon. They knew her as Cousin Minnie Pearl. During all my years in Nashville, Minnie treated me like a little schoolboy. She picked on me and kidded me and poked fun at me and loved me and encouraged me and had faith in me. I was very saddened by the news of her stroke a few years ago, so I called Henry Cannon, Minnie's husband of fifty or more years, and he said, "Larry, come on over to the house and visit with Minnie."

It was Valentine's Day, 1991. I stopped at a local supermarket and bought a heart-shaped box of chocolates and drove to the Cannon residence.

"She may not recognize you, Larry," Harry warned me. "Don't let it hurt your feelings. She hasn't said anything to anyone in a couple of days. But she can hear you and see you, and sometimes she talks a little."

"Minnie Pearl," I said, "you are my sweetheart, and I love you. It's Valentine's Day and I brought you some chocolates and you and I are gonna eat 'em."

That sweet old lady looked up at me and smiled and said, "Larry Gatlin, you're a nut."

I fed Minnie Pearl candy for about fifteen minutes. We smiled and laughed, and I told her jokes and she nodded, and I wiped chocolate from her mouth. We had a great time. She didn't say anything else, just "Larry Gatlin, you're a nut." She's right. I am a nut, and I really believe that a sense of humor is one of the things that has brought me through some very difficult times. Minnie Pearl had a sense of humor. Even when she was almost totally incapacitated by the stroke, she was funny. I learned a lot from that Valentine's Day visit. She left us in March of 1996.

3. Lesson on Forgiveness: Willie and Connie Nelson

Many years ago at one of Willie Nelson's Fourth of July wingdings, I got very drunk and very loaded and very rude to Connie, Willie's wife at the time. I only vaguely remember the awful incident and wouldn't have remembered it all if a buddy named Bob Hammer from Oklahoma City hadn't called it to my attention.

One night in Dallas, Hammer said, "Gat, what are you gonna do about that Willie deal?"

"What Willie deal?"

"You know, about being rude and crude to Connie."

Well, I did not know what he was talking about, so he enlightened me. Something about stumbling out of a bathroom with my pants unzipped and some rude, crude untimely utterances from a very bad drunk–addict. Well, I was mortified. Willie was one of my heroes and, even more importantly, Connie was and is a wonderful lady.

I immediately called Darrell Royal and asked if he knew about all of this. He did; Willie had told him. (I turned as white as a sheet. *Dear God, I've really done it this time.*) I asked Darrell if he would set up

Me and Willie at a "guitar pullin'" at the Royal's house

a meeting with Willie so I could apologize. Darrell said he would and, a few months later, at the Darrell and Willie Golf Tournament in Houston, he arranged for me to speak with Willie privately on Willie's bus.

I apologized, explaining I had been drunk and loaded. I told him I realized that was not a very good excuse but asked if he would forgive me and also asked for his permission to apologize to Connie.

Willie said, "Larry, we've all done things like that and worse. I know you didn't mean it. (I'm winging it here—I don't remember the exact words.) Don't worry any more about it. And feel free to talk to Connie."

We hugged, and I thanked him and went back inside to the big concert and found Connie. Again, I asked for forgiveness and again it was given.

The weight of guilt and shame and embarrassment were lifted because those two nice people practiced the art of forgiveness (and it is an art). In this crazy world, forgiveness is the key to peace of mind because some drunk or some saint or some motorist or some

266

talk show host is always gonna be out there and be dead wrong and bent on messing up somebody else's day. I hope I am as big as Willie and Connie Nelson were the next time someone behaves dead wrong toward me or my family.

4. *Lesson in Humility: Mick Jagger*

I was running late for the 3:00 Wednesday matinee at The Gatlin Brothers Theatre. I was naked (not the pretty sight it once was, thanks to gravity and middle age), drying off after my shower, watching CNN. The news guy said, "Mick Jagger and the Rolling Stones have been paid $13 million by Bill Gates for the use of their hit song 'Start Me Up' to promote Microsoft's new product, Windows '95. The song will only be used for one month."

My mouth flew open. *Thirteen million dollars for one month.* "That's insane," I said out loud. I dried off, got dressed, and drove to the theater, where I fumed for another hour. I was singin' and smilin' on the outside, but I was fumin' on the inside. In the middle of the gospel segment, where Steve and Rudy and I go out into the audience to do old gospel favorite requests for about two hundred fifty paying customers, my mind was on Mick Jagger and the Rolling Stones and $13 million.

While I was singing "Amazing Grace" and smiling to beat the band, I was fuming. *Dear God*, I was saying to myself (and not in a reverent way), *how can it be that those reprobate rock 'n' roll, immoral, dope smokin', druggie booze heads are making $13 million for one song for one month and my brothers and I are working our hearts out to make a living and pay bills, singing for two hundred fifty people at a three o'clock matinee?"* I was not a happy camper, but I plodded on—"Amazing Grace! How sweet the sound."

Somewhere in the middle of the song I heard a small voice, not audible, but real nonetheless: *Larry, My child, Mick Jagger is none of your business. I have given you these two hundred fifty people. Sing for them. Smile at them. Feed them and love them as I have loved you. Take care of your own business and leave Mick Jagger to Me.*

It was a moment of grace—a moment of enlightenment and of

peace. After we finished the gospel segment, I introduced comedian Royce Elliott (a very funny and very nice man), and then went back to my dressing room. When I walked in there was an envelope on the floor. I opened it and read:

> Last week I attended one of your shows at The Gatlin Brothers Theatre. You and Steve and Rudy sang a beautiful version of "Great Is Thy Faithfulness" and my heart was truly blessed. I have just had a double mastectomy, and the doctor says that I only have a few months to live. I am no longer afraid of death. You and your brothers are a great blessing to me. The song helped me to cope with this situation and I thank you. God bless The Gatlin Brothers.
>
> Sincerely,
> A Grateful Fan

I fell to my knees on the floor of my dressing room and cried and thanked God and then cried some more.

I asked God the question, "Who am I to question Your ways? You who scattered the stars and spoke the universe into existence. Father, forgive my arrogance, pride, anger, and unbelief!"

It was a humbling experience. Humility—what a concept! On occasion, for me at least—what a reality. Hey, Mick. Sorry I spoke ill of you. Forgive me, please, and congrats on the $13 million.

4. Lesson in Unconditional Love: Janis, Kristin, and Josh

As I have looked over this book, I realize I have not really written very much about Janis and Kristin and Josh. Janis and I always tried to raise our kids like we were raised—to fear God and love their neighbors. We tried to keep them out of the spotlight. In other words, we were trying to let them be normal, whatever that means. In keeping with that philosophy, I'm not going to go into all of our family stuff. If they want to write their own accounts of life in the Gatlin house, I say, go for it.

We've had a bunch of great times together, but, suffice it to say, we also had a few rough ones. Of all the great blessings of my life, I am most grateful to God for Janis and Kristin and Josh's unconditional love. I was altogether unloving and unlovable. I was mad and drunk and loaded and mean. I did not abuse them physically—ever. But the mental abuse, the anger, the vile language, and the mean spirit I exhibited for six or eight years was hard for them to understand, I'm sure. But they loved me through it all—unconditionally.

On the cross, Christ said, "Father, forgive them, for they do not know what they do."

My kids always said, "Father, we forgive you for you know not what you do."

Unconditional love—what a concept. In our case, what a revelation, what a reality.

5. Lesson on Agreeing to Disagree—Peacefully: President Bill Clinton

Cal Thomas is one of the great writers in America today; I've read his column for years. I met Cal and his wife, Ray, at the Republican National Convention in San Diego in 1996 at some big gathering of muckety-mucks in some big hotel. Unknown to me, he was and is a big Gatlin Brothers fan, and unknown to him, I was and am a big Cal Thomas fan. Our meeting in San Diego gave us the opportunity to pat each other on the back and tell each other how wonderful we thought the other one was.

A few weeks after our meeting, Cal invited Janis and me to attend the National Prayer Breakfast in Washington, D.C., with him and Ray, and I eagerly accepted. The night before the breakfast Cal and Ray hosted a nice dinner for three hundred people at the Hilton, where the keynote speaker gave a wonderfully inspiring talk. Cal asked me to sing, so I did my old standby, "Great Is Thy Faithfulness." (When in doubt, sing "Great Is Thy Faithfulness.")

The next morning at the breakfast, Dr. Benjamin Carson, a noted pediatric neurosurgeon from Johns Hopkins University and Hospital, gave an inspiring speech about opportunity in America and doing the best you can do. Sounds like the same old stuff, but it wasn't. Dr. Ben put it in a new perspective. He was terrific.

Then it was President Clinton's turn. I sat up and listened. I wanted him to say something awful. I wanted him to say something political.

I wanted him to step on his tongue. I wanted him to mess up so I could feel good about being on the other side of the political fence from him. He didn't do it. He pretty much threw away the speech he had prepared and spoke extemporaneously, from his heart, about being repairers of the breach. He quoted Isaiah, and then he got to it. I will paraphrase.

He said, "The poor are in the breach. They are falling through the cracks in our society, and government cannot fix all the cracks and help all the poor people. We must all help to raise the poor up, with jobs and education and . . ."

He sounded like a Republican. More importantly, he sounded like a caring human being with good sense and not just a bleeding heart with no plan except to throw money at the problem. He did not lecture. He was not political. He was not partisan in any way. He just talked, almost like a father to his children. Then he said, "There are others in the breach. The folks in Bosnia and Haiti and other parts of the world who are living in fear of war. We in America must do what we can to heal the breach and bring peace to these people."

Then he got down to it. "We politicians are in the breach. We spend so much time fighting each other and accusing each other, we do not do the job we were sent here to do. We have become callous and cynical and hard. We have fallen into a hole."

It was wonderful. I was inspired and very moved.

Later that day, when I was in Jim Free's office, I sat down and wrote a letter:

> Dear Mr. President:
> I've never liked you—until today. I've spoken ill of you on
> many occasions. Please forgive me. Although we will never
> see eye-to-eye on every political question, I give you my
> word that if you will lead this great country in the same
> spirit that you showed this morning, I will follow you and
> cheer you.

I've forgotten everything I said, but I really meant it all. Finally, I promised to pray for him every day.

I gave the letter to Jim Free, and he delivered it to the president at the White House. A few weeks later, I got a reply. While I do not think it would be appropriate to quote the entire letter, since it was personal correspondence, I don't think President Clinton would mind if I hit some high points.

First, the president said he had been a Gatlin Brothers fan for a long time, and he invited me to drop by and see him when I was in Washington. I was surprised and grateful. Then he got to it. He quoted Paul. Now we see through a glass darkly, but we shall know as we are known. He spoke of how we are all on our path to the same destination and that we all make mistakes, but we have to pick ourselves up and go on.

I really appreciated the letter and sentiment, and since that day I have felt more of a kinship with my new "pen pal," President Bill Clinton. You know, folks, the Lord Christ Himself said, "He who is without sin among you, let him throw a stone at her first."

Well, that leaves me out of the rock fight. I am just a sinner saved by God's grace. So I have to constantly overcome my natural tendency to accuse and judge other people, to take their inventory and tell them how they should live their lives. I think there must be a way to stand up for one's convictions without pontificating and being pompous. I'm working on being committed to a cause without being a radical or a zealot. All too often I have caused the breach with a word spoken without thought of love, or with an action taken without really considering the ramifications.

Well, I have criticized the president for four years, and when I think he is wrong in the future, I will not hesitate to voice my opinion. But I will try to do it in the spirit of love and not in the spirit of hatred or anger or political partisanship. I will try to be a healer of the breach and not the one who makes it wider and more difficult to repair.

6. *Lesson on Courage: Naomi Judd*
Early in December of 1991 the sound of the telephone ringing woke me from a sound sleep.

"Larry, this is Naomi Judd. We need your help." It was about 1:00 or 2:00 A.M. the day before the Judd's final concert at Murphy

Center in Murfreesboro, Tennessee, and Wynonna had lost her voice. "Can you give me the doctor's name? You know, the one who helped you with your voice problems?" Mama Judd asked.

I immediately got out of bed to get my phone book and gave her Dr. Robert Ossoff's home number. Naomi thanked me, and I went back to sleep, after saying a prayer for God to restore Wynonna's tremendous voice for the big concert.

The next night a sold-out crowd and a pay-per-view audience of over six million—were treated to great singing and great playing and great songs and to a sort of lovefest. Everyone in the big arena that night knew it was a very special time. Naomi and Wynonna had thanked Dr. Ossoff and me for our help in getting her voice back, and I just smiled as she tore the place up on "Love Can Build a Bridge."

Several months later Dr. Robert Schuller of the nationally syndicated television program *The Hour of Power* called and asked if I knew Naomi. I told him I did.

"Larry, I would love for her to be on the *Hour*. I think she is wonderful."

I assured Dr. Bob that Naomi was a wonderful spirit-filled lady and that I would call her. She was not at home when I did, but I left her a message.

Fast-forward. In October of 1992 I got a call from Dr. Schuller's assistant, asking if I would do *The Hour of Power* with Naomi Judd. She had told them she would do it only if I'd come and sing and support her.

I was very flattered. I mean, here's a lady who has sung on countless TV shows, for two or three presidents, and for millions of people all over the world, and she said she wanted me to support her. I was afraid the logistics would not work out. Steve and Rudy and I were to be in Minneapolis the Saturday night before the filming of the 9:00 A.M. Sunday service in Orange Grove, California, so the logistics were a nightmare (almost impossible to get from Minnesota to California by 10:00 A.M.).

Well, Dr. Schuller and God (maybe not in that order) worked it out so that a very big, very fast, private airplane was sitting in

Me, Naomi Judd, and Dr. Robert Schuller

St. Paul, Minnesota, with its nose wheel pointed west and a vacant seat with my name on it (and equipped with chicken salad sandwiches and potato chips and Cokes and chocolate chip cookies. My thanks to Mr. and Mrs. Bob Pond for the plane and the goodies).

We got into the Orange County, John Wayne Airport very late, around 1:00 or 2:00 in the morning, and I was hurried off to a hotel for four or five hours of sleep.

The next day was one I will remember forever. I love Dr. Schuller, and I am always blessed by his words of wisdom, by the choir and organ music, and by the overall sense of being in God's house, especially that particular house of God, The Crystal Cathedral.

Dr. Schuller said a few words to introduce me, and I sang "Great Is Thy Faithfulness," and then sat down next to Naomi.

Next Dr. Schuller said some nice words about Naomi and Wynonna and their career together and then he introduced her.

The next ten or fifteen minutes were among the most unforgettable of my life. Naomi is beautiful inside and out—and she is funny!

At the risk of not being 100 percent accurate, I'm going to paraphrase what she said that morning.

"Dr. Schuller, some people from your office called me more than a year ago and asked me to be on the *Hour of Power*. Well, it's taken me a year to check you out, and you're OK."

The audience roared with laughter, as did Dr. Schuller.

"Dr. Schuller, before I go any further, there's something we need to remember. Eve is the only woman in history without a past."

Everyone laughed again.

Then she said seriously, "I have a past and part of it is not too pretty."

A holy quietness fell on the congregation as she told her story. (I will not try to tell it all here. I could not do it with the power and conviction that Naomi did that morning.)

Naomi told the audience of five thousand to six thousand people at two services in the Cathedral and a TV audience of millions how she had gotten pregnant when she was seventeen years old and how she had wrestled with what to do about her unborn child. Then she said something like this: "I knew that I could get rid of the life within me. I knew there were people in our small town who could 'do the job,' but I chose to go through with the birth and to keep the child. Her name is Wynonna."

The very spirit of Almighty God poured out a blessing of love and rejoicing on that place that I can still feel right now.

When Naomi was finished, the audience erupted in a standing ovation. Not for Naomi Judd, the world famous singer, but for Naomi Judd, the life giver, the nurturer, the provider, the mother.

When she sat down next to me, I hugged her and thanked her for letting me be a very small part of that incredible event. I whispered to her, "Naomi, you have probably just saved thousands of unborn children with your courage and your faith."

"I hope so," she said as she smiled back at me.

The Judds' final concert in Murfreesboro had been terrific. Some say it was their finest hour, and I would agree it was unforgettable. But I think Naomi Judd's finest hour was a beautiful morning in 1992 in Garden Grove, California, when she stood in front of millions and declared her belief that life is a gift of God to be cherished and protected.

7. *Lesson on Not Holding a Grudge: Bill and Gloria Gaither*

In May of 1991, I got a call from my friend Bill Gaither, the great gospel songwriter. He said, "Larry, come over to the studio next Tuesday and help us sing 'Where Could I Go but to the Lord' with James [Blackwood] and Hovie [Lister] and J. D. [Sumner] and Howard and Vestal [Goodman] and all your old gospel friends."

I said, "I'd love to," and so I did.

It was wonderful to be with so many of my heroes and friends. We were all brought together to sing one song and do a video for Bill. Well, we sang for a while and we laughed for a while and had a big time.

We broke for lunch, and after I ate, I walked back into the studio and sat down on the piano stool. A few minutes later, Eva Mae LeFever came out of the kitchen and sat down beside me. I said, "Eva Mae, I have not heard you play piano in a long time. Play something for me."

As she played, people started to trickle back into the studio from the kitchen. Jake Hess started singing the song Eva Mae was playing, and I realized something magical was happening. I motioned to the control room to "roll tape" (control room speak for "start the videotape"), and I asked the cameraman to start taping. They did, and Bill came out to assume his rightful place as leader of our little sing-along.

James Blackwood sang, Jake Hess sang, Howard and Vestal sang, George Younce sang, and Glen Payne sang. Then Hovie Lister played piano and finally I—a cripple-throated, broken-hearted but happy, Larry Gatlin—tried to sing. It was before my first throat surgery and the "boulders" in my throat would not let me do a very good job. But I tried to sing "I Bowed on My Knees and Cried Holy."

Fast-forward, one year later. Bill Gaither's first *Homecoming* video, with our group sing-along, was a big hit in gospel music and a tremendous financial success. Well, I just sucked my thumb. I really got mad at Brother Gaither. I was the one who got the ball rollin' that day and gathered the folks around the piano and got the technicians and camera people to start the recording machines and video cameras. No credit for the video and no money. I was really hot.

For three long years I would turn the TV off or change channels when an ad for another in a seemingly endless line of Gaither *Homecoming* videos would come on. I would curse Bill Gaither and everybody concerned. (Wow, what a good Christian attitude, Larry! I'm really proud of you.)

I was stewing. One day I was watching TV and one of the Gaither deals came on: Jake Hess sitting around a piano singing, "Prayer Is the Key to Heaven." I started to turn if off but since I love Jake and I love the song, I decided to listen. I sat there and cried like a baby. It was so beautiful and wonderful and uplifting, and it brought back many fond memories. I said to myself, "Larry, you are really being stupid and childish and very un-Christ-like. You need to call Bill and straighten this thing out." Well, I never did.

Then one night in 1995, I was sitting in bed reading when the phone rang. It was Gloria Gaither, Bill's wife, a very talented singer, songwriter, and author.

Well, anyway, Gloria said to me, "Larry, do you remember that idea I told you about three years ago? You know, the Steinbeck project?"

I confessed only vaguely remembering, so she brought me up to speed on the idea of turning John Steinbeck's *To a God Unknown* into a musical. She wanted me to write the music, and I told her it sounded like a great idea. Then I said, "Gloria, I really want to talk to you about the Steinbeck deal but before I do, I need to talk to Bill."

When Bill took the phone and said "Hi, Larry," I got a lump the size of Rhode Island in my throat.

"Hi, Bill. I've been needing to call you for a long time, but I was too chicken."

"What's the problem, Larry?"

"Well," I said, "I need to ask you to forgive me. I have been mad at you for three years about the *Homecoming* video deal."

"What are you talking about?"

"Well, I got my feelings hurt when nobody gave me any credit for the sing-along. I was the one who got the whole deal started that day with Eva Mae and Jake and James, and I'm the one who told the camera guys and the sound guys to roll tape. You got all the credit and all the money, and I got a bronze plaque to put on my wall. I've been mad at you for the last three years. I was wrong, Bill, and I'm sorry. It was really your deal, and I wasn't very Christ-like."

It was quiet on the other end of the phone for a couple of seconds. Then Bill Gaither said, as only he could, "Larry, I always wondered how the whole sing-along got started while I was eating a sandwich in the kitchen. I forgive you, brother, and I love you.

We talked for a while and then I asked Bill to put his wife back on.

Gloria and I decided we would do the Steinbeck project. I had not been writing any songs while in Myrtle Beach. Dead stop. No creative outlet at all for me. But I was open to the opportunity.

Gloria sent me a copy of her adaptation of *To a God Unknown*, and I started reading it. It's a wonderful piece of literature, albeit one of Steinbeck's more obscure works. I began to hear music and words, and I began to see scenes in my mind. My creativity began to work again. I wrote three or four songs within the first few days of reading the manuscript, and I was finally, miraculously, no longer at dead stop.

All at once one night, alone in my bed (Janis was in Austin at the time), I had a real spiritual awakening. The sky did not open up. There were no tablets of stone. There was no finger writing stuff on my wall. Just the still, small voice of God telling me that when I do not create, I begin to die.

I had read a wonderful book a year or so earlier, *The Artist's Way*, which says all of us have some kind of creative ability, and it is part of our calling as human beings to use that ability to cocreate with the Great Creator. The book also says that to not do so cuts us off from that creative part of ourselves and God. I had been creating nothing. I had allowed my "internal censor," as the book calls it, to tell me that as a songwriter I was finished, that my new gig was to

play golf during the day, then show up at The Gatlin Brothers Theatre and sing. Well, I was doing just that, and I was miserable.

Thank God for Bill and Gloria Gaither. Working on that project
got me kicked off high center—or low center—and put me back in
the creative mode. We all met in Monterey, California, in September of 1995 and drove around Steinbeck country as we discussed
the project.

About seven months later Bill called and said, "Hey, Larry, why
don't we do a Gatlin Brothers video and get together all your old
heroes and sing and tell stories and have a great time."

I said, "Brother Bill, that is a great idea. You go put it together,
and I will be there." (Obviously none of this would have happened
if I hadn't finally talked to Bill about the barrier between us.)

In April of 1996 Steve and Rudy and I went to Alexandria, Indi-
ana, to film *The Gatlin Brothers Come Home*. We enjoyed one of
the greatest evenings of our lives with James Blackwood; Jake Hess;
Hovie Lister; J. D. Sumner; Glen Payne; George Younce; Vestal and
Howard Goodman; The Wills Family from Arlington, Texas—Bob,
Calvin, and Lou; Calvin Newton; Jim Murray; Jim Hamill; Ben Speer;
our mom and dad and our sister, La Donna; Lily Fern Weatherford;
and many others.

We sang and talked and laughed and cried and praised God and
had a camp meeting for more than four hours. (I think heaven is
gonna be a lot like that glorious night.)

After everyone had hugged and said good-bye, some of us gathered at a little hamburger joint across the street from the hotel. I
came in late and sat down next to James Blackwood and across from
his nephew, Winston (R. W. Jr.).

The conversation eventually got around to the airplane crash that
killed James's nephew and Winston's father, R. W. Blackwood, and
Bill Lyles. I listened as James explained the events of that terrible
day back in 1954 in Clanton, Mississippi, and my mind went back
to a small white house at 250 Westridge Street in Abilene, Texas,
and a little heartbroken boy, crying his eyes out over the death of
two of his heroes.

James explained that for many years he had questioned God and that he had almost shaken his fist at the sky in anger. But finally he just surrendered. Then the Holy Spirit of God whispered in a still, small voice: *James, I am in charge, not you. Be at peace. This is not the end of the story. Be at peace.*

As James told me the story, a piece of life's puzzle was put into place by the hand of God. Every time I have the urge to shake my fist at the sky in an effort to box with God, I stop short and remember what James told me that night: "God is in charge, not you. Be at peace, Larry. This is not the end of the story. Be at peace."

8. Lesson on Counting My Blessings: Myrtle Beach

I question almost daily why I am in Myrtle Beach. We have done some good work, and we have tried real hard to make it a success. But so far the theater is not working the way we hoped it would. We need some more people in the seats.

Our house is nice, and there's great golf and the beach, but still I'm in what my friend Jack Boland used to call a "state of divine discontent." I know there is something more I'm supposed to be doing.

Old Moses had to spend forty years in the backside of the desert before he got to go back to Egypt to lead the children of Israel to the promised land. Well, let's face it. Myrtle Beach is not exactly the backside of the desert. I mean, ninety golf courses, the beach, fresh seafood, a beautiful theater, sleepin' with Janis in the same bed every night. I know, you're saying, "Yeah, Larry, that's the backside of the desert all right."

For almost three years I've prayed every day that God would give me the insight to understand the Myrtle Beach situation. In other words, "God, could we please do this my way? Could we please get out of here if we're not going to draw more than seven hundred people per night? Can I please go home to Austin and play golf with Darrell and Ben and Willie? And can I go to Cisco's for breakfast every morning and talk to Louis Murillo and Clovis, and look at the Hill Country and the bluebonnets? Can I be a big star again, God? Can I get out of Myrtle Beach, God? Can I please, God, huh? Huh? Please?"

The answer has always come back: *Yes, you can quit and move on, but that is not My will. That is yours. I want you in Myrtle Beach, South Carolina, at The Gatlin Brothers Theatre, at least for now.*

John Cote and David Bishop, our partners in The Gatlin Brothers Theatre, have dealt honestly and fairly with us, and we are trying to work it all out.

I have a feeling that when Moses sat on Mount Horeb and watched the children of Israel go into the promised land, he was grateful to God for his backside of the desert experience. As I sit in my dressing room at The Gatlin Brothers Theatre, viewing the future in my mind's eye, I, too, see the promised land, and I am grateful for this backside of the desert experience.

I've learned that the backside of the desert does bloom with blessings. Moses met his wife in the backside of the desert. He met his father-in-law, Jethro. Moses also met God in the burning bush on the backside of the desert. Talk about a blessing!

My backside of the desert also has its blessings:

Janis and I have met some fine folks—the Bishops, the Cotes, the Pardues, the Lees (golfing buddies of ours at Man-o-War, The Witch and the Wizard)—and the community has really been nice to us. Glen Hall, Clinch Hayward, and the folks at Waterford and the Jacksons and the golf courses, restaurants, and other businesses have opened their arms to us.

I have written this book while in Myrtle Beach and also a collection of short stories about my old friend Paul Whitley from Waggoner Ranch in Texas.

I have also written what I think is the best music of my life for a new musical, *Texas Cafe*. A little background here.

In April and May of 1994, Sue Atkinson, director of the Bristol Riverside Theatre in Bristol, Pennsylvania, helped me mount a production of my first musical, *Alive and Well: Living in the Land of Dreams*. The show has more than forty songs, and it was big and boisterous and confusing. Two critics hated it, but four loved it, as did the people who paid to get in. Every night they would ask, "When's it going to New York? Where can we get the record?"

Well, it didn't go to New York, and there is no record, yet—maybe someday. Sue has a good eye and a good ear and a great heart; we proved we could do it, and it was a success. I will always be grateful to Sue and to Jo, Ann, Lori, Bob, David, Keith, and all the cast and crew of *Alive and Well*.

In the spring of 1998 *Texas Cafe* opened at the Bristol Riverside Theater in Bristol, Pennsylvania. This one has a real book, the songs are all original, and I've learned what to do and what not to do. *Texas Cafe* is going to be a bigger success, and this one's going to New York, and there will be an album. All of this has happened while I was in Myrtle Beach. (Backside of the desert? Not so, Larry.)

Most important of all, my golf handicap has gone from 10 to 5 in Myrtle Beach!

The painful part of my Myrtle Beach experience is that so far The Gatlin Brothers Theatre is not the financial success that the brothers and our partners hoped it would be. Add that to the fact that I am an American by birth and a Texan by the grace of God, and I was away from Texas for twenty-one years and have been in Myrtle Beach for three more. I miss Texas.

But don't get me wrong. It's been great fun. I wouldn't trade anything for the new friends we've made in Myrtle Beach.

CHAPTER 19

Curtis Strange, Steve Gatlin, Ben Crenshaw, and me at Pebble Beach for the A.T. & T. (Nice sweater!)

THE BEST GAME IN LIFE: GOLF

Every night at our show at The Gatlin Brothers Theatre, I let our friends in the audience ask questions. I prompt them by giving them the questions and then I ask them to repeat each back to me.

This usually involves a couple of obvious questions, like "Larry, are you married?" and "Do you have any kids?" and then I say, "The final question people always ask me is: 'Larry, do you play a lot of golf?'"

And the people repeat after me: "Larry, do you play a lot of golf?"

"No, we don't," I answer. "Just every morning about 9:30." Everyone laughs and I tell them a little bit about the great courses we have played and the great players we have played with.

This chapter is about golf. If you don't like golf, then skip right over it or browse through the other stories. If, however, you love golf as I do, dig right in. Some of my fondest memories in life are of Augusta and some of the wonderful things I've seen there. Ben Crenshaw's first Masters victory in April of 1984 is one of them.

In April of 1984 Janis and I were vacationing in the Caymans. As I watched the tournament on the TV screen in the hotel bar (one of the few places on the island with satellite sports coverage), Janis said to me, "Why don't you go back a day early and go to Augusta for the Sunday round?"

I almost jumped out of my chair. What a wonderful gesture on her part. She knew that I was pulling for Ben Crenshaw to win it and that I was pulling for Tom Kite only slightly less. They are both great players and great friends of mine.

Anyway, I jumped on the plane and flew to New York City and then to Atlanta and then to Augusta (nice routing, huh?). Early Sunday morning Ben played the fifteenth, sixteenth, seventeenth, and eighteenth holes, which had been rained out the day before. Then he and my brother Steve, who was staying with Ben during the tournament, picked me up at the airport. Steve and I dropped Ben off at the house then went for some breakfast. We picked Ben up at about 10:30 or 11:00 and drove to Augusta National.

It was a day I will remember fondly all my life. My dear friend Ben Crenshaw won the 1984 Masters, and my other dear friend, Tom Kite, played valiantly and came in sixth. I think Tom Watson, another friend, came in second. Tom Kite was the first one to come into the scorers' tent to congratulate his former teammate and current friendly adversary, Ben Crenshaw.

After everyone had left and evening was falling over a now-silent Augusta National, Ben came out of the press tent with a gentleman in a green jacket.

"Mr. Yates," Ben said, "these are my friends Larry and Steve

Gatlin. Is it okay for them to come into the locker room while I get my stuff?"

"Why surely," Mr. Charlie Yates replied in a Southern drawl. "You Gatlin boys are old gospel singers, aren't you?"

"Yes, sir, we are," Steve and I replied.

"Just a closer walk with thee," the old gentleman sang softly as we joined in on the harmony. "Grant it, Jesus, is my plea . . ."

This was our introduction to Charles Yates, the oldest living member of Augusta National Golf Club, golfer, and human being extraordinaire. (Mr. Yates was the British Amateur champion in 1939.) On that occasion he invited us to come to the next year's Friday night "gathering," one of the great traditions of the Masters.

Then Steve and I went home to the rental house, and Ben went to the Champion's Dinner with Charles Yates. When Ben got home around 11:30, we all drank beer and channel-surfed for two or three hours and watched every replay we could find of Ben's great victory.

The next day we flew Ben to Atlanta in our plane so he could catch a plane home to Austin to a hero's welcome. It was well deserved. He is a hero—and a great pal. Steve and I flew off to a concert somewhere, clutching copies of *The Augusta Chronicle* with the headline, "Crenshaw Gets Green Jacket."

The next year we attended Charlie Yates's little sing-along at Butler Cabin, just off the putting green at the end of the magnificent old clubhouse. The ole Pea Picker himself, Tennessee Ernie Ford, was a regular at the Butler gathering, as was a wonderful group called The Augusta National Quartet—four wonderful African-American gentlemen who worked at the club.

The Gatlin Boys fit right in. We knew most of Ernie's songs and most of the quartet's songs, and we sang "All the Gold in California," "Houston," and a song called "God Knows It Would Be You." I wrote the song for Janis but always dedicate it to Charlie's wife, Mrs. Dorothy Yates, and to Bettie Yonker, the front office manager, and Judy Dabney, the membership reservation secretary.

Ernie Ford was truly one of a kind in American music. He had a great voice. He could sing gospel hymns or patriotic songs or blues songs or funny songs. He could just sing, period. I loved the sound of the huge bass voice on "Whispering Hope"—"Soft as the voice of an angel breathing a lesson unheard."

Folks, it was special. He was special. I miss him. Friday nights at the Butler Cabin have not been the same since Ernie's death.

And then there was Ben Crenshaw's inspiring victory in 1995. Everyone who knows anything about golf knows that Harvey Pennick, Ben and Tom Kite's longtime teacher and close friend, had died at ninety-something the week before, and Ben and Tom had been pallbearers at his funeral. Then Ben comes to Augusta not playing well at all and plays four rounds without a three-putt and wins the tournament. It was a spiritual thing.

I always gallery Ben and Tom on Sunday. I watch all our buddies through the week, but Sunday is for "Gentle Ben" and T. K. I stay with them through fifteen, and then I head for the CBS tower at the eighteenth green. I'm too short to see anything at sixteen, seventeen, or eighteen, so I just go to the tower and watch everything on TV monitors and the action under the tower at the eighteenth green.

Pat Summeral and Ken Venturi and I have shed some tears of joy together in the tower. Jim Nantz, my old U of H buddy, is doing a great job replacing Pat in the tower, by the way. (We still miss you, Pat.)

When Ben knocked in that little putt on eighteen to win and then just broke down (Carl Jackson, his trusty caddie, walked over to congratulate and help him gather himself), Ken Venturi and Jim Nantz both looked at me. We all had "big water" in our eyes.

After Ben signed his scorecard, he was walking toward Butler Cabin for the postvictory, green jacket ceremony, which is staged for the TV audience. There was a gauntlet of cheering fans. I was one of them. Julie, Ben's beautiful wife, looked up and saw me and said, "Ben, there's Larry."

He broke away from the group of guards and the throng of people and walked up to me. We threw our arms around each other and laughed and cried, and I congratulated my buddy. He went on to Butler Cabin for the TV ceremony, then returned to the practice putting green for the *official* green jacket ceremony with the members of Augusta looking on.

Ben said, "I had an extra club in my bag today. Mr. Pennick was with me on every shot. Thank you all, and God bless you," it was a moment for the ages.

Charlie Yates escorted Ben to the press tent and Mr. Jack Stephens ended the festivities, and we all just mingled for a while. Then Steve and Rudy and I began to make the rounds to say our good-byes. We still had to drive back to Myrtle Beach that night. We stopped to say good-bye to Bettie Yonker and Judy Dabney and then, as we were leaving, Steve spotted Ben on a golf cart with Charlie Yates. Steve hollered and Ben asked Mr. Yates to stop. We talked again and then all proceeded together to Butler Cabin. Ben went downstairs to freshen up and change clothes for the Champion's Dinner, which was to be held a few minutes later in the dining room in the beautiful old clubhouse. We were standing on the front porch of the cabin when Charlie Yates started singing: "Brightly beams our father's mercy, from the lighthouse ever more."

We joined in.

"But to us He gives the keeping, of the lights along the shore. Let the lower lights be burning. Send a gleam across the waves. Some poor fainting struggling seaman you may rescue, you may save."

(For about thirteen years now we've been singing that song with Charlie Yates, and we look forward to it every year.) As we were singing Mr. Stephens walked up to Butler Cabin and began to listen to our little quartet. When we finished, he said, "You boys *are* going to join us for the Champion's Dinner, aren't you?"

I was stunned. "Well, Mr. Stephens, that is very kind of you, but we don't want to be in the way."

He looked at me and said, "Larry, Ben would want you boys to be there, and the members of Augusta want you to be there too."

"Well, sir, the boys don't even have jackets or ties." (I always wear a jacket and tie for Sunday's round—just a little tradition of my own.)

"We'll take care of that, Larry," Mr. Stephens said. Well, let me tell you, jacket and ties appeared out of the clear blue sky.

Ben and Julie and all the Austin contingent—Julie and Scotty Sayers and some more of Ben's friends—were there, and the waiters quickly set another table for the Gatlin brothers. After dinner, Ben stood and made some remarks and asked to be excused. (Their pilots were under some kind of constraint regarding sleep and flying and flight times, so all the Austin folks needed to get to the airport.)

Mr. Stephens said, "Ben, your friends the Gatlin brothers would like to sing a special song before you go."

We stood and sang "The Eyes of Texas":

> *The eyes of Texas are upon you—all the live long day.*
> *The eyes of Texas are upon you—you cannot get away.*
> *Do you think you can escape them,*
> *From night 'til early in the morn.*
> *The eyes of Texas are upon you*
> *'til Gabriel blows his horn.*

Ben flashed us a "hook 'em" horns, we all hugged, and they left for the airport. A bit later, Mr. Stephens asked us to sing a couple of songs but jokingly admitted that as an Arkansas native, he was not too pleased with our selection of "The Eyes of Texas."

We immediately stood and sang—"The eyes of Arkansas are upon you . . ."

Mr. Stephens laughed out loud and said we were forgiven. We sang "Houston" and "All the Gold in California" and the members of the Augusta National Golf Club joined in and sang and clapped and laughed. It was a real honor to be there. We revere and respect the Augusta National, and we will always be grateful to Ben, Mr. Jack Stephens, Mr. Charlie Yates, and the membership of the greatest golf club in the world for allowing us to be part of that wonderful evening. (And a special thanks to Mr. Pennick. He not only taught Ben Crenshaw and Tom Kite to play golf, he helped teach them to be gentlemen, sportsmen, and just downright great guys.)

Other memories from Augusta include Arnold Palmer commanding "Arnie's Army" through "Amen Corner." And Jack Nicklaus winning in 1986. And a not-so-fond memory of Curtis Strange, knocking it in the water on the No. 13 and 15 holes to lose the tournament after fighting back from an opening round 82. (Curtis has had a

Me, "Big Jack," Steve, and Rudy. What a player this man is!

tough time for a couple of years, but he's a fighter and will be ok.) And Raymond Floyd knocking it in the water on No. 11 and on the second playoff hole with Nick Faldo.

I will cherish the memory of all these moments. I will also remember my little "76" there last May to beat Brother Steve and Brother Rudy out of five bucks apiece. The first time we played there many years ago I didn't make a divot until the eighth hole. Then I made a divot with a 3-wood I could have buried an elephant in. Lord, the memories.

● ● ●

In 1978 Rudy Michael Gatlin—His Rudeness, Cousin Rusty, Old Nub-Gub—began the MDA Gatlin Brothers Golf Tournament (now known as the Chili's Gatlin Brothers Golf Tournament), an annual event, which over the last twenty-plus years has raised millions of dollars for the Muscular Dystrophy Association.

Roy Clark came to the Gatlin Brothers Golf Tournament in April 1997 and put on a one-man show as only Roy can do it. It was not his first time to help us at the tournament. He's been there several times.

After four or five songs, Roy came and sat down with me at our table in the ballroom where he performed to a packed house. We talked about the old days and old friends and music and the fact that God had mercifully let us both live through the insanity of the '70s and '80s, and we talked about dreams that had come true and some that had not.

After a while, Roy looked at me and said with a Roy Clark smile on his face, "Gat, I'm goin' to bed. I'm sleepy." (Roy's been on the road for forty-five years. He's in constant demand. People are always pulling at him to do one thing or another or be one place or another, and I appreciate very much that he took the time to help us.)

I hugged him and said, "I love you."

He hugged me back and told me he loved me too, and went off to bed.

The Chili's Gatlin Brothers Tournament has meant a lot to the Muscular Dystrophy Association, the city of Dallas, and the Gatlin brothers, personally. There are a lot of people out there with big hearts who have helped over the years to make the MDA Gatlin golf thing a huge success. Randy Smith, Anita Stephenson, and Rudy have done a fabulous job.

Time and space will not allow me to replay for you the twenty years of tournaments and good times we've had doing them, but I would be remiss if I did not mention some of the people who came and helped us out—Roy Clark, Vicki Carr, Stephen Stills, Louis Grizzard, The Nitty Gritty Dirty Band, Charley Pride, Alex Harvey, Kenny Davis, Dicky Betts, Larry Carlton, Red Steagall, The Texas Playboys, Janie Frickie, Williams & Ree, George Chambers and the Country Gentlemen, and many more.

Thanks to all of you, we're making progress in fighting this terrible disease.

• • •

Another tournament filled with memories is the Gerald Ford Celebrity Golf Tournament in Vail, Colorado. There were always

Mrs. Betty Ford and me at the Gerald Ford Tournament in Vail

old friends there, and we met new ones every year. Former U.S. Ambassador Leonard Firestone, what a wonderful man he was. Former Notre Dame coach Lou Holtz, a nut and great guy. Bryant Gumbel—of course we knew B. G. from the *Today Show* and from his golf tournament in Florida for the United Negro College Fund. Bob Hope was always there, and he was always wonderful.

On the occasion of our first Gerald Ford tournament in July of 1989, Steve and Rudy and I performed at the gala, and right in the middle of our performance, the Spirit moved me to do something special for Mrs. Ford.

Moving center stage, I looked down at President and Mrs. Ford, who were seated in the front row, and said, "Mr. President, this is the very first time we have been able to attend your tournament and it is wonderful. Thank you for inviting us again after we have turned you down so many times. I owe you an apology, Mr. President.

"On one occasion when I called the day before the tournament and canceled, I said I had the flu. Well, sir, that was a lie. I was laid up in a hotel in Houston, drunk and sick and coming down from a three-day cocaine binge after our performance at the Houston Rodeo. Sir, please forgive me for lying to you. That wonderful lady sitting next to you, Mrs. Betty, is one of the reasons I am here tonight—sober. Because she had the courage to face her problem with alcohol and bring it all out into the light of day, the rest of us ole drunks have been able to step out of the shadows into the light. So, Mr. President, I'm grateful you asked us to play in your tournament, but I'm here because of Mrs. B."

The audience went nuts. Having said all that, I said, "Mrs. B., may I have this dance?"

At that I ran into the audience and Steve and Rudy kicked off "Houston (Means I'm One Day Closer to You)." Betty Ford, the patron saint of all alcoholics, and Larry Gatlin, a five-year (at that time) sober, recovering alcoholic, danced up and down the aisle at the Vail Performing Arts Center to the smiles, applause, and good wishes of all those in attendance.

● ● ●

Golf has been good to the Gatlin brothers. All the people—Arnold Palmer, Jack Nicklaus, Ben Hogan, Sam Snead, Gene Sarazen, and Byron Nelson—so many of the greats. Playing Cypress Park and Pebble Beach with Jack and Ben, and playing St. Andrews with Sir John Carmichael, a knight of the British Empire (for thirty years service in Khartoum), and Lee Trevino, Ben Crenshaw, Tom Kite, and Curtis Strange.

In the summer of 1992 at Pebble Beach Golf Club, Tom Kite won the U.S. Open Championship. We did not get to be there with him on that great occasion. We were somewhere on the road, but we were gathered around a TV set on the bus or in a hotel room. (I can see it, but can't remember exactly where we were.) We cheered every shot and prayed for every putt to go in.

Tom was destined to win. He gritted his teeth and set his jaw, pulled out that old Persimmon head driver on the last hole, and just blasted a perfect drive out there toward the big tree in the middle of the fairway and then brought it home to victory. It was terrific, Tom. (Or was it Tom Terrific?)

Tom and Christy Kite, Janis and L.G. backstage at The Palace

A few months later, when Janis and I joined Riverbend Church in Austin, Tom and Christy Kite were the first ones to come over and hug us and welcome us to this wonderful congregation of broken, wounded, messed up, but healing pilgrims.

"Welcome home," Tom said as he shook my hand and hugged my neck. By golly, when the U.S. Open champion welcomes you as a church member and back to Texas, you are finally home.

$\mathscr{T}$HE
PRODIGAL SON

I was a young man who had the best of everything—
I was the first born of a hard workin' man.
But I was not satisfied with the best of everything
So I took my possessions in my hand.
I traveled far and wide, and I tasted worldly pleasure
But deep inside I was lonely without measure.
I wound up in Las Vegas nearly dead.
Then I raised my eyes toward heaven and I said:
I will arise and go back to my Father's house
I will beg him to forgive me for the fool I've been.
I will arise and go back to my Father's house.
I would gladly be a servant if he'll take me back again.
—The Prodigal Son

Today, as I was riding in my car to the Westlake Library to try to find a quiet place to work, something dawned on me. This book is really the end of the new beginning. The new beginning had its birth on December 9, 1984, and the intervening thirteen-plus years have begun a new chapter in my life. So, for me this effort is a milestone—a benchmark—a road sign. It's almost like saying, "Well, that's all well and good, but what now?"

The honest answer to "What now?" is "I don't know!"

Before I even make an attempt at "What now?" I think I need to tie some kind of string around the "Well, that's all well and good" part.

Throughout the book I have referred to the story of the prodigal son. The part I love the most is when the prodigal was far off and his father ran toward him.

One morning I crawled on my hands and knees, totally insane from the effects of cocaine and alcohol, and prayed, "God, if You don't help me, I'm going to die." I was trying to get up out of the pigpen. All I did was pray that one simple prayer, and immediately, while I was still far off—the Father, God Almighty—ran toward me, and a series of events and people and places was set into motion that would eventually, thankfully, lead me back home.

Home—isn't that a wonderful word? Doesn't it bring to mind peace, healing, forgiveness, love, and reconciliation? I prayed one simple prayer, and the Father did the rest.

Dear friends, my purpose here is not to proselytize or espouse any doctrine or theology. My purpose is not to enlist you in any organization or group. My mission is simply this: tell the story, and let God do the rest.

If you are sitting in the pigpen of worldly despair and hopelessness, get up, and take one small step toward the Father. He will do the rest. And while you are still far off, He will run toward you with open arms of love, forgiveness, and plenty. He did it for me, and since God is no respecter of persons—according to His word—He will do it for you.

One day Jack Boland and I were talking, and I said I was afraid of this or that; I was ranting about something. He laughed out loud and said, "Larry Gatlin, it will be a wonderful day in your life when you realize you no longer need to defend yourself!"

I thought, *duh—what? No longer defend myself? Are you crazy? This world eats up those who don't defend themselves. The music business eats up those who do not protect themselves.* I ranted and raved, and Jack just smiled.

It took a while, but I later understood what Jack meant and have tried to apply it to my daily life. Bit by bit, little by little, I have made progress from that day to this. This once-lost prodigal son has been restored to sanity and, in the process, found a little heaven on earth.

OK, this world ain't perfect. But of this I'm certain: there is far more that is right in the world than is wrong, and all we have to do is look around us to see that.

There is no better place. There is no better nation. There is no better time to be living than now. It's something many of you have already realized. It's something I have finally realized too. For this once-lost prodigal son who went off into a far country, this little heaven on earth is one place—at this moment, at this time in my life—I am very glad to call home.

And now for the "What now?" part. I'm going to trust that to God.

Once I asked Jack Boland, "Why in the middle of what seemed to be a good day, does awful stuff happen?"

In his mystic way he looked at me and said, "When awful stuff happens it is God bangin' on your hood trying to get your attention! God wants you to come up higher: search for higher truth, higher love, higher consciousness—the mind of Christ.

"Larry," he said, "God loves you so much that He allows awful stuff to happen so that you will get out of yourself and seek Him."

On yet another occasion I was complaining to Jack about something, and he simply said, "Larry Gatlin, you can put God in as small a box—or as big a box—as you want to." He paused and let me ponder that for a moment, and then he added, "Or you can take God out of the box altogether.

"Larry, if you want a small life, if you want to love small, dream small, and live small, keep God in a small box. If you want to live a little bigger, dream a little bigger, love a little bigger, keep God in a little bigger box. Or just don't keep God in a box at all if you want all that He has for you."

I was speechless.

A short time ago I asked my old pal D. J. McLachlan to try to help manage my career. I told D. J. I only wanted to concentrate on six things:

1. This book,
2. *Texas Cafe,*
3. The Gatlin Brothers Theatre in Myrtle Beach,
4. Some solo dates, such as symphonies and AA talks,
5. *Last Real Cowboy on Late Great Planet Earth*, that collection of short stories about my old friend Paul Whitley and the Great Waggoner Ranch,
6. And last, but not least, the Gatlin Group, a marketing and merchandising company Janis and I have started.

By doing this, I put God in a box. I'm not sure what size box it is, but it is a box. I pretty much said, "God, this is my plan, this is my agenda, this is what I want my life to be—so take it."

Oh, the arrogance of such a statement. Who am I to tell Him, "Hey, God, here are the six things I want my life to consist of. Bless them and bring them to pass"? Who am I to trot out my little shopping list in front of the God who scattered the stars and planets and suns into their perfect places in the sky?

Who am I to limit the God of the universe? In the last few days I have heard God Almighty bangin' on my hood. He got my attention so I also realized that a six-item shopping list for the rest of my life may not be enough.

I'd like to close with the words of my song "One Dream Per Customer":

> *Is life a simple matter of one dream per customer*
> *Or are you allowed all you dare to dream?*
> *And if you dream a nightmare,*
> *   should you pray to just stop dreamin'*
> *Or could it be that nightmares*
> *   aren't as bad as they first seem?*
> *And if you dream a wondrous dream*
> *that comes true to the letter*
> *Does it mean that's as far as you get to go?*
> *If that's the way it is, God's playin' tricks on His children*
> *And since God does not play tricks*
> *The answer is no.*

So wake up, dreamer, it's time you realize
The best dreams you'll ever dream
You'll dream with open eyes.
So step out on your faith
However small it may seem.
'Cause it's not a simple matter
Of one dream per customer.
You're allowed all you dare to dream.

Stir up the fire within you
And step out on your faith
However small it may seem.
'Cause it's not a simple matter
Of one dream per customer.
You're allowed all you dare to dream.

To you, dear friends, I say: Dare to step out on faith. Dare to listen to God banging on your hood with the admonition to come up higher. Dare to trust God to bless you "pressed down, shaken together, and running over." Dare to dream big and think big and live big.

Take God out of the box.

Have a great day. In fact, have a great life. It's all the same price: free. The price has already been paid by that Jesus Man.

I know you have seen those deals on TV, "The following is a paid political announcement," and then some guy starts spewing venom about his opponent. Well, the following is an unpaid, nonpolitical endorsement, and there is no venom—only love.

There is a place in the mountains of North Carolina that is very special to me and I believe very close to the heart of God. It's called The Pavilion. Gilles and Lillian de Jardine are the driving force behind The Pavilion. They are mystical spirits, full of love and understanding. They are disciples of Christ through Jack Boland and the program of recovery and renewal. The healing that they teach and practice at The Pavilion is based on Jack's interpretation of the Gospel of Christ and on the enlightenment God has given them, and that is considerable. The Pavilion is not a drug and alcohol treatment center like The Betty Ford Center or the CareUnit of Orange County. It is more of a total life renewal center—a place of peace and healing that is very special. I am not going to go into all the "stuff" about The Pavilion on these pages, but I would like to tell you that when Gilles and Lillian do their good cop–bad cop number on a person, that person is changed forever.

Gilles de Jardine has a wonderful gift. He can be the most loving little "meanie" in the world. He can see through all the pretenses that people throw out, and he cuts right to the chase. I've heard him say stuff like, "OK, you can cut all the crap now and tell us how you really feel."

Gilles tears people up—lovingly. He makes 'em mad and makes 'em scream and holler and vent, because he knows that only by cutting through all the lies in our lives, do we get to the real self, the self we are when we are by ourselves, in the dark.

Then after the little French Canadian pit bull, Gilles, has got you whimpering in the corner or screaming in the middle of the room, sweet Lillian comes to the rescue and brings her special gift—the gift of healing and peace and understanding and love. Lillian de Jardine is without question one of the most gifted healers on earth. She has been touched by God, and she gives of her gift to everyone she meets. Together, by the power of God and the example of Christ and the witness of the Holy Spirit, these two incredible people put people who have fallen apart back together.

I'm on the board of directors for The Pavilion, and I'm going over there sometime in the near future to do a week or so with the pit bull and the angel because I know I'm not all I can be—yet. Since there is no limit, no boundary on God's grace and riches, I want more. Gilles and Lillian are now helping me mine those riches.

So, how are you doing? Is your life wonderful and happy and joyful and free? If it is, God bless you. I'm happy for you. If, on the other hand, your life is out of control, dial 1-800-392-4808—The Pavilion. Your life will change for the better. I promise you that.

I wrote almost seven hundred pages for this book. The editor said I could only have about 325 pages. I've had a big life. I could have written one thousand, two thousand, or ten thousand pages, but that is just not to be. So, I've tried to think of some folks who are not in the book (the editor took you out, not me). So here goes . . .

I. Family

All the Doan Clan (my mama's folks), Aunt Bessie (what an angel, and her boys Jimmy Ray and Cliff . . . I've already told you about Tom. And the Gatlin Gang (my daddy's folks) Forrest and Roberta Moss, my father- and mother-in-law. Thanks for letting me marry your daughter. And to the memory of your son, Tulsa District Attorney David Lyle Moss, my dear friend who died too soon. (No offense intended, God . . . we thank You for David's life.)

II. Friends

Aunt Jewel and Uncle Bill Lundsford. Rev. and Mrs. Wesley J. Lange and their boys, Gary and Bobby. Holmes Henderickson and all our Harrah's family. The "real" Ewings of Dallas, "Big Sam," Gail and Jimbo, Tancy, and my little brother Fin (you are a real piece of work, podnah, and I love you and Beth and Finley and Charlie and little Gail). Bill and Wylodean Saxon and The Garner Brothers, Jim and Jack. To Dr. Gerald Mann, my friend and pastor at Riverbend Church, I'm grateful to God for you. You feed me something rich from God's Word every time I hear you speak. I love you, Gerald Mann. (You, too, Lois Mann. God help you put up with that zany preacher man you married.)

III. Teachers

Miss Ann Louise Jones, Miss Mary Jane Gentry, Mr. Ben Nix, Dr. Charles Peavy, Dr. Bill Lindsley, Mrs. Juanita Furr.

IV. *Teammates and Players*

Mike Campbell, Danny Brinlee, Don Carr, Keith Ethridge, Mike Golden, Mike Flynt, Lynn Hormsey, Ricky White, Pat Brown, Skippy Spruill, Mike Moore, Larry Priddy, Tris Bars, Jack Green, Tommy New, Ernie Mac Reynolds, Danny and Leo Rodriguez, Milton Thompson, Gilbert Vasquez, Eddie Vaughn, Randy Walker, Fritz Wernley—too many more to name . . . great guys all.

V. *Coaches*

Jack Newsom, Joe Swann, Martin Duncan, Jerry Thormahlan, Bill Herron, Bill Yeomen, Melvine Brown, Ben Hurt, Bobby Baldwin . . . again, too many to name . . . Great guys all.

VI. *Hunting Buddies*

Blaine MacAlister, Dan Bodecker, The Tyler Rose, Earl Campbell.

VII. *Music Types*

My band—Steve Smith, Phil Fajardo, Shannon Ford, Ralph Geddes, Mike Smith, and Bill Holloman. What a great bunch of guys and musicians. Johnny Mathis—what a great friend you've been to me, John. I love to hear you sing, I love to play golf with you, I love that New Orleans shrimp dish you cook for me when I'm in L.A., and most important, I cherish our friendship. Van Cliburne—Van, you are a wonderful spirit . . . so was your mom, Rilda Bea . . . we all miss her. See you in Fort Worth. The rest of The Blackwood Quartet—Bill Shaw, the great Irish tenor; and Jackie Marshall, the zany and multitalented piano player. And The Statesmen—Denver Crumpler, the sweet-singing tenor; Doy Ott, the quiet one, the great baritone songwriter and arranger; Jim "Big Chief" Wetherington, the full-blood Indian from Ty, Georgia.

VIII. *Hollywood Cowboys*

Roy Rogers—The King of the Cowboys—thank you for coming to hear us sing at the Big Fair in '89, and thanks for showing us through your fabulous museum. Gene Autry—The Singing Cowboy—Thank you for all your kindness to me over the years.

IX. A Real Cowboy

Paul Whitley . . . Paul, I know you're on the other side of the river, and I know you left some good horses on this side for all your buddies. Don't know when I'll see ya . . . but I know I will. Hope you like the book Last Real Cowboy on the Late Great Planet Earth, that I wrote sorta about you. (I had to make up some stuff, Paul, to fill in the blanks . . . the stuff you didn't tell me while you were sittin' around the fire at Cedar Top.)

X. Golf Courses
Barton Creek

To all the gang at Barton Creek Golf Club—Jim Bob, Mr. D., Bo, Brent, "Noggie," Muley, Isidio, Kenny, Glen, and all the staff and crew; you are the best. If everybody treated me as good as my wife, Walter Hagen, American Airlines, and you folks at Barton Creek, I'd never complain again. Thanks, and I'll see you on the first tee. You, too, Jeannie, girl.

Myrtle Beach

To the guys in Myrtle Beach at the Witch, The Wizard, and Man-O-War—Claude, Richard, Jeff, Tom, David, Wayne, Alan, Kathy, Grahm, Nick, Katie, Lee Lee—all of you. Ken Tomlinson at Tidewater and The Cauthons and Les Morris at Pawley's Plantation. And Nelson and Mary Emily Jackson and all the folks at Prestwick. And Glen and Jo Ann Hall and Clinch at Waterford. Thanks to you all.

The Honors

To all the gang at the Honors Course. Whitey Monster, Jim Jernigan, M. J., Juanita, Gene Gene, Maybelline and Frank (two of the best guys in the world; they're both on the other side of the river), Pete Parker (world-class sober saint) and Burkes Smith, the Burkamo, and George Parker, Pete's boy, another little brother, and to the boss Mr. John T. Lupton, thanks for everything. I'll see you all in the spring. Oh, yeah, J. T., if God ever sees fit to give me some real money, I pray that I use it generously and benevolently for the good of my fellow man the way you have. And, God, if You give me a couple billion, I'll be generous and benevolent. (God just said, "Larry, be generous and benevolent with what I've given you, and I'll give you more.")

The Pebble

To all the gang at the Pebble—Paul and Cindy Spangler, Lee Ann, R. J., Laird, Richie, and all the great guys and gals at Pebble Beach; what great times we've had there. We look forward to many more. There's no place on earth like Pebble Beach.

To the R.O.A.C.H.'s (Royal Order of Ancient Cable Hackers)— Jay O'Neill, Bob Hughes, Jack Crosby, John Saeman, Jay Ricks, Jim Fitzgerald, Doug Dittrick, and you, too, Alan Harmon (The Duke)— thanks for letting me pinch hit. It's been grand.

I could tell a hundred Billy Bob Harris stories and I haven't. (Probably a good deal for both of us that I didn't, huh, Billy Bob?) I've never had a better friend than William Robert Harris of Dallas, Texas.

Keep the faith, Larry.